Advance praise for LOST IN MEDIA

"In a media-saturated culture that bombards us daily with a jumble of corporate-driven messages about consumption and selfishness, conformity and isolation, it's fair to say that many of us are living our lives "lost in media." Amid this barrage, we seek a compass and decency and community. This book offers critical examinations of media messages—from advertising to Hollywood to journalism and tabloid news."

—Jeff Cohen, Director of Park Center for Independent Media, Ithaca College;

LOST
IN
MEDIA

minding the media

CRITICAL ISSUES FOR LEARNING AND TEACHING

Shirley R. Steinberg and Pepi Leistyna
General Editors

Vol. 7

The Minding the Media series is part of both
the Peter Lang Education list and the Media and Communication list.
Every volume is peer reviewed and meets
the highest quality standards for content and production.

PETER LANG
New York • Washington, D.C./Baltimore • Bern
Frankfurt • Berlin • Brussels • Vienna • Oxford

LOST IN MEDIA

The Ethics of Everyday Life

Tony Kashani &
Benjamin Frymer, *Editors*

PETER LANG
New York • Washington, D.C./Baltimore • Bern
Frankfurt • Berlin • Brussels • Vienna • Oxford

Library of Congress Cataloging-in-Publication Data

Lost in media: the ethics of everyday life /
[edited by] Tony Kashani, Benjamin Frymer.
p. cm. — (Minding the media; v. 7)
Includes bibliographical references.
1. Mass media—Moral and ethical aspects.
2. Social media—Moral and ethical aspects.
I. Kashani, Tony. II. Frymer, Benjamin.
P94.L67 302.23—dc23 2012032465
ISBN 978-1-4331-1367-3 (hardcover)
ISBN 978-1-4331-1366-6 (paperback)
ISBN 978-1-4539-0906-5 (e-book)
ISSN 2151-2949

Bibliographic information published by **Die Deutsche Nationalbibliothek**.
Die Deutsche Nationalbibliothek lists this publication in the "Deutsche Nationalbibliografie"; detailed bibliographic data is available on the Internet at http://dnb.d-nb.de/.

Front cover photograph by Aida Dargahi

The paper in this book meets the guidelines for permanence and durability of the Committee on Production Guidelines for Book Longevity of the Council of Library Resources.

Printed in the United States of America

Contents

Preface

David Ingram

THE ETHICS of everyday life is inseparable from the politics of everyday life. Today, the venerable coupling of individual character and democracy captured by this simple thought is threatened by a force that neither Aristotle, the luminaries of the Enlightenment, nor any of the classical defenders of civic republican virtue could have foreseen: what German critical social theorist Jürgen Habermas famously dubbed the "structural transformation of the public sphere." This transformation marks the historical shift when government propaganda and censorship, in collusion with corporate-sponsored and partisan mass media, began to manufacture our desires and to program our thoughts. This has dangerously altered the public arena in which educated, well-informed, and more or less independent-minded citizens of the late 18th century shaped public opinion through the exchange of arguments. With the rise of the security state and the neoliberal onslaught on all things public, what Habermas later referred to as the "colonization of the lifeworld by the system" has all but transformed family, school, and political life. These three pillars of everyday life—in which individual ethos is shaped by public discussion and critical reflection—have fallen victim to the vocational imperatives of a capitalist economy and the policing needs of a national (and international) security state apparatus. In the article included in this volume, educator and culture critic Henry Giroux explains that

> What is at stake in the intersection of commerce, advertising, and consumption is the very definition and survival of critical public cultures or those formative spaces and cultures where people learn the knowledge and skills of engaged citizenship and social responsibility. I am referring here to those public spaces predicated on the multiplication of spheres of daily life where people can debate the meaning and consequences of public truths, inject a notion of moral responsibility into representational practices, and collectively struggle to change dominant relations of power. Central to my argument has been the assumption that these corporate-controlled media institutions and the forms of advertising and consumption they promote do not deny politics; they simply reappropriate it. This is a politics that "actively creates one version of the social," one that exists in harmony with market ideologies and initiatives. Such a politics offers no resistance to a version of the social as largely a democracy of images, a public media extravaganza in which politics is defined through the consuming of images.

Today's neoliberal pundits try to sell us on the idea that democracy is all about letting consumer preferences dictate public outcomes. This idea of market democracy conceals a dark side about which one of its earliest exponents, Joseph Schumpeter, warned Americans over 70 years ago: the subjugation of private opinions to the manipulative forces of political and economic elites. In the absence of critical filtering and bundling via rational discussion, the incoherent "input" of private preferences yields no basis on which to determine public choice. (This is the skeptical message purveyed by conservative rational choice economists.) The result is that whatever "coherence" is injected into "informed" opinion has to be manufactured from top to bottom.

The impact corporate- and state-administered public opinion has had on government accountability has been widely discussed in recent years. Democracy is useless unless citizens are well informed by what their governments do "in their name." Freedom of information is therefore vital to holding government leaders democratically accountable to the people who elect them to do their bidding. Thanks to the war on terror, the security state has seen fit to impose prior restraints on freedom of information that go beyond government censorship of classified documents. Take, for example, the U.S. State Department's hyper-reaction to the WikiLeaks episode and the embedding of war correspondents and other journalists in safe, government-controlled debriefing pools. The government's newly created right to "spy" on the private conversations of citizens and to access private library records and cyber communications may furthermore discourage citizens from openly speaking their mind; citizens now fear being targeted by aggressive law-enforcement agencies on suspicion of engaging in conspiracy. All these government actions are taken in the name of preempting potential threats by "America's enemies," all part of the purported "war on terror."

The concentration and corporate ownership of mass media exhibit another threat to democratic deliberation. Thanks to the Supreme Court's catastrophic decision in *Citizens United*, Super PACs funded by wealthy elites and corporations can now spend unlimited amounts of money in promoting their interests. Given lax oversight in the quality of publicity they disseminate, these PACs can generate their own simulacrum of reality ("hyperreality," as Jean Baudrillard famously put it). The PACs manufacture whatever facts fit their ideological worldviews, placing their "reality" before the often uncritical public. Their niche sources no longer operate under the same constraints of independent factual verification as mainstream news outlets. The result, again, is a fragmented public whose *disjecta membra* inhabit clashing "realities" resistant to objective mediation.

Truth, as punk TV news pundit Stephen Colbert reminds us, has been replaced by "truthiness," or the "truth" one wants to hear. Colbert's satirical imitation of conservative talk-show pundits in the tradition of Fox's Bill O'Reilly performatively deconstructs the rhetorical strategies that invite audiences to abandon critical distance in directly identifying with the pundit as the final authority on what is true and real. As Jjenna Hupp Andrews observes in this volume:

> Both [O'Reilly and Colbert] structure their arguments by referencing anecdote instead of fact, by appealing to emotions over reason, and by using everyday language and syntax. (Colletta, 2009, p. 862). These techniques enable them to incite an emotional response of truthiness. . . . O'Reilly presents his performance not as a "performance" but as objective news analysis in a "No Spin Zone." Colbert, whose character is modeled on O'Reilly (among other conservatives), takes his performed opinions to the logical extremes and does not pretend to be objective. Colbert uses the "comic device of exaggeration" as a "rhetorical strategy of showing how an opponent's argument can lead to absurd conclusions if taken far enough". . . .

More than 60 years ago, German critical theorist Theodor Adorno dissected other rhetorical strategies by which mass media and the "culture industry" play upon the subconscious prejudices and emotional attachments of culture consumers. In doing so, he argued, these forces result in citizens abdicating critical judgment by deferring to the "pseudo-reality" proffered by the powers that be. The rhetorical use of stereotyping, formulaic repetition, and subliminal messaging used in TV and radio programming conspire to create in the minds of a passive public a sense of the totalitarian inevitability of a hierarchically structured status quo. This ultimately results in the masochistic denial of individual autonomy (ego destruction accompanied by infantile narcissistic gratification) and in a kind of sadistic voyeurism (witnessing the misery of misfits, minorities, and other outsiders). The Benetton advertisements discussed by Giroux in this volume perfectly illustrate how selling brand-label merchandise with images of death row inmates, starving children, and other denizens of its "shock publicity" is not at all intended to raise consciousness about the world's injustices (as hypocritically trumpeted by Benetton executives). Rather, the juxtaposition of these images alongside Benetton logos enables consumers to feel guiltless in buying into the very capitalist fashion industry whose correlative sweatshop system of wage exploitation produces such massive suffering.

The German critical theorist and father of cultural studies Walter Benjamin observed that the ability to mass reproduce images for popular consumption comes with a price: the isolation of the image from the historical context in which its full emotional power and significance shines forth. In today's corporate world, whatever power remains in the image serves solely to manipulate the viewer for purposes of propaganda and publicity; its power is emotionally and semantically truncated and redirected toward objects of gratification, thereby concealing the original significance of whatever site is depicted so as to blunt further questioning. We feel that we're fighting injustice by buying Benetton designer clothes without having to think about how Benetton and the entire global economic system of which it is a part *produce* injustice.

The state of mass media may not be quite as dire as I have presented it. Years ago French social critic Michel Foucault observed that dominant discourses with all of their exclusions and hierarchies tend to produce counter-discourses. Today we witness the Occupy Movement, which is as much concerned about expanding and deepening the public sphere as it is about fighting corporate capitalism and its stranglehold over democracy. Cyber technologies have also facilitated populist critiques of the status quo and have even proven useful in revitalizing the non-virtual public spaces of face-to-face demonstrations that were recently on display in connection with Arab Spring. But the jury is still out on the ambivalent yield of cyber technology for democracy. For all of their apparent charm in facilitating virtual interaction, popular websites such as Facebook do not encourage face-to-face critical debate and their platforms for communicating content are rigidly dictated from above. Furthermore, cyber technologies make the task of censorship and spying easier than ever before.

Yet the inability of governments and economic elites to contain the proliferation of counter-discourses on the web—however uncertain their informational reliability and critical depth—leaves room for guarded optimism on this score. To return to the eponymous subtheme of this volume, if we are not to be lost in media, then we will need a corresponding rationalization of our everyday lifeworld ethos. Realizing our public autonomy as citizens of a rational deliberating democracy will require a radical rethinking of what is right and good, one that redirects us away from our widespread passivity as private consumers of mass media toward an active pedagogy of critical media reception of the sort exemplified in these pages.

Foreword

Norman Solomon

IN THE 21st century, breathtaking changes in technology have empowered vast numbers of people to actively participate in social media and other dynamic forms of communication. Yet a few multibillion-dollar conglomerates with huge investments in evolving media—online, broadcast, cable, film and cutting-edge digital platforms as well as print—continue to exercise vast power over what mass audiences of Americans watch, hear and read every day. In tandem with massive advertising that conveys its own messages along with subsidizing certain types of media content, the present-day concentrated ownership of the means of media production and distribution is pivotal for the functionalities of de facto propaganda in our society more than a dozen years into this century.

We may be dazzled by the profusion of high-tech advances, from the latest versions of iPhones and iPads to Facebook and Twitter, but some time-worn basics remain central to the media world. Eight decades ago, President Franklin D. Roosevelt wrote to a press baron: "I have always been firmly persuaded that our newspapers cannot be edited in the interests of the general public, from the counting room."[1] Today, the counting room is still in command, though the green eyeshade has been replaced by sophisticated computer modeling to maximize profits. Instead of individuals named Hearst, Pulitzer, and McCormick, the impetus for media domination has fallen to the likes of venture-capitalist raiders and Wall Street firms. Since the turn of this century, amalgams of individual and corporate greed have ravaged the *Los Angeles Times*, the Knight-Ridder chain, and many other print outlets, while ruthlessly undercutting the quality of journalism in other mass media.

Today's "counting room" is the power behind the public thrones of media kingdoms, whether Google, Facebook, the *New York Times* or the constellations of major cable TV channels that are mostly owned by just a few mega-companies. All sorts of decisions, made every day behind closed doors, determine the increasingly overt ways in which online advertisers stalk us, whether we're doing a Google search, going to our Facebook page, or emailing our friends. The drive for profits is what shapes and circumscribes much—but not all—of the media world.

For better and worse, our lives are so intertwined with media that they cannot be disentangled. Understanding this entanglement gives us more potential to change it for the better. "Media activism" used to be an oxymoron—the media environment has long injected anesthetics into the body politic, resulting in numbed passivity—but recent decades have brought a sustained upsurge in astute media criticism and active engagement in challenging the media status quo. With creativity and determination, many millions of people are actively involved in communicating for purposes far more uplifting and life-sustaining than the pursuit of money and market share. We understand that communication is essential to our human possibilities. We study media to grasp its intricacies *and* to inform our actions.

A multilayered spectrum of media activism—including empirical research, study, criticism, debate, protests, political organizing, and creating independent media projects—is now flourishing outside traditional orbits of conformity. The landscape of media understanding and action has changed substantially in recent decades. For example, from its start in the mid-1980s, Fairness & Accuracy in Reporting (FAIR) has combined many aspects of progressive media work. Nearly thirty years after FAIR got underway, many organizations are engaged in some form of media activism across the United States. We're thinking a lot more clearly about media, and we're much more engaged in trying to transform the media universe.

Awareness of media power is necessary and insufficient. Our capacity to decode pervasive media messages that inculcate passivity is a prerequisite for effectively challenging them. The flowering of media activism requires the nutrients of information and analysis. This book will help more people to engage in understanding our media world and working with others to change it for the better.

Note

Franklin D. Roosevelt letter to Joseph Pulitzer Jr., *St. Louis Post-Dispatch Symposium on Freedom of the Press* (St. Louis: St. Louis Post-Dispatch, 1938); quoted in Robert W. McChesney, *The Political Economy of Media* (New York: Monthly Review Press, 2008), pp. 76–77.

Acknowledgments

We wish to thank Shirley R. Steinberg and Pepi Leistyna for creating such a timely book series for an important area, which is directly connected to public critical thinking and social change. We are very appreciative to have *Lost in Media* as part of the Minding the Media series with Peter Lang Press. We also want to thank David Ingram, one of the leading thinkers in critical theory, for generously taking the time to write an excellent preface to our book. We are fortunate to have our erudite contributors, providing cutting-edge discussions in every chapter of this book. We want to thank them all. Sophie Appel at Peter Lang deserves our special thanks. She has been an outstanding representative working with us to complete the design and structure of the project in a timely manner. We also want to thank Kimberly M. Radek, who singlehandedly formatted the manuscript. Without her help we would be lost.

We wish to thank our colleagues who have patiently reviewed the manuscript and articulated their superb words of reflections. Thank you Margaret Anderson, Norman Solomon, Mark LeVine, Jeff Cohen, Shoba Sharad Rajgopal.

Ben would like to thank a number of people for their support and empathy during a difficult period: Margaret Anderson, Sharifa Ahjum, Natasha Chen Christensen, my brother Paul, Leah Millstein, Aida Dargahi, Wendy Ostroff, Anna McClain, and Julie Lindberg. I would especially like to thank my mother for her strong support and encouragement which has meant so much.

Tony wants to acknowledge the patience and support of the love of my life Aida Dargahi, an outstanding academic and artist in her own right. My son Idan played an integral role by agreeing to be the model for the cover photo. My eldest son Javid was also, as always, supportive and reflective. My sons are sources of inspiration for me. My brother Ali, my father Reza, and my mother Shirin have always been instrumental in my success as an academic and a person in search of wisdom and balance.

Finally, we hope this anthology will be part of discussions about media and ethics in public spheres inside and outside the academy.

We wish to dedicate this book to those who embrace critical engagement and always want to do the right thing.

1 Introduction

Tony Kashani and Benjamin Frymer

Obscenity is a moral concept in the verbal arsenal of the establishment, which abuses the term by applying it, not to expressions of its own morality but to those of another.
—Herbert Marcuse (1971)

IN A SCENE in the underappreciated film *Bulworth* (1988), Warren Beatty's character, Jay Bulworth, a radicalized U.S. senator, responds to the objections of his use of obscene words on the air, while being interviewed on television as part of his reelection campaign. He provocatively raps the following explosive monologue:

Obscenity? The rich is gettin' richer and richer and richer,
while the middle class is gettin' more poor.
Makin' billions and billions and billions of bucks?
Well my friend, if you weren't already rich at the start,
well that situation just sucks.
'Cause the riches' mother fucker in five of us
is getting ninety-fuckin-eight percent of it
And every other motherfucker in the world is left
to wonder where the fuck we went with it.
Obscenity? I'm a senator. I gotta raise $10,000 a day every day
I'm in Washington.
I ain't gettin' it in South Central.
I'm gettin' it in Beverly Hills.
So I'm votin' in the Senate
how they want me to.
Then I been sendin' 'em my bills.
But we got babies in South Central
dyin' as young as they do in Peru.
We got public schools that are nightmares.
We got a Congress that ain't got a clue.
We got kids with submachine guns,
We got militias throwin' bombs.
We got Bill just getting' all weepy.
We got Newt blamin' teenage moms.
We got so many factories closin' down.
Where the hell did all the good jobs go?
Well, I'll tell you where they went.
My contributors make more profits.

> Makin', makin', makin'
> Hirin' kids in Mexico
> Oh a brother can work in fast food
> If he can't invent computer games . . . .
> Okay, okay, I got a simple question that I'd like to ask of this
> Network that pays you for performing this task.
> How come they got the airwaves?
> They're the people's, aren't they?
> Wouldn't they be worth 70 billion to the public today?
> If some money-grubbin' Congress didn't give them away
> for big campaign money?
> It's hopeless, you see.
> If you're runnin' for office without no TV.
> If you don't get big money,
> you get a defeat.
> Corporations and broadcasters make you dead meat.
> You been taught in this country there's speech that is free.
> But free don't get you no spots on TV.
> If you want to have senators not on the take,
> then give them free airtime; they won't have to fake.
> Telecommunications is the name of the beast
> that, that, that, that, that's eating up the world
> from the west to the east.
> The movies, the tabloids, TV and magazines,
> they tell us what to think and do and all our hopes and dreams.
> All this information makes America phat.
> But if the company's outta the country, how American is that?
>
> (Adapted from "Bulworth: Quotes," n.d., at IMDb.com)

What the above unprecedented and rare cinematic moment demonstrates is that American society, along with much of the rest of the world, is lost in an ethical wasteland, and much of it is deeply interconnected with global media. Media are ubiquitous. From the moment we wake up until we go to sleep (at least for most of the Western world and in developed nations), we have to engage with different kinds of media. Furthermore, reality is no longer what it used to be. After January 1,1983 (the official birthday of the Internet—when it was turned on), we have rapidly become accustomed to receiving and producing a mediated reality (subject to immediate change and alteration) through the lenses of media. In a highly commodified culture, any meaningful analysis of media forces has to move to the broader social and ethical terrain to understand the abstract forces pushing individuals away from their own selves, the capacity to form authentic values, and the very process of ethical development.

As David Ingram pointed out in the preface of this book, the ethics of everyday life and the politics of our lives are intertwined. And from this vantage point, media collectively play an integral role in shaping the world and the self. Building upon Henri Lefebvre's (2008) argument in *Critique of Everyday Life*, this anthology investigates the multiplicity of ways our everyday lives are lived through media. According to neoliberal ideology, the market is an ethics in itself and there is no need for ethical deliberations in everyday living because the market will determine right and wrong. The ethics of neoliberalism has permeated every facet of our lives. Moreover, this form of capitalistic ethics is facilitated, for the most part, by a globalized corporate media consortium. With this anthology, we are calling for a new ethics of everyday life, one that liberates the individual to think for him- or herself and shed the tendencies to become a docile consumer, instead transforming into an engaged cosmopolitan citizen. It is paramount to recognize the links between new media culture and ethics of everyday life.

In his chapter, "From Benetton to Murdoch: The Culture of Money, Shock, and Schlock," Henry Giroux discusses the morally corrupt culture of new mass advertising. By deconstructing Benetton's aggressive strategies, Giroux illuminates a significant shift in ethics of advertising toward normalization of shock aesthetics. He urges cultural workers and educators to assume moral responsibility in addressing the decline of democracy directly as part of a "global pedagogical movement."

Tony Kashani's chapter, "We Are All in This Thing Together: The Complex Ethics of Social Media Networking," is an inquiry into new media's impact on the ways in which people make ethical decisions in their everyday lives. He employs social contract theory to better understand the complexity of social media networking. Kashani sees possibilities of ethical responses by the global citizens to commercial culture of social media in order to transform a neoliberal agenda into a democratic and egalitarian project.

In his chapter, "Ritalin: Panic in the USA," Toby Miller provides an insightful and timely analysis of the formation of a moral panic surrounding the use and controversy of the ADHD drug Ritalin. Miller examines the formation of this moral panic in terms of its construction in popular culture/media, the role of the U.S. government, and conflicts of interest between competing professional health organizations. He therefore not only highlights an important new arena of bioethical contestation but also demonstrates the significant role of the expansion of ethics into larger cultural discussions and debates.

Douglas Kellner's "The Murdoch Media Empire, Journalistic Ethics, and the Spectacle of Scandal" is a critical examination of the global media oligarchy. By analyzing the media spectacle of Ruport Murdoch's *News of the World* "misdeeds," Kellner points out the paradoxical nature of neoliberal media's infrastructure, as Ruport Murdoch's tabloid becomes the hottest subject of the very sensationalist paradigm he helped create on a global scale. The chapter sounds a necessary alarm to engaged citizens everywhere to be aware of the implications such scandals have for the future of media and democracy.

"Media and Ethics: The Public Sphere, Truth Telling, and Practice of Freedom" is Ali Kashani's philosophical examination of the ethical relationship between media and the public. By utilizing Aristotelian notions of human social tendencies, Kant's response to "What Is Enlightenment?" and Habermas's ideas about the public sphere, Kashani examines the ethical responsibility of the media as facilitators of the new public sphere and the conditions that allow democratic debates to take place by the public for the public.

Benjamin Frymer's chapter, "Alienation in the Age of Spectacle Culture," examines the pervasive alienation in late capitalist societies by tracing the intellectual pathway in critical theory and philosophy culminating in Guy Debord's critique of "the society of the spectacle." Frymer not only places Debord's critique in the context of a radical analysis of alienation but also makes the argument that this entire trajectory in critical theory establishes fundamental links between alienation and the increasingly "abstract" character of modern/capitalist societies. Frymer argues that modern individuals become dominated by abstract systems and cultures of their own creation, becoming "lost in media" amongst other abstract realms of advanced capitalist culture.

Brian Klocke's chapter, "Neoliberal Media's Commodification of Occupy Wall Street and Radical Social Movements," engages in extensive empirical media research, yielding a fresh analysis of mainstream media coverage of the Occupy Wall Street movement. The chapter makes a critical argument about the neoliberal patterns and ideological character of mainstream news coverage. Employing both content analysis and ideology critique, Klocke provides insights into how media coverage of Occupy Wall Street largely reinforces the very ideas and social hierarchy the movement has opposed.

In her chapter, "With No Responsibility: The Colbert Show," Jjenna Hupp Andrews explores the cutting-edge satirical critique of contemporary news media by Stephen Colbert. Andrews unpacks the deadpan comedic notion of "truthiness," as introduced by *The Colbert Report*, offering a sobering critique of the ways of mainstream news media and punditry such as the Fox News' Bill O'Reilly and Sean Hannity "news" programs. She explicates the ways in which Colbert's unique form of satire works as a subversive element within the broader media landscape.

Kimberly M. Radek, in her provocative chapter, "The Devil Is in the Details: Christian Messages Gliding Unseen Within *Deep Blue Sea*, looks beneath the surface of Hollywood cinema to uncover the deeper messages embedded in its elaborate productions. By appropriating Shirley Steinberg's theories, Radek puts her critical spotlight on the horror film *Deep Blue Sea.* Radek provides a highly illuminating example of what Stuart Hall calls the "work" of representation, or the way cultural constructions impact audiences through the play of unseen ideological elements. In the case of *Deep Blue Sea*, she exposes the film's deep connections to conservative ideas and hegemonic Christian theology. Her discussion of the representation of gender reveals the deep connection between patriarchy and ultraconservatism.

Ajay Gehlawat's chapter, "Why *Harold and Kumar Go to White Castle*: The Representation of Otherness in Mainstream Teen Cinema," is a refreshingly negotiated reading of a film that is ostensibly a generic Hollywood ethnic teen comedy. Gehlawat offers a probing analysis of the film where he peels away the obvious layers and in the tradition of cultural studies reveals the subversive dimensions of the film, hence reflecting on the possibilities of Brechtian theater within the Hollywood system.

Finally, Native American scholar M.A. Jaimes Guerrero takes the film *Avatar* and Hollywood to task in "No-Win *Avatar*: Culture Clash in Pocahontas Revisited." Combining the theoretical insights of bell hooks and Tony Kashani, she sees *Avatar* as yet another Pocahontas story. Guerrero reminds the reader of the importance of film analysis as a political act.

We have chosen the above diverse perspectives deliberately to offer a discourse of critical media comprehension in the tradition of critical theory. The overarching objective for this volume is to foster new ethics for an engaged citizenry and to empower individuals to resist through their deep understanding of media culture.

References

Beatty, W. (Director) (1998). *Bulworth.* [Motion picture]. United States.

"Bulworth: Quotes," n.d., IMDb.com. Available at http://m.imdb.com/title/tt0118798/quotes?qt=qt0144762

Lefebvre, H. (2008). *Critique of everyday life* (G. Elliott & J. Moore, Trans.). New York: Verso.

Marcuse, H. (1971). *An essay on liberation.* Boston, MA: Beacon.

2 From Benetton to Murdoch: The Culture of Money, Shock, and Schlock

Henry A. Giroux

Benetton appropriated for one of its advertising campaigns actual news photos of social events that portray various calamities of the time. These include pictures of a bloodied Mafia murder victim, depictions of child labor, a terrorist car bombing and the bloodstained clothes worn by a Croatian student the day he was killed.

– C. Wright Mills (1980)

WHAT C. WRIGHT MILLS once termed "the cultural apparatus" matters even more 50 years later.[1] At the dawn of the 21st century, this apparatus has grown into a vast web of media monopolies, which serve to entertain global audiences, set fashion standards, provide information about the world, promote celebrity culture, create consumer desires, and occasionally offer insights about existing social problems while holding powerful individuals and institutions accountable. But they do more. They also function as teaching machines, producing and legitimating particular modes of identity while providing the framing mechanisms that drive the questions, interests, and values that shape a society. Through the sheer power of their size and ubiquity, the media and their digital extensions influence major institutions, influence the larger culture and reproduce particular social values; they also set standards, exert influence upon politics and often privilege the trivial over the substantive, the consumer over the citizen and the narrowest of interests over larger ethical and social considerations. As the old and new media take over the space of the public and private, they have become a more insistent and aggressive anti-democratic force corrupting politics, demeaning public goods, trading in campaigns of fear, substituting opinions for legitimate argument, and turning news outlets into spectacles of pain and perversion, if not worse. Think here of the preponderance of hate radio and television shows that feature the likes of Glenn Beck, Michael Savage, and Bill O'Reilly. And bear in mind the narcissistic messages endlessly paraded on realty TV shows. Listen to the often cruel and homophobic nonsense vomited up from the mouths of right-wing luminaries such as Michele Bachmann and Sarah Palin and how the mainstream media reports such invective as a serious species of argument. The scandalous example of Rupert Murdoch is a recent case in point where money and greed combined with a politics of corruption and shock to produce a culture of cruelty that tarnished everything it touched. Not only did News Corporation inundate the world with schlock tabloids, it also invaded the privacy and violated the dignity of the British royal family, various celebrities, and the victims of the 2005 terrorist attack in London by hacking into their voice-mail accounts. And by some accounts, it is guilty of the same criminal offense in the United States (Baker, 2011). But the most offensive hacking News Corporation has done is to hack into people's minds, filling their everyday lives with gossip, spectacles, the relentless sexualization of women, and incessant cheerleading for a market-driven society where all that matters is winning and making money. Unfortunately, what is often left out of existing narratives about the rise of big media and its commitment to shock and political conservatism is the role it plays as a form of public pedagogy, an educational force that demeans any viable notion of democratic values, relations, and critical agency. One way of understanding this reactionary form of public pedagogy is to examine the crucial, if not foundational role that trendy and "conscious" corporations like Benetton have played over the last 40 years in trading in an aesthetic of glam exposé that makes an appeal to addressing viable social issues.

The merging of spectacle, shock, and schlock in advertising has assumed increasing importance in societies where the media and other forms of screen culture become the most powerful repository for engaging and educating the wider public. In what follows, I want to turn to a brief history of Benetton and its practices as a way of understanding the current role that the media play in promoting a culture of sensation, fear, and cruelty that obliterates any remnant of social responsibility and a viable politics and pedagogy of representation. The Benetton model is important because it illustrates how the aestheticization of shock, difference, and glamour can be used and manipulated not only to attract a wider audience for its clothing line but also to misappropriate social consciousness as a way to bring attention to itself while subordinating important social issues to the brand-name power of the logo and the lure of the commodity.

Benetton and the Politics of Shock

Companies such as Benetton, the famous clothing manufacturer, have for decades used the proliferation of images and the celebration of diversity to create pedagogical practices that offer consumers a sense of unity and harmony within a world increasingly devoid of any substantive discourse of community and solidarity. It is in its concerted and often pernicious efforts to rearticulate the relationships among difference, human agency, and community that mass advertising increasingly succeeds in its promotional mission: to disguise the political nature of everyday life and appropriate the vulnerable new terrain of insurgent differences in the interests of crass consumerism.

With the rapid expansion of digital media, mass advertising has become the creator of a representational politics that powerfully challenges our understanding of what constitutes pedagogy, the sites in which it takes place, and who speaks under what conditions through its authorizing agency. When I first wrote about Benetton's advertising campaigns ten years ago, I suggested that the emergence of advertising as a global enterprise had generated a new form of violence against the public. Images that shocked people in the past had become "the most effective way of selling commodities" (Bailey & Hall, 1992). By this I did not mean simply that violence intrudes into designated public spheres as much as I was suggesting the presence of a "public whose essential predicate would be violence" (Payne & Taylor, 1992). Defining itself as a subverter of stereotypes, Benetton combined taboos, shock, and violence within a new aesthetic and mode of voyeurism that mediated between the pleasures derived from witnessing the sadistic and masochistic images. At the core of this violence were constituting principles that accentuated individualism and binary differences as central elements of the marketplace. Underlying this violence of the public was a notion of the social bereft of ethics, social justice, and any viable notion of democratic public culture. Put differently, mass advertising and its underlying corporate interests represented a new stage in an effort to abstract the notion of the public from the language of ethics, history, and democratic community. The rearticulation and intersection of advertising and commerce on the one hand, and politics and representational pedagogy on the other, could be seen in the emergence of Benetton as one of the leading manufacturers and retailers of contemporary clothing.

Today, much more so, I believe we are witnessing an unprecedented shift in American popular culture toward an utterly depraved form of aesthetics. Images that shocked one generation of viewers and then produced alienation and indifference in the next, have become even more sensationalized, as people eagerly and brazenly consume displays of aggression, brutality and death. In what follows, I suggest that this culture of cruelty is part and parcel of the growing influence of neoliberal policies across all sectors. A new and disturbing public enjoyment in the humiliation of others—far from representing an individualized pathology— now infects U.S. society as a whole in such a way that bespeaks the imminent death of the social state.

Since the early 1990s, Benetton has proven that trafficking in pain and human suffering is not only good for business but also good for providing a patina of legitimacy to the company as an artsy brand with philanthropic concerns.[2] Benetton's United Colors campaign appropriated shocking and visually arresting representations of violence and pain in order to sell clothes and attract global attention to its brand. In doing so, Benetton did more than conjoin the worlds of beauty and suffering; it also pushed a mode of commercial advertising in which the subjects of often horrendous misfortunes and acts of suffering disappeared into the all-embracing world of logos and brand names. For example, in 2000, it launched a campaign with images of convicts on death row. Claiming the ad was supporting an anti-death-penalty theme, Benetton launched the campaign in *Talk* magazine with a 96-page supplement called "We, on Death Row," in which it offered close-up photos of 26 condemned men from various states accompanied by sympathetic profiles. Focusing mostly on regrets and what they missed in the outside world, the ad campaigned offered no details of their crimes. For example, as Vicki Mabry (2009) reported, "Viewers never learn that one of the featured prisoners, Conan Wayne Hale, killed three teenagers in Oregon or that in a racially motivated crime Jeremy Sheets kidnapped, raped and murdered a black teenager in Nebraska. And the ads do not explain that Jerome Mallett killed a state highway officer in Missouri. But they do hear Mallett bemoan the fact that he's going to die. In the Benetton spots, Jones talks about the food he misses most, including his mother's homemade biscuits." Many of the relatives of the victims were outraged. The campaign stirred both outrage and an ensuing boycott of Benetton in the United States. Benetton eventually dropped the campaign and the famed Benetton photographer, Oliviero Toscani, eventually resigned. The death-row campaign took a deep interest in situating death, decadence, and violence as commodities and cultural icons, all in the interest of selling clothes.

Benetton takes a bold stance in attempting to use advertising as a forum to address highly charged social and political issues. Through its public statements and advertising campaigns, Benetton occasionally brings a dangerous, new dimension to corporate appropriation as a staple of its shock aesthetics. Inviting the penetration of aesthetics into everyday life, Benetton has utilized less deterministic and more flexible approaches to design, technology, and styling. Such approaches to marketing and layout privilege contingency, plurality, and the poetics of the photographic image in an attempt to rewrite the relationship among aesthetics, commerce, and politics. Instead of depoliticizing or erasing images that vividly, and in some cases, shockingly depict social and political events, Benetton attempted to redefine the link between commerce and politics by emphasizing both the politics of representation and the representation of politics. In the first instance, Benetton appropriated for one of its advertising campaigns actual news photos of social events that portray various calamities of the time. These include pictures of a bloodied Mafia murder victim, depictions of child labor, a terrorist car bombing, and the bloodstained clothes worn by a Croatian student the day he was killed. In the second instance, as part of a representation of politics, Benetton positions itself less as a producer of commodities and market retailer than as a corporate voice for a particular definition of public morality, consensus, coherence, and community.

As we move into the second decade of the 21st century, ethical considerations and social costs are eclipsed by market-driven policies and values. Images of human suffering are increasingly abstracted from social and political contexts and the conditions that make such suffering possible—and thus visually alluring. Moreover, as public issues collapse into privatized considerations, matters of agency, responsibility, and ethics are now framed within the discourse of extreme individualism. According to this neoliberal logic, individuals and the problems they confront are removed from any larger consideration of public values, social responsibility, and compassion. The collapse of the social and the formative culture that makes human bonds possible is now outmatched by the rise of a Darwinian ethic of greed and self-interest in which violence, aggressiveness, and sadism have become the primary metric for living and dying.

Death and violence have become the mediating link between America's domestic policy—the state's treatment of its own citizens—and U.S. foreign policy, between the tedium of ever-expanding workdays and the thrill of sadistic release. Disposable bodies now waste away in American prisons, underfunded schools, and overflowing shelters just as they litter the battlefields of Iraq and Afghanistan. America has become a permanent warfare state, with a deep investment in a cultural politics and the corollary cultural apparatuses to legitimate and sanctify its machinery of death. In a culture that increasingly disavows any sense of the origin, context, and legacy of violence, it is all the more important to question how we arrived at this historical conjuncture. Benetton should be considered a pioneer in the development of the new aesthetics of depravity and its subsequent debasement. We should understand its role not only because of its marketing success but also because of the complex position it negotiated at a transitional stage in U.S. culture.

Benetton: Small Beginnings and Global Controversies

All over the world, Benetton stands for colorful sportswear, multiculturalism, world peace, racial harmony, and now, a progressive approach toward serious social issues.[3] In 1965, Luciano Benetton and three siblings established a small business, Fratelli Benetton, near Treviso, Italy. Originally designed to produce colorful sweaters, the business expanded into a full range of clothing apparel and eventually developed into a $2 billion fashion empire producing 80 million pieces of clothing a year for 7,000 franchise stores in over 100 countries. Benetton's advertising campaign over the last two decades has been instrumental in its success in the fashion world. The advertising campaign is important not merely as a means for assessing Benetton's commercial success in extending its name recognition. It is also crucial for understanding how the philosophy of the company has attempted to reinscribe its image within a broader set of political and cultural concerns. In 1984, Benetton hired Oliviero Toscani, an award-winning photographer, to head its advertising campaign. Given a free hand with the advertising budget, Toscani's early work focused on culturally diverse young people dressed in Benetton attire and engaged in a variety of seemingly aimless and playful acts. Linking the colors of Benetton clothes to the diverse colors of their customers from all over the world, Toscani attempted to use the themes of racial harmony and world peace to register such differences within a wider unifying articulation. In 1990, Toscani adopted the United Colors of Benetton as a recurring trademark of the Benetton ideology. In 1991, Toscani initiated a publicity campaign that removed Benetton merchandise from the firm's advertising and started using its $80 million global ad budget to publish controversial and disturbing photographs in magazines and on billboards. Taking full control of the ad blitz, Toscani personally photographed many of the images that dominated the 1991 Benetton campaign. These included a number of compelling images that created a provocative effect: variously colored, blown-up condoms floating in the air; a nun kissing a priest on the lips; a row of test tubes filled with blood; and a newborn baby girl covered in blood and still attached to her umbilical cord. In 1992, Toscani embarked on his most dramatic effort to combine high fashion and politics in the service of promoting the Benetton name. He selected a series of highly charged, photojournalistic images referencing, among other things, the AIDS crisis, environmental disaster, political violence, war, exile, and natural catastrophe. These appeared in various journals and magazines as well as on billboards without written text except for the conspicuous insertion of the green and white United Colors of Benetton logo located in the margins of the photograph.

Benetton's shift in advertising strategy between 1983 and 1991 and the later shift in the new millennium need to be considered as part of a wider politics and pedagogy of representation. The earlier photographs representing children of diverse races and colors dressed in Benetton clothing have a "netherworld quality that gives the viewers the impression they're glimpsing some fashionable heaven." (Stevens, 1992). Depicted in these photographs of children hugging and holding hands is a portrayal of racial harmony and difference that appears both banal and sterile. The exaggerated precision of the models and primary colors used in the advertisements render racial unity as a purely aesthetic category, while eliminating racial conflict completely in this two-dimensional world of make believe. In addition, these colorful images appear almost too comfortable and seem at odds with a world marked by political, economic, and cultural conflict. In the early ads, difference is for the most part subordinated to the logic of the marketplace and commerce. At the same time, the harmony and consensus implied in these ads often mock concrete racial, social, and cultural differences as they are constituted amid hierarchical relations of struggle, power, and authority. Benetton's corporate image in this case seems strangely at odds with its own market research, which indicated that its "target customers—18–34-year-old women—are more socially active and aware than any generation that precedes them."[4] The switch in the ad campaign to controversial photojournalistic images reflects an attempt on the part of Benetton to redefine its corporate image. In order to define itself as a company concerned with social change, Benetton suspended its use of upscale representations in its mass advertising campaign, especially in a world where "denial in the service of upbeat consumerism is no longer a workable strategy as we are continually overwhelmed by disturbing and even cataclysmic events" (Squires, 1992). In an uncertain world of massive inequality and human suffering caught in the disruptive forces of nationalism, famine, violence, and war, such early representations linked Benetton's image less to the imperatives of racial harmony than to the forces of cultural uniformity and yuppie colonization. Moreover, Benetton's move away from an appeal to utility to social responsibility provides an object lesson in how promotional culture increasingly uses pedagogical practices to shift its emphasis from selling a product to selling an image of corporate responsibility. Benetton's increase in sales, profits, and the widespread publicity suggested that the campaign worked wonders.

The response to the campaign inaugurated in 1991 was immediate. Benetton was both condemned for its appropriation of serious issues to sell goods and praised for incorporating urgent social concerns into its advertising. In many cases, a number of the Benetton ads were either banned from particular countries or refused by specific magazines. One of the most controversial ads portrayed AIDS patient David Kirby surrounded by his family shortly before he died. Benetton used the colorized image of Kirby to sell jumpers. The Kirby ad became the subject of heated debate among various groups in a number of countries. In 1995, Benetton once again traded on the photographic juxtaposition of human suffering, the spectacle of human blood, and name-brand promotion by putting the Benetton logo next to a picture of the blood-stained clothes of a Croatian college student named Marinko Gargo, who was shot and killed by enemy fire in Bosnia–Herzegovina in July 1995. Claiming that the purpose of the ad was to enlighten the world about the Bosnian War, Benetton ignored critics who asserted that the company was once again capitalizing on and sensationalizing human tragedy for profit. In spite of the criticism and perhaps in part due to it, the company's sales doubled, reaching more than $1.8 billion in the United States alone. The Benetton name even infiltrated popular literary culture, with Douglas Coupland coining the phrase "Benetton Youth" in his novel *Shampoo Planet* (1993) to refer to global kids whose histories, memories, and experiences began in the Reagan era of greed and conspicuous consumption. *Adweek* reported that because of the success of the Benetton campaign, Toscani had become something of a commercial "star" and had been asked by American Express to develop marketing concepts for them. David Roberts, an analyst with Nomura International/London, claimed during this era that Benetton's "name recognition is approaching that of Coca-Cola."[5]

Benetton's practical response to the controversy was threefold. First, Benetton and its spokespersons reacted aggressively within a number of public forums and debates in order to defend its advertising policies by either condemning the criticism as a form of censorship or criticizing other ad companies for producing advertising that merely engaged in the most reductionistic forms of pragmatism. Second, it used the debate to reorder its identity as a corporate force for social responsibility. Third, it seized upon the controversy itself as a pretext for further marketing of its ideology in the form of books, magazines, talks, interviews, articles, and the use of celebrities such as Spike Lee to endorse its position in the debate. Benetton proceeded to articulate and defend its position in the popular press in material published in its own books and newspapers and even in campaign copy sent to its various retail stores. It also attempted to defray criticism of its ads by allowing selected executives to speak in interviews, the press, and various popular magazines. The three major spokespersons for Benetton were Luciano Benetton, founder and managing director; Oliviero Toscani, creative director; and Peter Fressola, Benetton's director of communications in North America. All three provided different versions of a similar theme: Benetton is not about selling sweaters, but social responsibility, and it is a company that represents less a product line than a lifestyle and worldview.

While serving as a senator to the Italian Parliament in the early 1990s, Luciano Benetton emerged as the principal ideologue in the Benetton apparatus. He was chiefly responsible for defining the structuring principles that guided Benetton as both a corporate identity and an ideological force. His own political beliefs appeared deeply rooted in the neoliberal language of the free market, privatization, the removal of government from the marketplace, and the advocacy of business principles as the basis for a new social imaginary. Hence, it is not surprising that in addition to defending the ads for evoking public awareness of controversial issues, Luciano Benetton readily admitted that the advertising campaign "has a traditional function...to make Benetton known around the world and to introduce the product to consumers" (Sischy, 1992). More than any other spokesperson, Luciano Benetton articulated the company's position concerning the relationship between commerce and art and served as a reminder that the bottom line for the company was profit and not social justice.

Fressola, on the other hand, focused on Benetton's ideological position, claiming that the ad campaigns did not reflect the company's desire to sell sweaters. He argued, "We're not that stupid. We're doing corporate communication. We're sponsoring these images in order to change people's minds and create compassion around social issues. We think of it as art with a social message" (Squires, 1992). Of course, the question at stake here was whose minds Benetton expected to shape. In part, the answer lay in its own advertising material, which made it quite clear that "various studies have shown that...consumers are as concerned by what a company stands for as they are about the price/value relationship of that company's product."[6] There was nothing in Fressola's message that challenged the legacy of the corporate use of communications to advance, if only tacitly, "some kind of self-advantaging exchange."[7]

The moral high ground that Benetton wished to occupy appeared to be nothing less than an extension of market research. When questioned about the use of the Benetton logo imprinted on all of the photographs, Fressola, Toscani, and other spokespeople generally responded by evading the question and pointing to the use of such photographs as part of their support for art, controversy, and public dialogue around social issues. But the presence of the logo was no small matter. In light of their market research, which stressed what Raymond Loewy calls the need for designer corporate symbols to index visual memory retention, the presence of the Benetton logo indicated a powerful advertising motive. It asserted that, regardless of the form taken by the brand logo, the purpose of advertising was to subordinate all values to the imperatives of profit and commercialization. Loewy's argument explains this mentality: "We want anyone who has seen the logotype, even fleetingly, to never forget it, or at least to forget it slowly."[8] The company's response to criticism provided a powerful indictment of both Benetton's socially responsible rationale and the claim that Benetton was engaging in a new form of corporate communication. By refusing to disrupt or challenge designer logos, communication in these terms did nothing more than link the commodification of human tragedy with the imperatives of brand recognition, while simultaneously asserting the discourse of aesthetic freedom and the moral responsibility of commerce. This was captured in part by a statement that appeared in Benetton's fall/winter 1992 advertising campaign literature:

> Among the various means available to achieve the brand recognition that every company must have, we at Benetton believe our strategy for communication to be more effective for the company and more useful to society than would be yet another series of ads showing pretty girls wearing pretty clothes.[9]

Toscani went further by separating his economic role as the director of advertising from what he called the process of communication, claiming rather blithely, "I am responsible for the company's communications; I am not really responsible for its economics."[10] Toscani appealed in this case to the moral high ground, suggesting that he was left untarnished by the commercial context that informed the deep structure of his job. Should we assume that Benetton's market research in identifying target audiences had nothing whatsoever to do with Toscani's creative endeavors? Or, perhaps, that Toscani found a way to avoid linking his own corporate success to the rise of Benetton's name recognition in a global marketplace? Toscani was well aware of the relationship between representation and power, not to mention his own role in giving a new twist to the advertising of commodities as cultural signs in order to promote a particular system of exchange. In its advertising campaigns of 1990s and forward, Benetton developed a strategy of containment through advertising practices using journalistic photos that addressed consumers through stylized representations whose structuring principles were shock, sensationalism, and voyeurism. In these images, Benetton's motives were—and continue to be—more concerned with selling particular products than with offering its publicity mechanisms to diverse cultures as a unifying discourse for solving the great number of social problems.

Representations of Hopelessness

> *Many people have asked why we didn't include a text that would explain the image. But we preferred not to because we think the image is understandable by itself.*
>
> —Luciano Benetton (quoted in Sischy, 1992, p. 69)

> *I think to die is to die. This is a human situation, a human condition....But we know this death happened. This is the real thing and the more real the thing is, the less people want to see it. It's always intrigued me why fake has been accepted and reality has been rejected. At Benetton, we are trying to create an awareness of issues. AIDS is one of today's major modern problems...so I think we have to show something about it.*
>
> —Oliviero Toscani (quoted in Sischy, 1992, p. 69)

In defense of the commercial use of sensational journalistic photographs, which included the aforementioned dying AIDS patient, a terrorist car bombing, a black soldier with a gun strapped over his shoulder holding part of the skeletal remains of another human being, and representations of convicted killers on death row, Benetton's spokespeople combined an assertion of universal values and experiences with the politics of realism. Arguing that such images served as a vehicle for social change by calling attention to the real world, Benetton suggested that its advertising campaign was informed by a representational politics in which the truth of such images is guaranteed by their alleged objective purchase on reality. From this perspective, shocking photos registered rather than engaged an alleged unmediated notion of the truth. This appeal to the unmediated truth effects of photographic imagery was coupled with a claim to universal truths ("to die is to die") that served to deny the historical, social, and political specificity of particular events. Ideologically, this suggested that the value of Benetton's photos resided in their self-referentiality, that is, in their ability to reflect both the unique vision of the sponsor and their validation of a certain construction of reality. Suppressed in this discourse was an acknowledgment that the meaning of such photos resided in their functions within particular contexts.

Before discussing specific examples from Benetton's more recent advertising campaigns, I want to comment briefly on some of the structuring devices at work in the use of the photojournalistic images. All of Benetton's ads depend upon a double movement between decontextualization and recontextualization. To accomplish the former move, the photos militate against a reading in which the context and content of the photo are historically and culturally situated. Overdetermined by the immediacy of the logic of the spectacle, Benetton's photos become suspended in what Stuart Ewen has called "memories of style" (1988, p. 248). That is, by dehistoricizing and decontextualizing the photos, Benetton attempts to render ideology innocent by blurring the conditions of production, circulation, and commodification that present such photos as unproblematically real and true. By denying specificity, Benetton suppresses the history of these images and, in doing so, limits the range of meanings that might be brought into play. At stake here is a denial of how shifting contexts give images different meanings. Of course, the depoliticization that is at work here is not innocent. By failing to rupture the dominant ideological codes (i.e., racism, colonialism, sexism) that structure what I call Benetton's use of hyperventilating (a realism of sensationalism, shock, and spectacle), the ads simply register rather than challenge the dominant social relations reproduced in the photographs.

This process and its effects become clear in analyzing one of Benetton's early controversial ads in which AIDS patient David Kirby is portrayed on his deathbed surrounded by members of his grieving family. On the one hand, this image suppresses the diverse lifestyles, struggles, and realities of individuals in various stages of living with AIDS. In doing so, the Kirby image reinforces dominant representations of people with AIDS, reproducing what Douglas Crimp, in another context, refers to as "what we have already been told or shown about people with AIDS: that they are ravaged, disfigured and debilitated by the syndrome [and that] they are generally...desperate, but resigned to their inevitable deaths" (Crimp, 1992, p. 118).

The appeal to an aesthetic of realism does little to disturb the social and ideological force of such inherited dominant representations. On the contrary, by not providing an analysis of representations of AIDS as a de facto death sentence, relying instead on the clichés enforced through dominant images and their social effects, the Benetton ad reproduces rather than challenges conventional representations that portray people with AIDS as helpless victims.

Benetton's use of photojournalistic images that are decontextualized from any meaningful historical and social context are then recontextualized through the addition of the United Colors of Benetton logo. In the first instance, the logo produces a representational zone of comfort, confirming a playfulness that allows the viewer to displace any ethical or political understanding of the images contained in the Benetton ads. The logo serves to position the audience within a muddled combination of realism and amusement. Public truths revealed in Benetton's images, regardless of how horrifying or threatening, are offered "as a kind of joke in which the reader is invited to participate (the 'joke' is how low can we go?), but its potential dangers are also pretty clear: today aliens from Mars kidnap joggers, yesterday Auschwitz didn't happen, tomorrow who cares what happens" (Hebdige, 1989, p. 83).

Of course, the joke here is that anything is for sale, and social commitment is just another gimmick for selling goods. In this type of representational politics, critical engagement is rendered ineffective by turning the photo and its political referent into an advertisement. If the possibility of social criticism is suggested by the ad, then this is quickly dispelled by the insertion of the logo, which suggests that any complicity between the viewer and the event it depicts is merely ironic. The image ultimately refers to nothing more than a safe space where the logic of the commodity and the marketplace mobilize consumers' desires rather than the struggle over social injustices and conflicts. For instance, in the case of the image of the bloodstained clothes of the Croatian student, the use of the Benetton logo juxtaposes human suffering and promotional culture so as to invite the viewer to position him or herself between the playfulness of commodification and an apocalyptic image rendering social change either ironic or unimaginable. This serves less to situate a critical viewer who can mediate social reality and its attendant problems than to subordinate this viewer to the demands and aesthetic of commerce. Blood circulates in this image as part of an economy of spectacle and fear. Capitalizing upon an aesthetic of irony coupled with a logic of fear, Benetton's representations of blood and human suffering depoliticize and dehistoricize those very images they mark as part of the economy of the social and political.

Recontextualization also appeals to an empty relativism that suggests that such images can be negotiated by different individuals in multiple and varied ways. Benetton claims that such photos generate diverse interpretations. Such an assumption rightly suggests that viewers always mediate and rewrite images in ways that differ from particular ideologies and histories; but when such an assumption remains unqualified, it overlooks how specific contexts, relations of power, and alignments with machines of culture privilege some readings over others. In other words, while individuals produce rather than merely receive meanings, the choices they make and the meanings they produce are not free floating. Such meanings and mediations are, in part, formed within wider social and cultural determinations that propose a range of reading practices that are privileged within dominant and subordinate relations of power. The reading of any text cannot be understood independently of the historical and social experiences that constitute how audiences interpret and identify with other images, modes of representation, and knowledge.

In Benetton ad campaigns, the viewer is afforded no sense of how the aesthetic appeal to realism works to mask "the codes and structures which give photographs meaning as well as the historical contingencies (e.g., patriarchal structures which normalize notions of looking) which give such codes salience" (Solomon-Godeau, 1991, p. 145). There is no sense of how the operations of power inform the construction of social problems depicted in the Benetton ads, nor is there any recognition of the diverse struggles of resistance which attempt to challenge such problems. Within this aestheticization of politics, spectacle foregrounds our fascination with the hyper-real and positions the viewer within a visual moment that simply registers horror and shock without critically responding to it. Roland Barthes has referred to this form of representation as one that positions the viewer within the "immediacy of translation" (Barthes, 1979, p. 72). According to Barthes, this is a form of representational politics that functions as myth, because it abolishes the complexity of human acts; it gives them the simplicity of essences; it does away with all complexity, without going beyond what is immediately visible; it organizes a world without contradictions because it is without depth, a world wide open and wallowing in the evident; and it establishes a blissful clarity: things appear to mean something by themselves without the necessity of mediation or critical analysis (Barthes, 1972, p. 143).

Furthermore, as Stuart Ewen (1988) eloquently explains, the consumer utopia of images and meaning making bereft of history and context ultimately lead to despair over the possibility of social change. He writes: "By reducing all social issues to matters of perception, it is on the perceptual level that social issues are addressed. Instead of social change, there is image change. Brief shows of flexibility at the surface mask intransigence at the core" (p. 264).

Isolated from historical and social contexts, Benetton's images are stripped of their political possibilities and reduced to a spectacle of fascination, horror, and terror that appears to primarily privatize one's response to social events. That is, the form of address both reproduces dominant renderings of the image and translates the possibility of agency into the privatized act of buying goods, rather than engaging forms of self-awareness and social determination. This appears evident in the fact that, while the images have changed, Benetton's approach to advertising over the past 20 year has basically remained the same, further indicating its position outside the realm of social struggle and political change.

Benetton: Twenty Years Later

Benetton recently claimed on its website, "Benetton Group's advertising campaigns are not only a means of communication but an expression of our time." The suggestion here is that Benetton simply reveals rather than produces and legitimates specific relationships between consumerism and the shock of the real. While Benetton has become tamer in recent years as its advertising campaign has parted ways with the shock ads it produced from the 1980s to the turn of the 21st century, it still maintains its core principles of highlighting a kind of cosmopolitan difference and a disingenuous concern with social issues as a vehicle to sell clothes. For example, in 2008, it launched a "global ad campaign called 'Africa works,' showing Africans working for themselves to beat poverty and promote equitable development."[11] Nothing is said, of course, about how capitalism and the very consumerism that Benetton promotes bear some responsibility for the global inequality that created the conditions associated with the individuals in these images. Corporate greed and the massive inequalities in wealth and power produced by neoliberal capitalism are absent from these sanitized narratives. Nothing is said about Western colonialism and the relationship the latter has to the images of hardships and struggles of Africans portrayed in the Benetton ads who have long suffered at the hands of corporations forever on the search for cheap labor and valuable resources. When social problems are not stylistically exploited, difference is colonized and stripped of any political importance in Benetton's ads. For instance, in its summer 2011 ad campaign, it juxtaposed young people of different races and ethnicities, always offsetting each other through the boldness of their contrasting skin colors and made all the more appealing through slightly edgy sterile images of either unity or images of transgression. In one ad, two young women are in their underwear kissing each other. The pleasure quotient of shock has not been dumped, just tamed a bit in the new face of Benetton. Difference as a powerful signifier of racism, hatred of immigrants, state terrorism, and debilitating modes of discrimination is bleached clean from these representations. History, contexts, politics, power, and ethics disappear into the consuming boutique of a depoliticized notion of aesthetic difference and political swamp.

The new pedagogy of mass advertising poses a central challenge to the role cultural workers might play in deepening their politics through a broader understanding of how knowledge is produced, identities shaped, and values articulated as part of a pedagogical practice that circulates within an economy of culture and power that exceeds traditional notions of how certain forms of agency are put into place. The struggle over meaning is no longer one that can be confined to programs in educational institutions and their curricula. Moreover, the struggle over identity can no longer be seriously considered outside the politics of representation and the new formations of consumption. Culture is increasingly constituted by commerce, and the penetration of commodity culture into every facet of daily life has become the major axis of relations of exchange through which corporations actively produce new, increasingly effective forms of address.

This is not to suggest that the politics of consumption in its various circuits of power constitutes an unadulterated form of domination. Such a view is often more defensive than dialectical and less interested in understanding the complex processes by which people desire, choose, and act in everyday life than in shielding the guardians of high modernism, who have always despised popular culture for its vulgarity and association with the masses.[12] What is at stake in the intersection of commerce, advertising, and consumption is the very definition and survival of critical public cultures or those formative spaces and cultures where people learn the knowledge and skills of engaged citizenship and social responsibility. I am referring here to those public spaces predicated on the multiplication of spheres of daily life where people can debate the meaning and consequences of public truths, inject a notion of moral responsibility into representational practices, and collectively struggle to change dominant relations of power. Central to my argument has been the assumption that these corporate-controlled media institutions and the forms of advertising and consumption they promote do not deny politics; they simply reappropriate it. This is a politics that "actively creates one version of the social," one that exists in harmony with market ideologies and initiatives (Hebdige, 1989, p. 89). Such a politics offers no resistance to a version of the social as largely a democracy of images, a public media extravaganza in which politics is defined through the consuming of images.[13]

Everyone concerned about the fate of democracy on a national and global level needs to reformulate the concept of resistance usually associated with these forms of public pedagogy and colonization. Such a formulation has to begin with an analysis of how cultural pedagogy works by problematizing the intersection of power and representation in an ever-expanding realm of images and culture. Representations reach deeply into daily life, contributing to the increased fragmentation and decentering of individual and collective subjects. Not only are the categories of race, gender, sexuality, age, and class increasingly rewritten in highly differentiating and often divisive terms, but the space of the social is further destabilized through niche marketing that constructs identities around lifestyles, ethnicity, fashion, and a host of other commodified elements. Take, for example, the Walt Disney Company's recent campaign, Disney Baby, in which Disney representatives visit maternity wards, give prospective parents "a free Disney Cuddly Bodysuit and ask mothers to sign up for e-mail alerts from DisneyBaby.com" (Barnes, 2011). Disney estimates that this baby market may be worth $36.3 billion annually and is working on a loyalty program, for instance, in which pregnant women might receive free theme-park tickets in return for signing up for email alerts (Barnes, 2011). News Corporation may be guilty of transforming news into propaganda, buying off some members of the British police and corrupting politics, but Disney surely has to give up its claim to innocence when it is equally guilty of corrupting the minds of generations of children, beginning the process as soon as they are born.

Central is the issue here of how power has become an important cultural and ideological form—that is, how power deploys culture and culture deploys power—particularly within the realm of popular culture. Educators, parents, young people, and others need a new map for registering and understanding how power works within various cultural apparatuses to promote modes of education that inscribe desires and identities as well as create multiple points of antagonism and struggle. Also in serious need of consideration is the creation of a new kind of pedagogical politics and pedagogy, organized through guiding narratives that link global and local social contexts, provide new articulations for engaging popular culture within rather than outside new technologies and regimes of representation, and offer a moral language for expanding the struggle over democracy and citizenship to ever-widening spheres of daily life.

Clearly, more is at issue here than understanding how representations work to construct their own systems of meaning, social organizations, and cultural identifications. All of us concerned about the fate of democracy need to take up the challenge of encouraging educators, students, and others to acknowledge our and their complicity in the discourse and pedagogy of market-driven knowledge, images, institutions, and social relations while at the same time bringing the needs and desires if not scandal of hope mobilized by such practices to a principled and persistent crisis. This is not meant to invoke a vulgar critique of the real pleasures of buying, nor to underestimate the diverse ways in which people negotiate the terrain of the market and reappropriate goods through oppositional practices. Nor is it meant to suggest that people are just dupes of market-driven pedagogies. Rather, these conditions require recognition of the political and pedagogical limits of casino capitalism, the power of corporate-controlled mega-media institutions to saturate a society with their beliefs, the role of powerful financial interests and the ultra-wealthy in creating institutions responsible for their active involvement in creating new identities, values, and social relations stripped of any ethical or civic considerations. How else to explain why hedge-fund managers, billionaires such as Bill Gates, and rich conservative foundations are aggressively trying to privatize schools and turn higher education into an adjunct of the corporation. These are all the last outposts of a society in which the spaces for real democratic public spheres and a formative democratic culture reside. Individual and collective agency is about more than buying goods, and social life in its most principled forms points beyond the logic of the market as a guiding principle. It is up to cultural workers and other progressive educators to address this challenge directly as part of global pedagogical movement. Remembering Benetton is not simply an act of nostalgia for a particular advertising campaign. It is, more importantly, a lesson in the role education can play when a corrupted part of the cultural apparatus such as the News Corporation trades in propaganda, violence, commercialization and commodification while repudiating the essential role it might play in providing the information, values, news, narratives, and formative cultures that are essential to a substantive democracy.

Notes

This chapter was originally published on July, 27, 2011, on www.truth-out.org, available at http://truth-out.org/index.php?option=com_k2&view=item&id=2331:from-benetton-to-murdoch-the-culture-of-money-shock-and-schlock

1. See, for instance, *The Politics of Truth: The Selected Writings of C. Wright Mills*, selected by John H. Summers (New York: Oxford University Press, 2008), especially the chapter "The Cultural Apparatus."
2. Some of the issues in this section are drawn from my "Consuming Social Change: The United Colors of Benetton," a chapter in my book *Disturbing Pleasures: Learning Popular Culture* (New York: Routledge, 1994), pp. 3–24.
3. Quoted in Benetton's spring/summer 1992 advertising campaign copy, p. 5. See also Reinhardt, Edwards, & Duganne (Eds.), *Beautiful Suffering: Photography and the Traffic in Pain.*
4. Benetton's spring/summer 1992 Advertising campaign copy, p. 4.
5. Quoted in Noreen O'Leary, "Benetton's True Colors," *Adweek* (August 24, 1992), p. 28.
6. Benetton spring/summer 1992 advertising campaign copy, p. 2.
7. See Warnick, *Promotional Culture*, p. 181.
8. Quoted in Ewen, *All Consuming Images*, p. 247.

9. Benetton fall/winter 1992 advertising campaign literature, p. 2.
10. Oliviero Toscani, quoted in Ingrid Sischy, "Advertising Taboos," p. 69.
11. For an example of these images, see http://www.benetton.com/africaworks-press/en/image_gallery/2_1.html
12. On the dialectics of consumerism, see Mike Featherstone's *Consumer Culture and Postmodernism* (Newbury Park, CA: Sage, 1991); and Mica Nava's *Changing Cultures: Feminism, Youth and Consumerism* (Newbury Park, CA: Sage, 1992).
13. I have taken this idea from the transcript of the television show *The Public Mind* with Bill Moyers (New York: WNET Public Affairs Television, 1989), p. 14.

References

Bailey, D., & Hall. S. (1992). The vertigo of displacement. *Ten8*, *2*(3), p. 15.

Baker, R. (2011, July 21). Murdoch U.S. scandal brewing. WhoWhatWhy.com. Available at http://whowhatwhy.com/2011/07/21/murdoch-us-scandal-brewing/

Barnes, B. (2011, February 6). Disney looking into cradle for customers. *New York Times*, A1. Available at http://www.nytimes.com/2011/02/07/business/media/07disney.html?pagewanted=all

Barthes, R. (1972). *Mythologies* (Annette Lavers, trans.). New York: Noonday.

———. (1979). Shock-photos. In R. Barthes (Richard Howard, trans.), *The Eiffel Tower*. New York: Hill & Wang.

Coupland, D. (1993). *Shampoo planet*. New York: Washington Square Press.

Crimp, D. (1992). Portraits of people with AIDS. In L. Grossberg, C. Nelson, & P. Treichler (Eds.), *Cultural Studies*. New York: Routledge.

Ewen, S. (1988). *All consuming images: The politics of style in contemporary culture*. New York: Basic Books.

Featherstone, M. (1991). *Consumer culture and postmodernism*. Newbury Park, CA: Sage.

Giroux, H. (1994), Consuming social change: The United Colors of Benetton. In Giroux, *Disturbing pleasures: Learning popular culture*, pp. 3–24. New York: Routledge.

Hebdige, D. (1989). After the masses. In S. Hall & M. Jacques (Eds.), *New times: The changing face of politics in the 1990s*. London: Verso.

Mills, C. W. (2008) *The politics of truth: The selected writings of C. Wright Mills* (Selected by John H. Summers). New York: Oxford University Press.

Mabrey, V. (2009, February 11). Catalog of killers. *Sixty minutes*. Transcript available at http://www.cbsnews.com/8301-3475_162-200723.html

Nava, M. (1992). *Changing cultures: Feminism, youth and consumerism*. Newbury Park, CA: Sage.

O'Leary, N. (1992, August 24). Benetton's true colors. *Adweek*, 28.

Payne, A., & Taylor, T. (1992). Introduction: The violence of the public. *Public 6*, 10.

Reinhardt, M., Edwards, H., & Duganne, E. (Eds.). (2007). *Beautiful suffering: Photography and the traffic in pain*. Chicago, IL: University of Chicago Press.

Sischy, I. (1992, April). Advertising taboos: Talking to Luciano Benetton and Oliviero Toscani. *Alternatives*, 69.

Solomon-Godeau, A. (1991). *Photography at the dock: Essays on photographic history, institutions, and practices*. Minneapolis: University of Minnesota Press.
Squires, C. (1992, May). Violence at Benetton. *Artforum 30*, 18–19.
Stevens, M. (1992, December 11). Change the world, buy a sweater. *Chicago Tribune*, 33.
Warnick, A. (1991). *Promotional culture*. Newbury Park, CA: Sage.

3 We Are All in This Thing Together: The Complex Ethics of Social Media Networking

Tony Kashani

One doesn't have here a power which is wholly in the hands of one person who can exercise it alone and totally over the others. It's a machine in which everyone is caught, those who exercise power just as much as those over whom it is exercised.

—Michel Foucault (1980)

THE NEW MEDIA are ubiquitous, all knowing, and Godlike. Social media, whether we like it or not, affect our lives to one degree or another. On July 7, 2005, a series of coordinated terrorist attacks hit three Underground trains and a bus, as the morning rush hour was ending in London. Fifty-two people lost their lives and many more were injured. This was a tragedy of epic proportion, to be sure. How did the world learn about this spectacular incident? The transport system was shut down and many people were trapped in the tunnels. The media had to wait to gain access to the site. But before the conglomerate media could ignite the spectacle-making engine, the evacuees equipped with camera-phones had taken pictures of the carnage and started the distribution process. The popular social media outlet Flickr, generally known for birthday and wedding photos, was especially instrumental in facilitating this organic "amateur" photojournalistic response. In less than 24 hours, people around the globe were aware of the attacks and were sharing photos, anecdotes, and opinions, in effect dictating the terms to the British government and the traditional media (Shirky, 2009). It goes without saying that much information was also hopping on Twitter and Facebook. The power of social media networking cannot be underestimated. In some ways, we cannot escape having to choose what to do about information and knowledge that enters our consciousness vis-à-vis social media in our everyday life. But are we looking at the ethics of social media? In this concise treatment, I will examine the evolution of social media and the ethical implications in relation to human culture.

Social Contract

Given that almost all human beings are social animals and we all have desire and aptitude to form communities, it's fair to use the theory of social contract to gain a better understanding of ethics of social media. According to this theory, the social contract defines the scope and limits of morality; therefore, it's morally right to obey the rules of the contract and morally wrong to transgress those rules (Rachels, 2003). We can logically conclude that our moral obligations begin and end with the rules of the contract that members of our civil society have agreed upon.

The 17th-century influential British philosopher Thomas Hobbes defined morality as the solution to practical problems that self-interested human beings are confronted with as they try to thrive within the societies in which they live (Rachels, 2003). According to Hobbes, if there were no social rules and no commonly accepted calculus to make sure the rules were obeyed and enforced, then we would be finding ourselves in chaos. This is analogous to the Wild West in the 19th-century U.S. or today's free zones in countries like Pakistan, where people do as they please with no regard to state laws. Hobbes had a name for this; he called it "the state of nature." But given the age of neoliberalism we find ourselves in, with Hobbesian ideas of self-interest politics and the increasing complexity of human interconnection being stark realities, this calculus is highly problematic. How does one adhere to the ethical rules when others think there are no ethics and there is only the marketplace? Furthermore, how does one get a grip in what Zygmunt Bauman (2008) has called "liquid times"? In the digital paradigm, things change with lightning rapidity and they are fluid. Facebook changes its policies with regularity and in turn its procedures for sharing information, which in turn affect the ethics of such sharing. Given the role Facebook is playing in global history as a platform for civil society to express thoughts, disseminate information, and organize, it occupies an important place on the social contract map. How does one agree to the terms that are subject to change in the age of speed?

In contrast to Hobbes, the 18th-century moral philosopher Jean-Jacques Rousseau had some other ideas. I think it will pay dividends if we look at Rousseau's ideas a bit. A central issue of Rousseau was how an individual could retain his or her freedom, whilst at the same time accepting the terms of a social contract, and the requirement that an individual is bound by the wishes of society as a whole. He was no egoist. How did he propose we do this? Rousseau spoke of a notion known as the "general will." His argument for general will is a normative one. He argued that an individual must give himself or herself totally, including all his/her rights, to the whole community (Rousseau, 2004). The presupposition is that the general will is sovereign, and individuals find their own freedom by conforming to it. People who think in terms of general will assume that to set aside one's individual, personal will, and to accept the general will, is to discover one's higher aspirations and moral freedom. Theoretically speaking, in a democracy, social norms operate this way. But what happens in actual practice is the subject of my inquiry here.

What Actually Happens

It is a fact well known to social scientists, if not the general public, that the relative anonymity of the Internet brings out the worst ethics in (some) people in many instances. If one spends an hour navigating the popular social site YouTube, reading the comments left in response to various video uploads, one can read some of the vilest human communications ever recorded in the virtual universe. And this is not necessarily content driven, as the most benign uploads can also attract racist, sexist, homophobic, xenophobic, and pathologically disturbed comments by those who hide under the conduit of their handle names. Are punishment and the fear of punishment the only things that deter people from choosing to do the wrong thing? To be sure, vulgarity does not dominate the social media world. But why does so much ugliness flush out when people know they can get away with it? What cultural forces teach such behavior to the less-developed members of our society? What is culture in the first place?

Culture is defined in the *Dictionary of Sociology and Related Sciences* as follows:

> A collective name for all behavior patterns socially acquired and transmitted by means of symbols; hence a name for all the distinctive achievements of human groups, including not only such items as language, tool-making, industry, art, science, law, government, morals and religion, but also the material instruments or artifacts in which cultural achievements are embodied and by which intellectual features are given practical effect, such as buildings, tools, machines, communication devices, art objects….As culture is transmitted by processes of teaching and learning, whether formal or informal, by what is called "inter-learning," the essential part of culture is to be found in patterns embodied in the social traditions of the group, that is, the knowledge, ideas, beliefs, values, standards and sentiments prevalent in the group (Fairchild, 1970, p. 80).

Suppose we use the above as a working definition in this inquiry. Then what are the forces that are embodied in the social traditions of the group (i.e., a society) that generate the knowledge, ideas, beliefs, values, and standards for that society? I have argued that Hollywood, for instance, is a cultural force that teaches people history, philosophy of living, gender roles, codes of behavior, and tastes for entertainment among other things (Kashani, 2009). But with the emergence of social media as a collective cultural force, we are witnessing a convergence of Hollywood-like media with *new media*, particularly social media. Whether we look at it from a Hobbesian or Rousseauian lens, new social contract terms are generated by the collective power of social media. It is as if a piece of news has to go through the new media filtering process before it is accepted as solid and "reliable" news. Furthermore, one can argue that reality is, in many ways, interposed by new media, if not for everyone, for many people on the planet—this is particularly true in the U.S.

When Facebook was *Time* magazine's cover story in May 2010, it had nearly 500 million users (Fletcher, 2010). Gregory Lyons, a top analyst at the global marketing firm iCrossing, predicted that if the current trends continue, Facebook would reach the magical number of one billion users in August 2012 (Wasserman, 2012). It announced that it exceeded that number in October 2012 (Fowler, 2012). In 2012, YouTube claimed that on the average four billion videos were viewed on the site each day (Reisinger, 2012).

I would argue that social media such as Facebook and YouTube are (global) cultural forces of unprecedented magnitude in history of humankind. One look at the dramatic scenes from the uprising in Egypt proves the networking power of such media. Many people mistakenly have dubbed the Egyptian revolution the "Facebook Revolution," given how activists used the networking power of Facebook to inform and organize. In actuality, Facebook and YouTube were simply platforms upon which real people, risking and some losing their lives, facilitated an unlikely democratic revolution. The video clip, captured by a cell phone, showing the government car running into the nonviolent protesters and in turn injuring many people was viewed nearly two million times in one week after it was uploaded on YouTube. The other most-watched video was that of the protester shot and killed by the police in a street in Alexandria. A quick reading of the overwhelming number of comments reveals good ethics on behalf of most of the responders. People recognized a fight for justice and freedom and for the most part supported the organic uprising of the young Egyptians.

The Ideology-Shifting Forces of Social Media

When discussing social media ethics, we are necessarily considering human behavior according to the dominant ideology. There are of course free thinkers who participate in social media activities, but my observations tell me they are in the minority. The most pervasive ideology that cuts across political affiliations (e.g., Democrats and Republicans) is that of neoliberal capitalism. Given that neoliberalism is the dominant discourse on a global scale, it is important that we understand its logic and politics in order to see its impact on people's moral behavior. The advocates of neoliberal ways are holding key influential positions in government, finance, military, culture industry, and education in the U.S. and other influential countries such as Germany and the U.K. Different media, such as news media, television, and cinema, play integral roles in this paradigm of technologically driven capitalism, and human beings are indeed impacted directly. It seems that we are no longer individual citizens but packages of perception. Not unlike our politicians who are sold to us as brands, we too are "brands." We are increasingly becoming interconnected to the extent that what we do impacts our position in the workplace, and it's not always a positive impact. There is a great potential there to excavate forces for social change.

In the U.S., almost all media are owned and operated by neoliberal capitalists and ideologues, giving American citizens a constructed worldview that attempts to take away their agency and transform them into docile consumers. But it is not that simple. This is a contested terrain. Many people find ways to resist and react in the ways that Michel Foucault (1980) called "counter-conduct." This condition begs a question: how can concerned citizens confront this powerful wave and get the nation back on a democratic trajectory? There are examples that prove to us that may be a possibility. The Occupy Movement, for instance, is debating collectively the various responses to the above question. The buzz words such as "99 percent vs. 1 percent" use the logic of capitalistic media to grab the public attention and have proven effective. The traditional media do not cover the debate, but social media with naturally a democratic access, take over this task. In some ways, as the London bombing coverage vis-à-vis Flickr demonstrated, the ethics of social media obligates, morally, the citizen social media users to turn the tables and set the agenda for all media.

Pew Research's Project for Excellence in Journalism recently published a report on news coverage through YouTube (2012) which concluded that nearly 35 percent of most-searched-for subjects were news events. Additionally, this 15-month study revealed that nearly 40 percent of most-watched news video clips were produced by ordinary citizens with no professional or academic background in journalism. As published on Pew Research's site for the Pew Research Center's Project for Excellence in Journalism (2012), some of the main findings of this study were the following:

- The most popular news videos tended to depict natural disasters or political upheaval—usually featuring intense visuals. With a majority of YouTube traffic (70%) outside the U.S., the three most popular storylines worldwide over the 15-month period were non–U.S. events. The Japanese earthquake and tsunami was No. 1 (and accounted for 5% of all the 260 videos), followed by elections in Russia (5%), and unrest in the Middle East (4%).
- News events are inherently more ephemeral than other kinds of information, but at any given moment news can outpace even the biggest entertainment videos. In 2011, news events were the most searched term on YouTube four months out of 12, according to YouTube's internal data: the Japanese Earthquake [*sic*], the killing of Osama bin Laden, a fatal motorcycle accident, and news of a homeless man who spoke with what those producing the video called a "god-given gift of voice." Yet over time certain entertainment videos can have a cumulative appeal that will give them higher viewership.
- Citizens play a substantial role in supplying and producing footage. More than a third of the most watched videos (39%) were clearly identified as coming from citizens. Another 51% bore the logo of a news organization, though some of that footage, too, appeared to have been originally shot by users rather than journalists. (5% came from corporate and political groups, and the origin of another 5% was not identified.)
- Citizens are also responsible for posting a good deal of the videos originally produced by news outlets. Fully 39% of the news pieces originally produced by a news organization were posted by users. (The rest of the most popular news videos of the last 15 months, 61%, were posted by the same news organizations that produced the reports.) As with other social media, this has multiple implications for news outlets. Audiences on YouTube are reshaping the news agenda, but they are also offering more exposure to the content of traditional news outlets.
- The most popular news videos are a mix of edited and raw footage. Some pundits of the digital revolution predicted that the public, free to choose, would prefer to see video that was unmediated by the press. The most viewed news videos on YouTube, however, come in various forms. More than half of the most-viewed videos, 58%, involved footage that had been edited, but a sizable percentage, 42%, was raw footage. This mix of raw and edited video, moreover, held true across content coming from news organizations and that produced by citizens. Of videos produced by news organizations, 65% were edited, but so were 39% of what came from citizens.

- Personalities are not a main driver of the top news videos. No one individual was featured in even 5% of the most popular videos studied here—and fully 65% did not feature any individual at all. Within the small segment of popular videos that are focused on people, President Barack Obama was the most popular figure (featured in 4% of the top videos worldwide). These ranged from speeches posted in their entirety to satirical ads produced by his political opponents.
- Unlike in traditional TV news, the lengths of the most popular news videos on YouTube vary greatly. The median length of the most popular news videos was 2 minutes and 1 second, which is longer than the median length of a story package on local TV news (41 seconds) but shorter than the median length on national network evening newscasts (2 minutes and 23 seconds). But the variation in the length of the YouTube videos stands out even more. While traditional news tends to follow strict formulas for length, the most popular news videos on YouTube were fairly evenly distributed—from under a minute (29%), one to two minutes (21%), two to five minutes (33%) and longer than five (18%).

This is about setting agendas. According to the *agenda-setting theory*, which has a merit in today's media-driven society, the media aren't always successful at telling us what to think, but they are quite successful at telling us what to think about (McCombs & Shaw, 1972). The Pew study shows that with proper ethics, everyday people can simply set their own agenda and choose what to think about. The organizing power of social media such as YouTube, Twitter, Flickr, and Facebook in tandem with the inevitable media convergence cannot be overestimated. Social media are forces that can transform a dominant ideology by utilizing the very same ideology's advanced capitalist tools. One caveat that merits our consideration is that the powerful media forces will try to mitigate citizens' efforts in setting the agenda by partnering with various new media. There are examples we can look at such as NBC's partnership with Facebook in covering the London 2012 Olympics and potential future cooperations. On the other hand, after 16 years of trying to dominate the Internet news paradigm by partnering with Microsoft, NBC decided to call it quits. In the U.S., the Democratic Party has been trying very hard to co-opt the organically grown Occupy Movement with mixed results. It is important to note that the party bosses have been relying on social media outlets for the most part to obtain desired acquiescence. They are banking on successful tactics of the past such as the Internet-driven Obama presidential campaign to pay off in this case too. Will it happen? The cat may be out of the bag in this case; and history has proven that when an idea's time arrives, no force can stop it.

Conclusion

Social media such as Facebook, LinkedIn, Twitter, and YouTube have cultivated a new private life for many of us. For many people around the globe (not the majority of humanity, to be sure, given the huge digital divide between developed nations' citizens and their counterparts in developing countries), the "private" and "public" have converged via social networking. In the United States more than 66 percent of adults are active members of social networking sites (Skelton, 2012). The fact of the matter is that Facebook and company have facilitated a paradigm where their users are perfectly comfortable sharing their most intimate private moments with perfect strangers who happen to be their "friends." To cultivate an open-book attitude is the goal for those who are looking to benefit from the genuine interests and feelings people share with one another. Multinational corporations understand quite well that information is the most valuable commodity in the age of neoliberalism. In some ways, Facebook users make a Faustian deal with corporations, knowing full well their information is shared and studied for future exploitation. But they also understand that their information is shared and studied elsewhere. For example, cell-phone service providers that offer us so-called smart phones to manage our lives have direct access to much more sensitive information than the Facebook managers would. With social networking media we, the users, have some degree of control in what and how much of our information can be revealed. Furthermore, we have the power of imagination and creativity to find ways of counter-conduct and utilize social media for better ethics and social transformation.

Given the complexity of new media and the sophistication of global citizens, it is a colossal mistake to declare the corporate juggernaut of globalization and mindless consumerism the winner. This race has only begun and there are many contestations to come. To be political and ethical is to develop new faculties of critical perspective and becoming informed citizens who wish to actively participate in creating a new media culture that helps societies get closer to the Greek invention known as democracy. Once we close the digital divide and empower even more citizens around the globe, resistance and active response will become part of everyday life of the world citizen, and he or she can, in the spirit of cosmopolitanism, practice unassailable ethics for an egalitarian world. What role will social media play in this narrative? We have a moral obligation to learn and teach about the complexities of new media, and in turn utilize social media to play the appropriate ethical role in the theater of everyday life.

References

Bauman, Z. (2008). *Liquid times: Living in an age of uncertainty*. Malden, MA: Polity.

Fairchild, H. P. (1970). *Dictionary of sociology and related sciences*. New York: Littlefield, Adams & Company.

Fletcher, D. (2010, May 31). Facebook: Friends without borders. *Time*, 32–38.

Foucault, M. (1980). *Power/knowledge* (C. Gordon, Trans.). New York: Pantheon.

Fowler, G. (2012). Facebook: One billion and counting. WSJ.com. Available at http://online.wsj.com/article/SB10000872396390443635404578036164027386112.html

Kashani, T. (2009). *Deconstructing the mystique: An interdisciplinary introduction to cinema*. Dubuque, IA: Kendall/Hunt Press.

McCombs, M., & Shaw, D. L. (1972). The agenda-setting function of the mass media. *Public Opinion Quarterly*, *36*, 176–185.

Pew Research Center's Project for Excellence in Journalism (2012, July 16). YouTube & news: A new kind of visual news. Available at http://www.journalism.org/analysis_report/youtube_news

Rachels, J. (2003). *The elements of moral philosophy*. New York: McGraw-Hill.

Reisinger, D. (2012, May 21). YouTube users uploading 72 hours of video each minute. Cnet. Available at http://news.cnet.com/8301-1023_3-57438332-93/youtube-uploading-72-hours-of-video

Rousseau, J. J. (2004). *The social contract and discourses* (G. D. H. Cole, Trans.). London, U.K.: Orion House.

Shirky, C. (2008). *Here comes everybody*. New York: Penguin.

Skelton, A. (2012, March 9). Social demographics: Who's using today's biggest networks. Mashable.com. Available at http://mashable.com/2012/03/09/social-media-demographics/

Wasserman, T. (2012, January 12). Facebook to hit 1 billion user mark in August. Mashable.com. Available at http://mashable.com/2012/01/12/facebook-1-billion-users/

4 Ritalin: Panic in the USA

Toby Miller

> *How has it come to pass that in* fin-de-siècle *America, where every child from preschool onward can recite the "anti-drug" catechism by heart, millions of middle- and upper-middle class children are being legally drugged with a substance so similar to cocaine that, as one journalist accurately summarized the science, "it takes a chemist to tell the difference"?*
>
> —Mary Eberstadt (1999)

RITALIN IS a popular pharmaceutical that keeps young people quiet and focused but attracts intense opprobrium. Beginning with an account of the dimensions of Ritalin's use in the United States and controversies surrounding it, I outline how this might be understood in moral-panic terms, examining the role of the psy-function and conflicts of interest, coverage in popular culture, and the response of government. Now, in many cases, progressives have criticized moral panics, recuperating moral-panic folk devils as semiotic guerrillas struggling against authority. In this instance, however, the scene is too complex and multifaceted for that theorization. There are no good guys; there is lots of panic, from all political-economic quarters (some of it justified), and none of it straightforward.

Use and Attendant Controversy

In 2004, attention deficit hyperactivity disorder (ADHD) medication sales in the United States added up to over $2.7 billion, thanks to more than 33 million prescriptions. Sales rose to $3 billion in 2006, with the most popular being Ritalin. Ritalin induces moral apoplexy because it works similarly to cocaine, though more slowly. A link has been established between its medical applications and recreational drug use, starting in Sweden in the 1960s, where it was subsequently removed from distribution. The U.S. Drug Enforcement Administration (DEA) designates it as a Schedule II substance, a categorization that stigmatizes drugs as liable to lead to abuse.[1] In 1995, the DEA declined to lower regulatory controls because of the drug's capacity to suppress appetite, induce wakefulness, and make people happy.[2]

Peter Breggin, one of the most visible contemporary critics of pharmacological psychiatry, stigmatizes Ritalin as an "iatrogenic drug epidemic" that generates mindless obedience, suppresses emotions and ideas, and diminishes self-esteem.[3] Other critics suggest that the psychologisation and therapisation of teaching have produced a rush to Ritalin. Schools in the United States have supposedly become mental health institutions, threatening parents with removal of their children from classes if the children attend without medication. Political conservatives attribute this trend to egalitarian educational philosophies, which they allege can make teachers responsible for students' performance against a presumed *tabula rasa* of equal innate ability. They contend that this tendency, along with pharmacology's displacement of old-style physical sanctions as a means of disciplining children, has encouraged educators to put their charges on Ritalin. Alternatively, it has been suggested that "high-stakes" testing—with funds allocated to school districts based upon improved student test scores—compels educationalists to recommend Ritalin to heighten performance. Indeed, property values, jobs, and salaries can depend upon grades. Meanwhile, critics accuse the United States government of exacerbating the trend by creating incentives to define pupils as disabled through special-education programs that support low-income parents and schools once children are diagnosed with ADHD. This becomes a concern of progressives, too, as they note the medicalisation of education and the advent of "teachers as sickness brokers for ADHD" via a formal role allotted by psychiatry, something duly exploited by pharmacorps' assiduous use of websites to promote products in ways that masquerade as disinterested informational clearinghouses. The Ohio State Board of Pharmacy has expressed worries that these programs heighten stimulant prescriptions, while both CBS's *Eye on America* and the DEA disparagingly refer to Ritalin® as "the fourth R in schools." In 1999, the Colorado Board of Education resolved to discourage teachers from recommending Ritalin. In 2000, the drug's manufacturer, Novartis, along with the 20,000-strong parents' rights group Children and Adults with Attention Deficit Disorders (CHADD) and the American Psychiatric Association faced ultimately unsuccessful class-action lawsuits in Florida, New Jersey, California and Texas that charged them with conspiring to drive up demand for Ritalin and suppressing warnings about its risks to the nervous and cardiovascular systems.[4]

True believers argue that concerns about the drug are driven by illegitimate anxieties about the number and rate of diagnoses, pointing to its high therapeutic safety index, a figure derived from dividing a toxic dose by a therapeutic one. But Ritalin may produce anorexia; "intermittent drug holidays" are recommended to ensure normal growth; and there are concerns over its role in the etiology of tics and Tourette's syndrome. Long-term use (beyond 14 months) has barely been studied, as the pharmaceutical industry is mostly interested in measuring short-term effects of medications. In the period between 1990 and 2004, of the 2,353 drugs that the Food and Drug Administration approved and required pharmacorps to study via post-sales research, just 6 percent were scheduled for further investigation by the industry.[5]

Moral Panics

The mixture is there, from all sides of science, politics, and commerce, for a moral panic. Moral panics are usually short-lived spasms that index ideological contradictions about economic inequality. Exaggerating a social problem, they symbolize it in certain groups, predict its future, then conclude or change. Part of society is used to represent (and sometimes distort) a wider problem—youth violence is a suitable case for panic about citizenship, systemic class inequality is not; adolescent behavior and cultural style are questionable, capitalist degeneracy is not; rap is a problem, the situation of urban youth is not. Particular kinds of individuals are labeled as dangerous to social well-being because of their "deviance" from agreed-upon norms of the general good. Once identified, their life practices are then interpreted from membership of a group and vice versa. Often generated by the state or the media, then picked up by interest groups and social movements (or vice versa), the impact of moral panics is generally disproportionate to the "problems" they bring into being. The dual role of experts and media critics in the constitution of moral panics sees the former testify to their existence and the latter sensationalize and diurnalise them—making the risks attributed to a particular panic seem like a new, terrifying part of everyday life. The cumulative impact of this alliance between specialist and popular knowledge is a heightened sense of risk about and among the citizenry in general. When U.S. television ratings are measured— each February, May, July, and November—news programs allocate massive space to supposed risks to viewers. The idea is to turn anxiety and sensation into spectatorship and money. The epithet once used to deride local television journalism in the United States—"if it bleeds, it leads"—today applies to network news, where the correlation between national crime statistics and crime coverage shows no rational linkage. The drive to create "human-interest" stories from blood has become a key means of generating belief in a risk society through moral panics about personal safety. Even when crime rates plunge, media discourse about crime rises: as the number of murders declines, press attention to them does the opposite. Similarly, school drug use may diminish, but audiences believe it increases.

The Ritalin controversy in the United States occurs at a meeting point of neoliberalism, Social Darwinism, and religiosity; the perfect storm for generating a moral panic. The distinction between therapy and enhancement becomes difficult to sustain, with ADHD's classroom *impairment* and Ritalin's classroom *improvement* mutually defining one another, in ways described by staff of the President's Council on Bioethics as "subjective" and "fuzzy." Such topics became a matter of legal redress when some medical students who failed their National Board of Medical Examiners tests claimed this was due to ADHD and sued the board for additional exam time—unsuccessfully, because the courts found that their completion of medical school indicated they could perform at an above average level intellectually. Many litigants have used the Americans With Disabilities Act against dismissal for poor work performance caused by ADHD but have lost virtually every court case. The National Collegiate Athletic Association, on the other hand, allows athletes with proof of ADHD to take stimulants. Put another way, when medicalised, these drugs are legitimate; when used as pathways to transcendence they are not.[6]

The Psy-function and Conflicts of Interest

Part of this panic derived from a crisis within the psy-function. Pediatricians and family practitioners write most prescriptions for Ritalin in the United States, thus removing it from the exclusive clutches of psychiatrists (the traditional gatekeepers of mind-altering drugs), who in turn argue that this leads to over-prescription. Of adolescents treated for depression in Oregon in 1998, 60 percent were prescribed drugs not by psychiatrists but pediatricians. In North Carolina in 1999, the figure was 72 percent. In addition, psychologists seek the right to prescribe medication and psychiatrists seek to discredit them. It's significant that the American Medical Association and the American Psychiatric Association ban members from participating in U.S. torture, but the American Psychological Association does not. For much of the 1990s, the military granted psychologists the right to prescribe medication, and they hope to have this renewed by participating in interrogations. This is happening in a context where health maintenance organizations

(HMOs) have undermined previously hegemonic powerbrokers through a discourse of bureaucratic-managerial commodification. There has been a rapid decline of insurance-company support for family therapy since the advent of wholesale managed care versus fee-for-service in the mid-1990s. HMOs want to erase symptoms and reduce long-term, face-to-face and in-patient treatment. They will only fund four to six therapeutic appointments before the use of pharmacology, paying psychiatrists much more for follow-up visits to evaluate the impact of drugs than to meet a child's family. Lance Clawson, a fellow at the American Academy of Child and Adolescent Psychiatry, suggested on C-SPAN in 2003 that the refusal of HMOs to fund sufficient meetings with physicians encouraged the early prescription of Ritalin. The drug has had its own makeover as a cost-cutting policy technology, a substitution effect for what had become an annual hospital cost to insurance firms of $30 billion for children.[7]

Other conflict-of-interest concerns have also caused controversy. In reaction to organic bottom-up patient groups that have been successful in goading and criticizing medical capital, big pharma has established and sponsored pseudo-civil-society arms of their publicity campaigns (Rose, 2006, p. 142). CHADD is one of many front organizations masquerading as organic consumer groups that lobby on behalf of their key sub-structural base—in this case, the pharmaceutical sector—by claiming to deliver "science-based, evidence-based information."[8] In the words of the *British Medical Journal*, the reality is that entities "[o]stensibly engaged in raising public awareness about under-diagnosed and undertreated problems" are part of corporate marketing and surveillance campaigns, creating comprehensive media platforms of experts, victims and advocates. The United Nations International Narcotics Board has issued a warning about CHADD's responsibility for the rate of Ritalin consumption.[9]

Popular Culture

Ritalin has also attracted major media attention, contradictorily tied to neoliberal marketing struggles over youth that parallel Ritalin's chronology. By the late 1960s and early 1970s, popular magazines were locked in a contest with color television for audiences. They reacted by addressing young people both as readers (through stories on popular culture) and as problems (through generational stereotyping). This practice continued as the cultural industries promoted the existence of catchy-sounding generational cohorts to advertisers ("the Greatest Generation," "Baby Boomers," "Generation X," "Generation Y," and "Generation Rx") with supposedly universal tendencies and failings. When the Partnership for a Drug-Free America (free of recreational drugs, not corporate ones) released a report on teens in 2005, the bourgeois media leapt at the neologism "Generation Rx" as part of an emergent moral panic over prescription abuse—without noting this was just the second occasion such substances had been included in a national survey.[10]

Pop-psychology books have also picked up on anxieties from the anti-psychiatry movement about both the disorder and its drug, represented by such denunciations of Ritalin as *The Myth of the Hyperactive Child, and Other Means of Child Control* by Peter Schrag and Diane Divoky (1975); Gerald Coles' *Learning Mystique* (1987); and Scientology founder and science-fiction writer L. Ron Hubbard's repeated attacks (Breggin, 1998, p. 31). The genre drew new strength in the 1990s in the wake of Prozac's popularization and associated debates about antidepressants, via Breggin's *Toxic Psychiatry* (first published in 1991) and *Talking Back to Ritalin* (1998), Lawrence Diller's *Running on Ritalin* (1998), Thomas Armstrong's *The Myth of the A.D.D. Child* (1997), and Richard De Grandpre's *Ritalin Nation* (2000). The debate has trickled into popular literature as well through Robin Cook's novel *Acceptable Risk* (1996).

Not surprisingly, from the 1970s, horror stories about Ritalin began appearing in the bourgeois U.S. press, as part of its drive to identify appealing topics unrelated to old definitions of news. In the late 1980s, there were articles critical of ADHD and Ritalin in the *New York Times*, the *Wall Street Journal*, the *Washington Post*, and the *Los Angeles Times*, and a segment on ABC's *Nightline* (Breggin, 1998, pp. 180, 183). *Good Housekeeping* magazine queried "the rush to Ritalin," dubbing it "kiddie cocaine" and suggesting that "at the slightest sign of trouble—a child keeps running back and forth to the water fountain, has an unruly week pushing other kids on the playground, or plays drums on his desk with pencils—parents are circled by the school's teachers, psychologists, and even principals, all pushing Ritalin" (Russell, 1997). Between 2000 and 2003, Ritalin made guest appearances on *Dateline NBC*, CNN's *Larry King Live* (featuring George Bush Minor's dyslexic brother and ADHD-diagnosed nephew explaining why Ritalin must be abjured), *48 Hours*, and *Eye on America* from CBS, and Cleveland's WKYC-TV. These programs screened investigative reports and idiot punditry on Ivy-League Ritalin abuse and drug dealing, emergency-room visits, and school complicity. PBS and A&E ran documentaries, with "journalist" Bill Kurtis intoning that Ritalin was challenging "the very essence of childhood itself." The *New York Post* headlined CHADD as a "Ritalin pusher" and the *New York Times* noted the panic.[11] Activist Jim Hightower referred to "babies on drugs" and other critics dubbed it the "chemical cosh" or "a cane-for-the-brain."[12] The war on drugs' slogan was accused of transmogrifying into "not medicating your child is unethical."[13] And *Newsweek* went from an unfortunately worded endorsement of Ritalin as "one of the raving successes in psychiatry" to warning that it "may be causing some hidden havoc…in an impatient culture."[14]

Government

The first congressional report on behavior-modification drugs and children was inspired by Ritalin as far back as 1970, while hearings were prompted in 2000 by a story in the *Washington Post* entitled "Omaha Pupils Given 'Behavior' Drugs," which raised the specter of mind control and merged with popular concerns about diet to suggest a more "natural" treatment.

The House of Representatives Subcommittee on Early Childhood, Youth and Families of the Committee on Education and the Workforce queried whether "youthful rambunctiousness" or "serious stressors like divorce or neglect" saw Ritalin erroneously prescribed. Congressman Bill Goodling said it "may be the biggest drug problem we have in the country, and it drives me up the wall to see little children get hooked so early" (House of Representatives, 2000, pp. 7, 9).

A scientific study in 2000 stated that in the previous decade, the prescription of stimulants as treatment of ADHD in U.S. children aged five to fourteen had increased dramatically, with use by those aged from two to four growing threefold between 1991 and 1995. These findings were confirmed by subsequent research.[15] The National Institute of Mental Health reacted strongly, rejecting prescription to large numbers of preschoolers (which the DEA had never approved) and funding a large research project to evaluate that group. Skeptics argued that their findings would eventually legitimate the practice. In one New York case, a local school district had informed the Child Protective Services Unit that parents had refused to put their child on the drug. The CPSU then accused the parents of child abuse—a charge that was not sustained in court and which led to 11 states insisting teachers not mention Ritalin or ADHD to families. Then the House's Government Reform Committee heard testimony from Lisa Marie Presley on behalf of the Church of Scientology that children were being "drugged," and ADHD was an invention that obscured the real problems of allergies, lead, hearing, and eyesight. It was, in the words of the Church's Citizens Commission on Human Rights, "[p]sychiatry's cash cow diagnosis" and had helped to kill Kurt Cobain.[16]

In 2003, the House Education and the Workforce Committee introduced a Child Medication Safety Act to protect parents from schools' requiring them to have their children medicated. It was sponsored by several leading Republicans, including then-speaker Dennis Hastert. *USA Today* proposed a national debate on the growing gender gap in educational attainment, under the headline "Girls Get Extra Help While Boys Get Ritalin," blaming the decline in male scholastic performance on the dominance of female teachers, the absence of "advocates," and the easy availability of Ritalin, as opposed to holistic, pedagogical answers to their difficulties. This was part of a clever reversal of arguments for gender equity, a standard move by the right to reassert patriarchy by deconstructive sleight of hand and a return to longstanding anxieties about the impact of female role models on young men.[17]

Conclusion

David Healy, a former secretary of the Royal College of Psychiatry, suggests that Ritalin and its kind "lie midway between magic bullets and snake oil," and the noted pharmacological researcher Julie Zito asks, "[h]ow do you even know who the kid is anymore?" when multiple prescriptions expose children to "a potpourri of target symptoms and side effects"[18] At the same time, the science in support of therapeutic rather than pharmacological interventions is gathering strength—with the American Psychological Association and the American Academy of Child and Adolescent Psychiatry favoring behavior modification as first steps since 2006 and clinicians blaming "permissive or uncertain child-rearing" for ADHD. Meanwhile, the latest jag for big pharma is paying doctors to talk up the likelihood of bipolar disorder among children—a bold untapped market/diagnosis—even as the Child Medication Safety Act of 2003 is designed to "protect children and their parents from being coerced into administering a controlled substance"[19] Concerns about mental health, educational success, drug use, and corporate commodification have joined left and right in a bipartisan panic culture, orchestrated around a little pill's impact on turning little people into big citizens. Unless the nature of corporate–state relations is fundamentally questioned as part of the debate about ADHD and its treatment, this panic will prove unproductive. But there are no ultimately sympathetic folk devils in need of recuperation in this story. The devils are objects, not people. Instead, this moral panic features unpleasant conflicts of interest, involving everyone from corporations to civil society and the professions.

Notes

This chapter was previously published in *Cultural Studies Review*, *14*(2), 103-112, (2008).

1. The DEA designation guarantees good data on levels of prescription, as the state sets an annual quota on the production of Schedule II substances in response to pharmaceutical industry requests and the amount of sales by pharmacies; see Lawrence H. Diller, *Running on Ritalin: A Physician Reflects on Children, Society, and Performance in a Pill* (New York: Bantam, 1998), p. 27.
2. Michelle Jarboe, "Black Market for ADD Drugs," Youthradio.org, August 29, 2006; "Really Desperate Housewives," *Economist*, 9 December 2006, p. 64; Eileen Barry, "N. E. Is Leader in Rate of Ritalin Purchases," *Boston Globe*, 14 May 2002, p. A1; Brian Vastag, "Pay Attention: Ritalin Acts Much Like Cocaine," *Journal of the American Medical Association, 286*(8), 2001, pp. 905–906; Christiane Poulin, "Medical and Nonmedical Stimulant Use Among Adolescents: From Sanctioned to Unsanctioned Use," *Canadian Medical Association Journal/Journal de la associationmédical canadienne,165*(8), 2001, pp. 1039–1044; Diller, *Running on Ritalin*, p. 348, n. 86; National Institute on Drug Abuse, NIDA InfoFacts: Methylphenidate (Ritalin) (Bethesda, MD, 2006).
3. P. R. Breggin, *Toxic Psychiatry: Why Therapy, Empathy, and Love Must Replace the Drugs, Electroshock, and Biochemical Theories of the "New Psychiatry."* (New York: St. Martin's Press, 1994), pp. 303–305, 309.
4. Lawrence H. Diller, "Just Say Yes to Ritalin," Salon.com, 25 September, 2000; K. Livingstone, "Ritalin: Miracle Drug or Cop-out?" *Public Interest*, *127*, 1997; L. Sax, "Ritalin: Better Living Through Chemistry?" *The World and I*, *15*, 2000, p. 286; John Murlowe, "Public Schools: Pushing Drugs?" *Investor's Business Daily*, 16 October 1997, pp. 1–2; Christine B. Phillips, "Medicine Goes to School: Teachers as Sickness Brokers for ADHD," *PLOS Medicine*, *3*(4), 2006, pp. 433–435; Gordon Tait, "Pathologising Difference, Governing Personality," *Asia-Pacific Journal of Teacher Education*, *29*(1), 2001, pp. 93–102; Alec McHoul & Mark Rapley, "Re-Presenting Culture and the Self," *Theory & Psychology*, *15*(4), 2005, pp. 442–444 and "A Case of Attention-Deficit/Hyperactivity Disorder Diagnosis: Sir Karl and Francis B. Slug It Out on the Consulting Room Floor," *Discourse & Society*, *16*(3), 2005, 419–449; House of Representatives, Subcommittee on Early Childhood, Youth and Families, Committee on Education and the Workforce, *Ritalin Use among Youth: Examining the Issues and Concerns*, 16 May 2000; Terrance Woodworth, *Ritalin—The Fourth R in Schools: Discussing the Use of Psychotropic Drugs for Youth: DEA Congressional Testimony before the Committee on Education and*

the Work Force: Subcommittee on Early Childhood, Youth, and Families, United States Drug Enforcement Administration, 16 May 2000; D. Leibowitz, "Parents Prosecuted for Taking Son off Ritalin," *Arizona Republic*, 8 August 2000; M. J. Layton & L. Washburn, "'Hyperactive' Kids: Victims of a Plot?—Lawsuit Alleges Scheme to Sell Ritalin," *Record*, 1 October 2000, p. 1; H. Wilce, "Is There Life After Ritalin?" *Independent*, 3 August 2000; Patrick Rogers, "Drawing the Line," *People*, 23 July 2001, p. 50; "Doctors, Lawyers Debate Ritalin," *United Press International*, 19 June 2001.

5. C. A. Powers, "The Pharmacology of Drugs Used for the Treatment of Attention Deficit Hyperactivity Disorder," in P. J. Accardo, T. A. Blondis, B. Y. Whitman, & M. A. Stein (eds.), *Attention Deficits and Hyperactivity in Children and Adults: Diagnosis, Treatment, Management*, 2nd ed. (New York: Marcel Dekker, 2000), pp. 477, 483, 489–490; Michelle Chen,"Drugmakers Hurry Sales, Delay Safety Studies," *New Standard*, 9 February 2007.
6. President's Council on Bioethics, "Session 3: Prescription Stimulant Use in American Children: Ethical Issues," 12 December 2002; Carl Elliott, *Better than Well: American Medicine Meets the American Dream* (New York: W. W. Norton, 2003); Lisa Belkin, "Office Messes," *New York Times Magazine*, 18 July 2004; Elizabeth F. Farrell, "Paying Attention to Students Who Can't," *Chronicle of Higher Education*, 26 September 2003, pp. A50–A51; Kendra Nichols, "The Other Performance-Enhancing Drugs," *Chronicle of Higher Education*, 17 December 2004, pp. A41–A42.
7. R. Schachar, R. Tannock, & C. Cunningham, "Treatment," in S. Sandberg (ed.), *Hyperactivity Disorders of Childhood* (Cambridge, U.K.: Cambridge University Press, 1996), pp. 435–436; "Doctors, Lawyers Debate Ritalin," United Press International, 19 June 2001;; Mischa Gaus, "Interrogations Behind Barbed Wire," *In These Times*, February 2007, p. 28; Edward Shorter, *A History of Psychiatry:From the Era of the Asylum to the Age of Prozac* (New York: John Wiley, 1997), p. 295; R. Waters, "Generation Rx," *Family Therapy Newsletter*, 2 May 2000; Rich Daly, "Hawaii Psychiatrists Try to Derail Psychologist Prescribing Bill," *Psychiatry News*, *41*(7), 2006, p. 4.
8. Children and Adults with Attention Deficit Disorders, *CHADD Annual Report 2004–2005*, 2005.
9. Ray Moynihan, Iona Heath, & David Henry, "Selling Sickness: The Pharmaceutical Industry and Disease Mongering," *British Medical Journal*, *324*, 2002, p. 886; also see Peter Conrad & Deborah Potter, "From Hyperactive Children to ADHD Adults: Observations on the Expansion of Medical Categories," *Social Problems*, *47*(4), 2000, p. 560.
10. Carolyn Kitch, "Generational Identity and Memory in American Newsmagazines," *Journalism: Theory, Practice and Criticism*, *4*(2), 2003, p. 188; Jenn Shreve, "Gen Rx," Salon.com, 15 July, 1997; "Generation Rx: National Study Reveals New Category of Substance Abuse Emerging," Partnership for a Drug-Free America, 21 April, 2005; Maia Szalavitz, "'Generation Rx' Label Dazzles Media," *AlterNet.org*, 26 April 2005.
11. Jonathan Leo, "American Preschoolers on Ritalin," *Society*, *39*(2), 2002, p. 58; House of Representatives, p. 14; Kurtis quoted in William McDonald, "Ifs, Ands or Buts of Drugs for Restless U.S. Children," *New York Times*, 9 April 2001, p. E8; Diller, *Running on Ritalin*, pp. 30–31; S. Sandberg & J. Barton, "Historical Development," in S. Sandberg (ed.), *Hyperactivity Disorders of Childhood* (Cambridge, U.K.: Cambridge University

Press,1996), pp. 3, 18–19; Douglas Montero, "Ritalin Pusher Changes His Tune on Schools," *New York Post*, 27 September 2002, p. 19; Kate Zernike & Melody Petersen, "Schools' Backing of Behavior Drugs Comes Under Fire," *New York Times*, 19 August 2001, p. 1.

12. Jim Hightower, "Babies on Drugs," *AlterNet.org*, 24 March 2000; Carol Midgley, "Kiddie Coke: A New Peril in the Playground," *Times*, 21 February 2003, pp. 2, 4; Johann Hari, "Change Our Schools, Not Our Children," *Independent*, 15 March 2007, p. 42.
13. Quoted in Sarah Schubert, Susan Hansen, & Mark Rapley, "'There *Is* No Pathological Test': More on ADHD as Rhetoric," *Journal of Critical Psychology, Counselling, and Psychotherapy*, *5*(3), 2005, p. 394.
14. Quoted in Mark F. Schmitz, Prema Filippone, & Elaine M. Edelman, "Social Representations of Attention Deficit/Hyperactivity Disorder, 1988–1997," *Culture & Psychology*, *9*(4), 2003, p. 394.
15. J. Zito, D. J. Safer, S. dos Reis, J. Gardner, M. Boles, & F. Lynch, "Trends in the Prescribing of Psychotropic Medications to Preschoolers," *Journal of the American Medical Association, 283*(8), 2000, pp. 1025–1030; Erica Goode, "Study Finds Jump in Children Taking Psychiatric Drugs," *New York Times*, 14 January 2003, p. A21.
16. J. Leo, "American Preschoolers on Ritalin," *Society*, *39*(2), 2002, p. 53; D. Leibowitz, "Parents Prosecuted for Taking Son off Ritalin," *Arizona Republic*, 8 August 2000; President's Council on Bioethics, "Session 3: Prescription Stimulant Use in American Children: Ethical Issues," 12 December 2002; Citizens Commission on Human Rights, "New Press Releases," 2003.
17. "Girls Get Extra School Help While Boys Get Ritalin," *USA Today*, 29 August 2003, p. 8A; Jordan J. Titus, "Boy Trouble: Rhetorical Framing of Boys' Underachievement," *Discourse*, *25*(2), 2004, pp. 145–169; Michael S. Kimmel, *Manhood in America: A Cultural History* (New York: Free Press, 1997).
18. David Healy, *The Antidepressant Era* (Cambridge, MA: Harvard University Press, 1997), p. 4; Zito quoted in Benedict Carey, "Use of Antipsychotics by the Young Rose Five-fold," *New York Times*, 6 June 2006.
19. Benedict Carey, "Parenting as Therapy for Child's Mental Disorders," *New York Times*, 22 December 2006; Gardiner Harris, Benedict Carey, & Janet Roberts, "Industry's Role in Children's Antipsychotics," *New York Times*, 10 May 2007; Act quoted in Stephen Petrina, "The Medicalization of Education: A Historiographic Analysis," *History of Education Quarterly*, *46*(4), 2006, p. 531, n. 42.

References

Armstrong, T. (1997). *The myth of the A.D.D. child.* New York: Penguin.

Barry, E. (2002, May 14). N.E. is leader in rate of Ritalin purchases. *Boston Globe*, p. A1.

Breggin, P. R. (1994). *Toxic psychiatry: Why therapy, empathy, and love must replace the drugs, electroshock, and biochemical theories of the "new psychiatry.* New York: St. Martin's Press.

—. (1998). *Talking back to Ritalin: What doctors aren't telling you about stimulants for children.* Monroe, ME: Common Courage Press, Monroe.

Coles. G. (1987). *Learning mystique*. New York: Pantheon Books.

Cook, R. (1996). *Acceptable risk*. New York: Berkley.

De Grandpre, R. (200). *Ritalin nation: Rapid-fire culture and the transformation of human consciousness*. New York: W.W. Norton & Co.

Diller, L. H. (1998). *Running on Ritalin: A physician reflects on children, society, and performance in a pill*. New York: Bantam Books.

Eberstadt, M. (1999, April 1). Why Ritalin rules. *Policy Review*, *94*, 24–40.

Economist. (2006, December 6). Really desperate housewives. *Economist*, p. 64.

House of Representatives, Subcommittee on Early Childhood, Youth and Families, Committee on Education and the Workforce. (2000, May 16). *Ritalin use among youth: Examining the issues and concerns*. Available at http://commdocs.house.gov/committees/edu/hedcew6-109.000/hedcew6-109.htm

National Institute on Drug Abuse. (2006). NIDA InfoFacts: Methylphenidate (Ritalin). Bethesda, MD: National Institute of Mental Health.

Poulin, C. (2001), Medical and nonmedical stimulant use among adolescents: From sanctioned to unsanctioned use. *Canadian Medical Association Journal/Journal de la association médical canadienne*, *165*(8), 1039–1044.

Rose, N. (2006). *The politics of life itself: Biomedicine, power and subjectivity in the twenty-first century*. Princeton, N.J.: Princeton University Press.

Russell, J. (1997, December). The pill that teachers push. *Good Housekeeping*, pp. 110–117.

Schrag, P., & Divoky, D. (1975). *The myth of the hyperactive child, and other means of child control*. New York: Pantheon Books.

Vastag, B. (2001).Pay attention: Ritalin acts much like cocaine. *Journal of the American Medical Association*, *286*(8), 905–906.

5 The Murdoch Media Empire, Journalistic Ethics, and the Spectacle of Scandal

Douglas Kellner

The press, designed for freedom's best defence,
And learning, morals, wisdom to dispense,
Perverted, poisoned, lost to honor's rules,
Is made the sport of knaves, to govern fools.
—Philadelphia *Public Ledger*, 1839

IN JULY 2011, dramatic revelations concerning misdeeds by Rupert Murdoch's *News of the World* (*NOTW*), one of the most successful tabloid newspapers in history, erupted, creating a vast media spectacle that was compared to Watergate and that threatened the existence of Murdoch's global media empire (Bernstein, 2011). Richard Nixon's Watergate crisis implicated the president in a series of scandals that led to the famous Senate Watergate Hearings, a major media spectacle of 1973, followed by his resignation from office, a first for a U.S. president. The cascading scandals in Rupert Murdoch's media empire were thus referred to in some circles as "Murdochgate" (see Bernstein, 2011), a series of outrages and crimes that are continuing to undermine his media power and empire in 2012 and the foreseeable future.

For years, there had been accusations that employees of Murdoch's various tabloid newspapers had hacked telephones to gain information and pay police and other informers for news stories. In 2007, a *NOTW* reporter, Clive Goodman, and a convicted hacker, Glenn Mulcaire, were sent to jail for hacking the cell phones of members of the Royal Family, and reports surfaced in subsequent years that celebrities like Hugh Grant, Sienna Miller, and Jude Law were also hacked, as well as figures connected to politics and sports, always an important domain of the spectacle. At the time, Murdoch and his minions claimed that the hacking was the work of a single rogue reporter and police and government inquiries accepted these claims.

On July 4, 2011, however, a British *Guardian* reporter, Nick Davies, who had been pursuing the hacking stories for years, broke the sensational revelations, with colleague Amelia Hill, that Murdoch's tabloid *NOTW* had hacked the cell-phone messages of Milly Dowler, a 13-year-old missing girl whose disappearance was a media sensation in 2002 (Davies & Hill, 2011). The *Guardian* reported that a *NOTW* employee had apparently hacked into Dowler's voice-message system; deleted messages, which gave her family and police hope that she was still alive; and used hacked material to write stories about this missing girl.[1] Dowler was found murdered, and the revelation that *NOTW* had hacked the murdered girl's phone and interfered with the police investigation created a British and global media spectacle in summer 2011.[2]

Furthermore, *Guardian* investigative reporting revealed that London police had indicated that more than 4,000 allegations of phone hacking of celebrities, politicians, the Royals, and ordinary people had been gleaned from convicted hacker Mulcaire's notebook, which contained over 11,000 pages of notes. Allegations that *NOTW* reporters hacked into cell-phone voice-mail systems belonging to families of U.K. soldiers killed in Iraq and Afghanistan and to families of victims of London terrorist attacks were especially explosive. Outrage grew from day to day as additional major figures in the Murdoch media empire were arrested, and Murdochgate became one of the major media spectacles of the moment, with far-reaching consequences.[3]

In the wildly successful *Harry Potter* films, the last of which was released just as the Murdochgate scandal was breaking in summer 2011, the *Daily Prophet* news tabloid provided a satire of a Murdoch tabloid, and one could see Murdoch himself as a figure for Voldemort, the evil villain whom Harry Potter was to vanquish. In any case, Rupert Murdoch's media empire has long been a major source of right-wing power throughout the English-speaking world. Differently branded as News International (U.K.) and News Corporation (U.S.), Murdoch's global media empire was said to have a market value of around $46 billion, with properties including some 175 newspapers worldwide, HarperCollins Publishers, 20th Century Fox and other movie studios, and television interests in China, Italy, Australia, and elsewhere, including major cable channels and distribution systems.[4] Murdoch was alleged to have a personal net worth of more than $7.6 billion, and was rated on the 2011 list of *Forbes*' richest Americans as the 38th richest person in the United States and the 117th richest person in the world.[5]

Rupert Murdoch had thus been at the center of the construction of global media companies using new technologies to create cable-satellite broadcasting empires and global news and information conglomerates. In the U.K. alone, Murdoch media properties comprise several leading newspapers, including U.K. establishment papers the *Times* and the *Sunday Times*, popular tabloids *NOTW* and the *Sun*, and control of Sky TV, along with a major stake in BSkyB, the two largest cable-satellite franchises in the U.K. At the time that the hacking scandal broke out, Murdoch had been seeking permission from the British government to purchase majority shares in the U.K. cable system BSkyB so he could effectively control cable television in the U.K. Although it appeared that the Cameron government was going to support Murdoch's bid to control British cable-satellite systems, on July 13, the Murdoch corporation dropped its $12 billion takeover bid as parliamentary opposition began to intensify after revelations of the hacking scandals.

In the United States, Murdoch owns many newspapers, including the *New York Post* and the *Wall Street Journal*, which he purchased in 2007 just before the newspaper industry went into economic free fall, losing millions in the exchange. Murdoch also controls 20th Century Fox films in the United States as well as Fox Television and Fox News, two of the most popular, profitable, and in the case of Fox News, powerful television channels in the world.

Murdoch's media empire contributed massively to the tabloidization of news and information in newspapers and journalism from the 1960s to the present and in broadcasting from the 1990s to the present.[6] His Sky TV and Fox News television channels highlighted sensationalistic stories with glitzy presentations, large graphics that tell people what to think, and the collapse of codes of news and entertainment—all framed from a right-wing conservative position. Murdoch's newspapers as well featured giant sensational headlines, short stories with gobs of tabloid trash and scandal, and pictures galore, including naked women in his Brit tabs. Thus, not only was Murdoch the major purveyor of an aggressively right-wing political slant on the news, but he also degraded journalism and helped create the tabloidization of news and information.

Indeed, it is ironic and fitting that Murdoch's media empire would be put in question and seriously undermined by the media spectacle of Murdochgate, as his newspapers, television channels, and Internet sites have been major forces since the 1980s in the tabloidization of news and information, highlighting scandals and wrongdoing of the rich, the famous, and the political class. In the United States, Murdoch's media had brought tabloid stories like the O.J. Simpson murder trial and Bill Clinton sex scandals into the center of news and journalism in the mid-1990s,[7] while importing codes of entertainment into journalism and, for some, seriously undermining traditional standards. His Fox News network became infamous as the voice of the right wing of the Republican Party, and in the U.K., Murdoch had the power to make and break politicians and even to choose governments as will be discussed further.

The following sections describe the Murdoch scandal, the ethical issues involved in Murdoch media corporation journalistic practices, and the threats to democracy residing in the Murdoch empire's power and ability to corrupt politicians and the state. Next, however, this chapter comments on the role of the media in democracies as conceived by theorists of democratic revolutions and republics in Western modernity, and how the corruption of journalism contributes to crises of democracy.

Journalistic Ethics and the Corruption of Democracy

> *A popular government without popular information or the means of acquiring it, is but a Prologue to a Farce or a Tragedy or perhaps both. Knowledge will forever govern ignorance, and a people who mean to be their own Governors, must arm themselves with the power, which knowledge gives.*
>
> —James Madison, 1822

A democratic social order, as was conceived in Western democratic revolutions in England, the United States, France, and other countries, requires a separation of powers so that no one institution or social force dominates the society and polity. The French philosopher Montesquieu called for emerging democratic polities to separate powers between branches of government as the English revolution of 1688 had done. The U.S. Constitution, developed after the American Revolution of 1776, in turn, separated the political system into the presidency, Congress, and the judiciary so that there would be a division and balance of powers among the major political institutions.

Yet democracy also requires an informed electorate that can participate in political affairs. Genuine democracy consists of the sovereignty of the people and thus government by, for, and of the people. For a free people to govern themselves, they must be adequately informed and able to participate in public debate, elections, and political activity. Freedom of the Press was therefore guaranteed by a Bill of Rights in the American, French, and other democratic revolutions of the 18th century order to assure that the press would be free from domination by any political force so that it could criticize the government and promote vigorous debate on issues of public concern, thus enabling the public to participate in political affairs.

Consequently, the dual democratic functions of the press in the United States were to provide a check against excessive power and to inform the people concerning the major issues of public interest in the U.S. constitutional order emerged after the American Revolution. A free press was thus vitally necessary to maintain a democratic society, and it is often claimed by champions of democracy that freedom of the press is one of the features that defines the superiority of democratic societies over competing social systems.

This concept of a free press was also extended to the broadcast media, which were assigned a series of democratic responsibilities in the United States by the Federal Communications Act of 1934 and by subsequent legislation and court decisions (Kellner, 1990). The democratic functions of the press and then the broadcast media were to provide information, ideas, and debate concerning issues of public significance to promote a democratic public sphere. Broadcasting was conceived as a public utility, with the airwaves established as part of the public domain, subject to regulation by the government to assure that broadcasting would meet its democratic responsibilities.[8]

In the 1980s, during both the Reagan administration in the United States and the Thatcher government in the U.K., much of this regulatory apparatus was dismantled, and giant corporations took over the major broadcast media, including television networks and the technological-institutional apparatus of cable and satellite broadcasting, which greatly expanded the reach of powerful cable news channels and gave entrepreneurs who owned and controlled them tremendous media power. Indeed, the consequences for democracy of the conservative deregulation policies in the United States, U.K., and elsewhere indicated that the result is an overwhelming concentration of power in the hands of corporate groups that now own powerful media empires, which they use to promote their own interests and agendas.[9] If media corporations such as the Murdoch empire utilize their powerful instruments of communication and information to advance their own corporate interests and those of politicians and policies that they favor, then the media have lost their democratic functions of serving to debate issues of sociopolitical interest and to serve as a check against powerful institutions like the state and corporation. When corporations like the Murdoch media empire choose which political party and government they prefer, the media loses its functions to serve as a critical watchdog against excessive government and corporate power and questionable government policies and corporate actions and instead serves its own partisan and commercial interests, as the Murdoch cabal has done for decades.

The ethical and political responsibilities of the press under a democratic order thus required a free and independent press to provide the information needed to produce a functional democracy. A democratic press should be part of a democratic system of checks and balances and the responsibilities of journalism involve both the need to inform the public and to expose lies and corruption from powerful institutions like the state and, today, corporations. Journalistic practices developed an ethic of objectivity and responsibility to tell the truth.

This chapter argues that the frightening media power accrued by the Murdoch media conglomerates has corrupted democracy and journalistic ethics and created a crisis of democracy in English-language countries in which the Murdoch media empire is especially influential. The following analysis describes how the Murdoch media empire came to corrupt democratic societies and journalistic ethics, focusing on the role of Murdoch's conglomerates in the U.K., where scandals have unfolded concerning computer and telephone hacking by the Murdoch conglomerate to obtain stories, including buying stories from the police and other official sources, putting government and police figures on the corporation's payroll to obtain information and favors, and controlling political parties and governments through their significant media power. This situation constitutes a crisis of journalism and democracy in the U.K., which involves some important political battles of the contemporary era that are described in the following sections.

Scandals of the Murdoch Media Empire

Behind the highly rehearsed faux candour of Murdoch senior and the bland evasions of his son, lies a story in which democracy—not just in the U.K., but in the U.S., Australia and elsewhere—has been consistently and wilfully undermined in pursuit, not simply of profit, but far more corrosively, of power. Lord David Putnam (2012) noted:

> For the past 30 years, the Murdoch empire has sought to undermine and destabilise elected governments, and independent regulators, in pursuit of a political agenda that, while hiding behind a smokescreen of free market orthodoxy, is in the end nothing less than a sophisticated attempt to optimise the power and influence of News Corporation and its populist, rightwing agenda.

With the unfolding of the hacking scandal concerning the Murdoch press in the U.K. in July 2011, old allegations circulated widely that staff from Murdoch's tabloid paper *News of the World* regularly hacked into cell phones, used private detectives, and bribed police officers so they could illegally obtain sources for stories, supplemented by new daily reports of other wrongdoings. From July 2011 into 2012, however, there were almost daily revelations of various scandals uncovered in which the Murdoch corporation produced its news stories through phone and computer hacking, paying off police and other authorities for stories, and involving itself in a wealth of illegal techniques of news gathering and associated crimes. The British government soon became deeply involved in the scandal when it was revealed that former *NOTW* editor Andy Coulson had been hired as director of communication by David Cameron and the ruling Conservative Party in 2007, despite his resignation after the Royal Family hacking political scandal, and helped run its media communications unit during the 2010 general election in which the Conservatives won, thus bringing a Murdoch fox into the British government henhouse.

Coulson's involvement in the hacking scandal had been alleged for some time, and he had resigned in disgrace as *NOTW* editor in 2007 due to the resulting fallout from the hacking of the British royals, but such a criminal past did not deter Cameron from hiring Coulson, who was long implicated in the foul practices of the Murdoch empire; obviously, Cameron and the Tories wanted to curry favor with the Murdoch media whose support they sought in the 2010 general election.[10] Yet when Coulson was formally arrested for his role in the hacking and in other illegal activities in July 2011, Cameron's Conservative Party government was threatened by its associations with the Coulson and Murdoch gang.

As the Murdoch phone-hacking scandal unfolded, focus centered on the media mogul Rupert and his son James Murdoch, chairman and chief executive of News Corporation, and the *NOTW* editor, Rebekah Brooks,[11] a fiery redhead and the youngest woman ever to edit a major U.K. periodical. In what appeared as a desperate attempt to limit damage, James Murdoch announced on July 7 that the 168-year-old *NOTW* tabloid would be shut down, as advertisers were abandoning the paper in droves and the uproar was growing. As noted, the Murdoch media colossus was currently involved in an effort that was being evaluated by the British government to gain full control of BSkyB cable/satellite system, and the Labour Party insisted that the issue be debated in the British Parliament, in the light of recent Murdoch corporation scandals. On July 13, Murdoch announced that News Corporation was withdrawing its proposal to take full control of BSkyB, and the same day U.K. Prime Minister David Cameron announced that a public government inquiry would be formed to investigate the affair under the charge of Lord Justice Brian Leveson, which will be discussed below.

When the scandal erupted in July 2011, Rupert Murdoch flew to London from a conference/vacation in Sun Valley, Idaho, and found himself at the center of a media circus of the type which his own press had long orchestrated. While he initially claimed he had returned to protect Brooks, who many in the British establishment were suggesting should resign as editor of *NOTW*, he was soon summoned to appear at a hearing in Parliament, along with Brooks and his son James. After first hesitating, they agreed to appear, as scandals were appearing daily, and one after another major *NOTW* figure, including Brooks, was arrested and charged in the criminal inquiry.

Accusations multiplied concerning police corruption and too-cozy relations with the Murdoch empire, and Paul Stephenson, the head of London's Metropolitan Police Service (a.k.a. Scotland Yard) resigned as uproar mounted over his failure to investigate alleged phone hacking by the Murdoch corporation and other wrongdoing after the 2007 convictions of some of Murdoch's employees. That under Stephenson's leadership, one of Andy Coulson's closest assistants at *NOTW*, Neil Wallis, was hired as public-relations advisor to the police also put Stephenson's judgment in question.[12] Wallis had a colorful background in tabloid journalism, hired by Murdoch's *Sun* at the time that they were waging all-out tabloid war against Elton John, a story which ended up with a record £1 million lawsuit paid out by Murdoch's paper.[13] Wallis went on to work with Murdoch's *NOTW* and had been implicated in hacking and other journalistic scandals at the paper, which critics felt should have disqualified him for a top London police P.R. position, but he was hired anyway, confirming again the incestuous and poisonous relations among the Murdoch corporation, the London police, and the British government.

Stephenson's resignation was followed by that of another high-ranking Scotland Yard cop, John Yates (a.k.a. "Yates of the Yard"), the U.K.'s counter-terrorism chief, who had worked and socialized with Wallis, and had apparently recommended that Wallis' daughter be given a job with the police. Both Wallis and Yates regularly socialized with employees of the Murdoch organization, giving their media empire access to the highest ranks of the police department and its media and public-relations apparatus.

It was clear that the Murdoch corporation had corrupted the British media, the political system, and now the police and legal system, all of which had failed to investigate and prosecute its earlier wrongdoings. Murdoch's media were employing the vilest methods to get stories and were kingmakers in the British system, while the state, police, and legal system were complicit in the Murdoch media empire amassing media and political power wielded in their own partisan and corporate interests, often operating outside the law.

In the 1980s, Murdoch's strong conservative inclinations had led him to support Margaret Thatcher, and his newspapers' all-out and vehement campaign against the British Labour Party, in the eyes of many, tipped the balance of political power to Thatcher and the conservatives.[14] While Murdoch had supported Thatcher and the conservatives in the 1980s, he broke with her successor, John Major, and supported Labour Party candidate Tony Blair in the 1997 general election, who after winning enthusiastically pushed Murdoch's interests and socialized with the Murdoch family.[15] Although Murdoch reportedly liked Blair's successor Gordon Brown, by contrast, other major News Corporation figures, and apparently Rupert himself, came to prefer David Cameron, whom the Murdoch papers ultimately supported and who beat Brown and the Labour Party in the 2010 general election.[16]

Thus, it appeared that England was suffering a major "legitimation crisis" at the time of the Murdoch media scandal and the English Riots of 2011, which I have discussed elsewhere (see Kellner, 2012).[17] In the 1960s, the United States was said to have suffered a legitimation crisis during the era of the Vietnam War when there was also heavy-handed police repression to deal with anti-war protestors, upheavals in ghettoes and poorer areas, growing divisions between rich and poor, and the scandals of the Nixon administration, resulting in Richard Nixon's resignation in the Watergate affair. The British government was now in full-scale legitimation crisis mode, as the Cameron government was soiled by its tawdry association with the Murdoch media empire. Further, Cameron's conservatives had carried out a right-wing agenda that cut social programs, education, and programs for youth, as well as a deficit-spending cuts agenda that benefitted the rich while harming the working and middle classes—all the while spending lavishly on expensive wars in Afghanistan and Libya.

The televised parliamentary hearing on July 19 was a global media spectacle of the highest order, as Murdoch, his son James, and Brooks were grilled by a British parliamentary committee. Although Murdoch injected near the opening of the hearing that this was the "most humble day of his life," he refused to take responsibility for the crimes of his corporation, and his answers ranged from doddering and vague, revealing his age and growing infirmity, to belligerent denials of any responsibility. James occasionally interrupted to try to answer questions but provided long technocratic and sometimes evasive answers, which later would be called into question. As the testimony was nearing its close, a British activist and comedian emerged to attempt to hit Murdoch with a shaving-foam pie but was diverted by a quick reaction from Murdoch's wife, Wendi, some 37 years younger than her husband. Mrs. Murdoch body-blocked the pie thrower, then picked up the messy shaving-foam plate and smashed it into the assailant's face, producing a minor piece of theater that received global media attention.

Following the British parliamentary inquiry, members of the Murdoch corporation questioned in public some of James Murdoch's answers, leading the once-heir-apparent to be resummoned to the British Parliament when it returned in the fall (Hill, 2011). James Murdoch was especially under fire for authorizing a £1 million-plus payoff to Gordon Taylor, chief executive of the Professional Footballers Association and a major figure in British sports, who had allegedly been hacked by *NOTW*, retaliated with a lawsuit, and was subsequently paid a large out-of-court settlement that British parliamentary questioners suggested was a bribe and hush money. James Murdoch also denied knowing details of a brief put out by a law firm, Harbottle and Lewis, working for News Corporation, which, James claimed, confirmed that the hacking was limited to one rogue reporter, whereas other executives in News Corporation claimed that Murdoch Jr. was familiar with details of the hacking brief and other company emails discussing widespread hacking problems in the company; moreover, Harbottle and Lewis claimed that the Murdochs misrepresented their work for the corporation.[18]

Meanwhile, there were announcements that the FBI and Department of Justice were opening inquiries into possible illegal activities of Murdoch's media corporation in the United States, and rumors circulated concerning the possible hacking of U.S. 9/11 families and dirty business deals done in the United States by Murdoch businesses. Indeed, by August 2011, there were reports that Murdoch employees had also engaged in computer hacking and even had a drone at their disposal in the United States—allegedly capable of taking pictures and hacking into telephone frequencies—that possibly violated U.S. navigation laws (the latter was reported on Keith Olbermann's August 3, 2011, *Countdown* TV show).

While the U.K. government had announced a commission of inquiry into activities of Murdoch's media empire and other media industries that may have employed similar criminal tactics, U.S. congressmen called for investigations into whether Murdoch's U.S. connections had engaged in similar tactics and whether Murdoch's corporations have broken other laws, as his media empire is rooted in the United States and Murdoch has obtained U.S. citizenship, making his businesses vulnerable to investigation through the U.S. Foreign Corrupt Practices Act. In Murdoch's native Australia, on September 13, the government announced a formal inquiry into the behavior of Murdoch's and other Australian media companies, generating investigations throughout the English-speaking world into Murdoch's heinous journalistic practices.

On August 1, London police arrested the former managing editor of *NOTW*, Stuart Kuttner, on suspicion of conspiring to hack cell phones and pay police officers. In a summary by Becker and Somaiya (2011):

> Mr. Kuttner, who is the 11th former *News of the World* employee arrested in the scandal surrounding the tabloid, personally authorized cash expenses until his retirement two years ago in his role as managing editor, said multiple current and former company employees, who, like most people interviewed spoke on the condition of anonymity because of the continuing police investigations and to avoid jeopardizing their ties with the company. Mr. Kuttner did not respond to requests for comment.
>
> A person familiar with the company's internal investigation said the regular infusions of cash, usually also authorized by newsroom editors as well as Mr. Kuttner, contributed to the newsroom's "wild West" atmosphere. The funds were used as advances on expenses and also to pay sources for articles, said the former journalists. So far a search by the company of the cash records has found more than $200,000 in payments to police officers from *News of the World*, according to two people with knowledge of the documents.
>
> The investigation of payoffs to the police is one part of what has become a three-pronged inquiry that began by focusing on the hacking of cell-phone voice messages and has also expanded to the hacking of e-mails. (Becker & Somaiya, 2011)

Members of Murdoch's media organizations were thus involved in complex cases of bribing police for information, hacking computers and cell phones, and corrupting government and police. In Murdochgate, we see media spectacle turn on one of its own major producers with unpredictable results, as through the fall and winter of 2011 and into 2012, allegations continued to emerge concerning knowledge of systematic wrongdoing throughout the Murdoch media empire. Individuals within the Murdoch corporation questioned the parliamentary testimony that James Murdoch gave, and on August 16, 2011, Clive Goodman, the only *NOTW* reporter to actually go to jail, published a letter claiming that knowledge of hacking was widespread in the Murdoch organization and discussed frequently at editorial meetings until editor Andy Coulson warned against public discussion of such illegal activity, which, in turn, created another media uproar and calls for new British parliamentary hearings (Lyall, 2011). And on August 23, it was revealed that Coulson continued receiving large payments from the Murdoch corporation after he went to work for David Cameron, as part of the Tory media team, which created even more scandals for the reigning British government.[19]

James Murdoch was called back to testify again before a British parliamentary committee on November 10, 2011, when two major figures in News International, the British Murdoch media conglomerate, contested his earlier testimony, indicating that he was unaware of widespread hacking at Murdoch companies.[20] James again denied knowledge of criminal activity at the family company, but British Parliament member Tom Watson argued that James and his staff were "all bound together by secrecy," and called Rupert Murdoch "the first Mafia boss in history not to know he is running a criminal enterprise," to which James Murdoch replied, "Mr. Watson, that's inappropriate." Yet the same month, there were revelations that Murdoch's media organizations had hired private investigators to conduct surveillance of two lawyers representing phone-hacking victims (see the following section), and stories continued to emerge concerning payoffs to police officers for information and other scandals concerning Murdoch and his media empire.

The Leveson Inquiry and Crimes of the Murdoch Media Empire

First it was the son, then it was his ministerial "cheerleader," and finally the father. The name in the Leveson frame has kept shifting all week, but, at the start of his evidence, Murdoch senior dropped an oblique hint that the spotlight could have further to shift. He recalled

> *how he had slipped in through a back door at No 10 to see the new prime minister immediately after the election. He then volunteered—apropos nothing—that "Andy Coulson was there."*
>
> *No one asked why a press officer was required at a secretive meeting, but this little offering was perhaps designed to encourage the thought that this* NoW*-editor-turned-spinner had been hand-picked to formalise the link between the heart of democratic power and the empire of the* Sun*. Last night Lord Justice Leveson made clear his displeasure at the way his judicial inquiry is being misappropriated for political ends, and the trail of destruction which the Murdochs have wrought in court this week is getting closer to Downing Street.*
>
> —Editorial, *Guardian*, 2012

Following the uproar over the Murdoch hacking scandal, on July 6, 2011, British Prime Minister David Cameron announced to Parliament that a government commission would be established to further investigate the Murdoch scandal. Although initially Cameron resisted calls to investigate Murdoch's media after Andy Coulson was arrested "on suspicion of corruption allegations," Cameron ordered parliamentary inquiries into the scandals. On July 13, Cameron appointed Lord Justice Brian Leveson as chairman of the inquiry, with a mandate to look into: (a) the specific claims about phone hacking at the *NOTW*, (b) the initial police investigation and allegations of illicit payments to police by the press, and (c) a further inquiry to review the general culture and ethics of the British media.

The Leveson Inquiry began hearings on November 14 and planned first of all to call scores of individuals who claimed to have been hacked and abused in multiple ways by the British press. The promising, sensational revelations into Murdoch's media empire and other media scandals for months to come would generate serious debates over ethics and journalism in the U.K. and indeed globally. The Inquiry, held at the Royal Courts of Justice in London, opened by calling the Dowler family, who recounted the painful story of how the hacking into their missing teenage daughter Milly's telephone and the deletion of messages so the Murdoch's tabloid *NOTW* newspaper could access new ones when her voice mail was full provided false hopes that their daughter was still alive. The family's hopes were eventually crushed when her murdered body was found.[21]

The Inquiry continued with movie stars and celebrities Hugh Grant and Steve Coogan, who both recounted harassment by tabloid media and anger at having their phones hacked and conversations reported in the Murdoch media. The two were followed by sports figures and other celebrities with similar stories. In the weeks to come, the Dowlers' lawyer, Mark Lewis, who was representing other victims of phone hacking as well, reported his consternation at finding out his phone was hacked, as were those of other lawyers who had investigated or defended clients against the Murdoch empire. The Leveson Inquiry brought in a panorama of celebrities who had been abused by the Murdoch and other media corporations, as well as an ordinary British family, the McCanns, who recounted their torment by tabloid media when their 3-year-old daughter went missing during a trip to Portugal. British tabloids went into a feeding frenzy of sensationalism about the case, including allegations that the parents were involved in their daughter's disappearance, a libelous charge that cost the offending tabloids vast amounts of cash.

Actress Sienna Miller told the Leveson Inquiry on November 14, 2011, of her distress when confidential details of her private life were published in the tabloid media, and she blamed those around her for leaking to the media, when, in fact, she learned later that the Murdoch and other tabloid media had systematically hacked her phones. *Harry Potter* author J. K. Rowling told the Inquiry (the same day) of the systematic harassment directed at her by the media over the years, constantly invading her privacy, even to the extent that notes from the media to facilitate interviews were put in her daughter's backpack. Formula One boss Max Mosley, the McCann family, Hugh Grant, and others recounted the pain of reading outright lies about them in the tabloid media and their inability to get the tabloids to retract the story or to get the public media regulatory body, the Press Complaints Commission (PCC), to respond to their complaints.

As the Leveson Inquiry hearings continued through December 2011 and into 2012, they were opening fascinating windows into the practices of British journalism, ranging from the tabloids to the *Guardian* and the BBC, providing rare insight into the production of news stories, journalism and ethics, the relationship between government, police, and the media, and issues of journalistic ethics, malpractices, and the public interest. Murdoch corporation employees were grilled on how their tabloid stories were produced, how private detectives and phone/computer hacking were deployed, and how the Murdoch corporation related to the police, government regulatory agencies, and public criticism of their media. (As many of those interrogated were under criminal investigation for telephone hacking, this theme was off-limits to the Leveson Inquiry for those facing criminal charges in the police investigations.) Lawyers representing victims of hacking and other invasions of privacy or libel related their experiences of being hacked, being followed by private investigators, and being intimidated by members of the Murdoch media mafia while representing their clients in potential lawsuits against the Murdoch corporation. Government regulators were grilled about how they had failed to prosecute or even publicly rebuke any members of the media establishment when complaints were brought to them, and rare public discussions were taking place concerning the failures of media regulation and how to better regulate the media.[22]

There were also daily discussions of proper journalistic ethics and responsibilities to the "public interest," a term that meant quite different things to different journalists, public officials, and academics. In terms of journalistic ethics, "public interest" implies that journalists have a responsibility to serve the public and not the state or corporations and to tell the truth. Yet former *NOTW* features editor Paul McMullan testified before the Leveson Inquiry that in the Murdoch media world the "public interest" was whatever interested the public and that "circulation defines what is in the public interest" (Rolle, 2012, #4).

After a break following the December 21 hearings, the Leveson Inquiry resumed activities on January 9, 2012. The year would, no doubt, see other scandalous revelations concerning Murdoch media wrongdoing and might be the year of judgment for Murdoch's media empire. Reports continued to surface in early 2012 concerning payments to victims of the Murdoch corporation hacking scandals. On January 19, 2012, a U.K. high court judge announced that Murdoch's *NOTW* had agreed to pay 37 phone-hacking victims—ranging from actor Jude Law to ordinary people—thousands of pounds in settlements, with estimates that settling the many other outstanding hacking legal suits would cost the company over £10 million (Sabbagh & Hill, 2011). This estimate may have been modest, as reports surfaced that many more were planning lawsuits including Cherie Blair, former Prime Minister Tony Blair's wife, and estimates emerged that the Murdoch corporation might have to pay more than $1 billion to hacking victims (Chozick, 2012).

Reports circulated that police were concerned that Murdoch corporation employees had destroyed emails that would serve as evidence in criminal proceedings, but there were also indications that a Data Pool 3 allegedly contained several hundred million of emails, possibly including ones that had been deleted and were of interest to criminal investigations. In Nick Davies' (2012) summary,

> For News International, Data Pool 3 is a nightmare. Firstly, no one know [*sic*] what is in there. All they can do is wait and see how bad it gets.
>
> Second, the police clearly believe it may yield new evidence of the crimes they set out to investigate—the "blagging" of confidential data from phone companies, banks, tax offices etc; the interception of voice mails and emails; the payment of bribes to police officers.
>
> Third—and most nightmarish—Data Pool 3 could yield evidence of attempts to destroy evidence that the high court and police were seeking. Data Pool 3 itself was apparently deliberately deleted from News International's servers. (2012, #8–#10)

On February 11, 2012, the BBC reported that eight journalists were arrested under Operation Elveden over alleged corrupt payments to police and public servants, including five from Murdoch's most powerful British tabloid the *Sun*. Police officers and members of the British defense establishment also had been arrested and charged with corruption (BBC, 2012).[23] British police continued to arrest Murdoch-organization journalists, and his employees were becoming angry that the Murdoch organization was providing information to police that were leading to the arrests (Sabbagh & O'Carroll, 2012). As the anger from the press room continued to mount, Rupert Murdoch himself visited the *Sun* offices on February 17, announced that 10 suspended journalists who had been arrested would be reinstated, and that a *Sun on Sunday* soon would be inaugurated. Its first edition was indeed published on Sunday, February 26, and the British media establishment cheered that the daring Murdoch had opened a new British tabloid Sunday newspaper when his newspaper empire was under attack, yet its publication seemed more like rearranging deck chairs on the *Titanic*, as scandals continued to multiply.

The next day, fresh allegations originated from police investigators that Murdoch's daily *Sun* tabloid had systematically paid large sums of money to "a network of corrupted officials" in the British police, military, and government (Lyall, 2012). Sue Akers, a deputy assistant commissioner for the

London Metropolitan Police, which was leading the criminal investigation into the Murdoch scandals, informed the Leveson Inquiry that hundreds of thousands of dollars had been paid out for news stories and salacious gossip and that payments had been authorized "at a very senior level within the newspaper." Strongly condemning the Murdoch organization, Akers testified that "There appears to have been a culture at *The Sun* of illegal payments, and systems have been created to facilitate such payments whilst hiding the identity of the officials receiving the money"(#5).[24]

Then, on February 29, 2012, it was announced that James Murdoch was stepping down as executive chairman of Murdoch's News International to focus on the corporation's global television business in New York, generating speculation that the Murdoch mafia was unraveling at the top and might well be reorganized without the Murdochs.[25] Amy Chozick (2012) reported in the *New York Times* that Chase Carey, News Corporation's chief operating officer, said at a Deutsche Bank media conference in Palm Beach, Florida, that within the company "certainly there are a number of parties who feel—would push to looking at a way to spin the publishing business separate from the rest." Murdoch insiders insisted that Rupert himself would not happily divest his beloved London newspaper from his media corporation, but there were growing pressures from members of Murdoch's News Corp. board of directors to do so.

Criticism of the Murdoch scandal continued to intensify. Chris Bryant, a Labour Party MP who had been paid £30,000 in damages by the Murdoch corporation in January to settle his *NOTW* phone-hacking claims, "told a Westminster Hall private members debate on media regulation on Tuesday that his 'poor researcher' had counted 486 lies told to parliament by News International, the police and other organisations about phone hacking and related investigations" (Deans, 2012, #2), speculating that the "phone-hacking scandal could turn out to be the biggest case of corporate corruption in the UK for more than 250 years" (#1). Bryant also noted that "Scotland Yard had been 'suborned' and effectively become a subsidiary of News International" (#4), highlighting my point about how the Murdoch scandals had led to a crisis of democracy in the U.K.

Indeed, testimony in the Leveson Inquiry during March 2012 continued to highlight the corruption of the British police, government, and media by Murdoch media corporations. Jeff Edwards, head of the U.K. Crime Reporters' Association, asserted that while working on the British tabloid, the *Daily*

Mirror, there was "no culture of bribing public officials"; by contrast, he claimed that he was fired from Murdoch's *NOTW* for refusing to bribe officials. In a *Guardian* summary of Edwards's background on the day of his testimony to the Leveson Inquiry, we read:

> Last month, Edwards told [BBC] *Newsnight* that while he was at the *Mirror* there was no culture of bribing public officials.
>
> However, he claimed that while he worked for the *News of the World* between 1980 and 1985 he was removed from his post as crime correspondent because of his refusal to pay police officers. He alleged:
>
> "Between 1980 and 1985 I was employed at the *News of the World* as their crime correspondent and I was removed from my post because of my complete and [*sic*] reluctance and refusal to pay police officers. I was told so and someone else was put into it who was prepared to take that action.
>
> "There was always, I thought, at the *News of the World* a culture of underhandness [*sic*], or corrupt practice."
>
> —O'Carroll, Halliday, & Baird (2012, #6–#9)

Even Murdoch's prestigious London *Times* was implicated in the scandal when it came out that a *Times* reporter had hacked into the email account of an anonymous police blogger ("NightJack"), and when he was outed, Murdoch's *Times*' reporter attempted to cover over the incident when it became a legal issue (Leigh, 2012). Not only were Murdoch's most prestigious U.K. newspapers like the *Times* getting implicated in the scandal, so too was the U.K. government. While initially, British Prime Minister David Cameron and his Conservative Party government had managed to slip out of the scandal despite the close relations between some of Cameron's top advisors, and the resignation of top police officials who had been too cozy with the Murdoch empire as 2012 unfolded, the Murdoch media scandals began to relentlessly implicate Cameron and his Conservatives. One amusing story revealed that *NOTW* editor Rebekah Brooks, twice arrested in the Murdoch scandals, had requested the loan of a retired horse from the London Metropolitan Police in 2007, and during the two years she had the loaner, Prime Minister David Cameron, among others, had ridden the horse (Hope, 2012).

While the episode might not involve criminal issues, after first dissembling, Cameron was forced to concede that he had indeed visited Brooks at *her* home and ridden the horse in question when Brooks was editor of Murdoch's *NOTW*. The incident rather clearly points to the cozy relation between the Murdoch syndicate, the London police, and the Cameron government.

Yet when Cameron came to the United States for meetings with President Obama during the second week in March 2012, the U.S. media failed to confront Cameron with his egregious connections with the Murdoch corporation and how he had brought in one of its major and heavily indicted thugs, Andy Coulson, to run his political communications operation.[26]

Urgency for government investigations into Murdoch media-empire scandals intensified again in late March 2012 after revelations emerged through an investigation by the *Australian Financial Review* that a Murdoch company, NDS, which

> employed a unit of ex-police officers—dubbed Operational Security—in the mid-1990s to pirate the smart cards of rival broadcasters Austar, Optus, and Foxtel in a bid to clear the way for News Corp to control Australia's lucrative pay-TV market. (Halliday, 2012a, #3)

The pirated cards were made readily available through a website of a hacker allegedly employed by NDS, and the availability of these cards to access its competitors' pay-cable services without paying damaged these broadcasters and helped Murdoch dominate cable television in Australia (Chenoweth, 2012).

The previous day, BBC's *Panorama* broadcast a show claiming that the same Murdoch company (NDS) cracked the code of a competing ONdigital provider of cable channels in the U.K. and made its source codes available for pirating—an action that undermined its rival.[27] The Murdoch corporation vehemently denied both allegations, but the scandals elicited the possibility of further government investigation of Murdoch corporation rogue business practices that could lead to fines and jail for Murdoch henchmen and that certainly would involve more bad publicity and legal aggravations.

As summer 2012 approached, Murdoch media scandals continued to multiply. On April 5, there were widespread reports that Murdoch's Sky News admitted that its reporters had hacked into emails while pursuing news stories, marking the first time that Murdoch's hacking scandal has spilled into his TV cable news empire. This bombshell came only two days after Murdoch's son James had resigned as the chairman of Sky's parent company, British Sky Broadcasting (BSkyB), pointing to growing chaos in the Murdoch media empire and suggesting that James was further weakened in his position in the family media colossus (Lyall & Somaiya, 2012). And news that lawyer Mark Lewis, who has been at the forefront of efforts to expose the Murdoch media empire scandals, was travelling to New York to begin discussions about lawsuits in the United States widened the global ramifications of the scandal (Pilkington, 2012b).

But one of the most dramatic spectacles of the Leveson Inquiry so far took place on April 24, 2012, with James Murdoch's appearance, followed by two days of testimony by Rupert Murdoch. Once again, James Murdoch blamed all of his associates for not informing him concerning the seriousness of the hacking scandals, and he denied again any knowledge or responsibility for the hacking and other scandals. But in the course of questions, emails were released that indicated that the office of the Cameron government culture minister and associates of the Minister Jeremy Hunt were sending emails to the Murdochs, indicating support for the Murdochs' full takeover of BSykB, which would give the family control over British pay-cable television and the digital future. Before the day was over, Hunt relieved an assistant, Adam Smith, of his job; Smith had evidently been chosen as go-between for the Cameron government and Murdoch mafia and had sent fawning emails to the Murdoch corporation, assuring them that their takeover was getting Hunt's and the Cameron government's support. This scandal, still unfolding, could have serious implications for the survival of the Cameron government, and Hunt would be called to testify at the Leveson Inquiry in May.

Rupert Murdoch's two-day testimony at the Leveson Inquiry was one of the crowning events of the whole procedure. On Murdoch's first day of testimony, he blustered on how he knew nothing of the hacking at *NOTW*, didn't really have much to do with the paper, didn't use his media and his political connections to promote his commercial interests, and didn't really have much political influence at all—claims that were generally scoffed at by commentators.[28] In another newsworthy story, Murdoch claimed that when he told British Labour Party leader Gordon Brown that he was switching his allegiance from Labour to the Conservative Party in the 2010 election, Brown told him: "Well, your company has declared war on my government, and we have no alternative but to make war on your company" —a claim that Gordon Brown immediately told the BBC was "wholly wrong" (Burns, 2012).

During his second day of testimony on April 25, Murdoch conceded to Robert Jay, the lead government questioner for the Leveson Inquiry, that there was indeed a cover-up of the extent of the hacking scandal at his News

Corporation and that he and James were among the victims! Patiently and quietly pushed by Jay to elaborate, Rupert revealed:

> I think from within the *News of the World* and—there were one or two very strong characters there, who I think had been there many, many, many years and were friends with the journalists. . . the person I'm thinking of was a friend of the journalists, drinking pal, and was a clever lawyer, and forbade them to go and see the evidence—or there had been statements reporting that this person forbade people to go and report to Mrs Brooks or to James. (cited in Rayner, 2012)

The "clever lawyer" was apparently Tom Crone, the former legal manager of *NOTW*, who immediately sent out a press release indicating that Murdoch's allegations that a "lawyer" had "forebade" journalists on the paper to take evidence of wrongdoing to Rebekah Brooks or James Murdoch was a "shameful lie" (O'Carroll, 2012b). Another of the "two strong characters" whom Murdoch suspected of leading the cover-up was apparently the former editor of *NOTW*, Colin Myler, who Murdoch suggested in his Leveson testimony, was part of the cover-up of the hacking scandal. Curiously, Rupert Murdoch suggested the cover-up was carried out by precisely the two men in his own organization who had disputed James Murdoch's claim that he had not been told about the extent of the phone hacking scandal at *NOTW* and who both insisted that they had explained the problem to James and had an email to prove it (which James forgets seeing).[29] Distancing himself from Myler when pushed by Jay, Murdoch said that his right-hand man, Les Hinton, had hired Myler, as if the miscreant had been forced on the innocent Murdochs.[30]

Political bombshells exploded on May 1, 2012, when a British parliamentary committee to which Murdoch had previously testified released a report claiming that Murdoch was "not a fit person" to run a global media empire.[31] The key paragraph reads:

> 229. On the basis of the facts and evidence before the Committee, we conclude that, if at all relevant times Rupert Murdoch did not take steps to become fully informed about phone-hacking, he turned a blind eye and exhibited wilful blindness to what was going on in his companies and publications. This culture, we consider, permeated from the top throughout the organisation and speaks volumes about the lack of effective corporate governance at News Corporation and News International. We conclude, therefore, that Rupert Murdoch is not a fit person to exercise the stewardship of a major international company.

The report was arguably aimed in part at another British government investigation by Ofcom, the U.K.'s media regulatory board, as to whether News International was a "fit and proper proprietor" of its media assets. A negative report by Ofcom could lead to calls for the Murdoch family to lose their lucrative license in BSkyB, their subscription service offering television, movies, sports, news and broadband, and telephone services. Further, as Bowers and Rusche (2012), suggest, the term "willful blindness," used several times in the parliamentary report to describe both James and Rupert Murdoch's behavior in the media scandals, "carries weight in US anti-corruption legislation," reflecting language in the U.S. Foreign Corrupt Practices Act and suggesting that, from a corporate governance perspective, those accused of willful blindness have not fulfilled their fiduciary duties and can be disciplined or removed from office (#13).

In particular, the parliamentary report accused James Murdoch of "a lack of curiousity [*sic*] . . . wilful ignorance even" of *News of the World* business practices that he was supposed to be in charge of. The report also accused Murdoch's key henchmen, Les Hinton, Colin Myler, and Tom Crone, of misleading the parliamentary committee in their testimony to it, and charging that Hinton was "complicit" in a cover-up of wrongdoing by the Murdoch corporation. The parliamentary report story was immediately headlined on the *New York Times*, the *Washington Post*, the *Los Angeles Times*, *Al-Jazeera*, and other global websites and evoked global outrage at the Murdoch empire. There were increased calls in the United States for further investigations of Murdoch's business practices in that country and for the FCC to investigate whether Murdoch was fit to broadcast in the United States (see Pilkington & Rushe, 2012a, 2012b). As mentioned above, the U.S. Foreign Corrupt Practices Act dictates that if a U.S.-based corporation like the Murdoch media empire is located in the United States, it is liable for crimes committed in foreign countries like the U.K. Thus, the report and renewed controversy concerning the Murdoch empire further imperiled Murdoch's control over his media conglomerates. As for who was fundamentally responsible for the scandal, British MP Tom Watson, who was on the parliamentary committee issuing the report and for years had been leading the charge to get the British government to properly investigate the Murdoch media empire, asserted:

> Everybody in the world knows who is responsible for the wrong-doing at News Corporation. Rupert Murdoch. More than any individual alive, he is to blame, mor-

> ally the deeds are his, he paid the piper and called the tune. It is his company, his culture, his people, his business, his failures, his crimes, the price of profits and his power. (Cited in Deans & Plunkett, 2012, #40)

As evidence it was panicking from the prospects of more testimony revealing the cozy relationships between the Conservative Party and the Murdoch corporation, the Cameron government requested that it receive advance access to the Leveson written inquiry evidence in the days to come (O'Carroll, 2012c).[32] Indeed, one of the most incriminating bombshells dropped concerning the close relationships between the Cameron government and the Murdoch media empire concerned revelations that the Tory Culture Minister Jeremy Hunt and his office had sent multitudes of personal emails to members of the Murdoch empire assuring them of support for the much-desired takeover of BSkyB. The $8 billion deal, once awaiting regulatory approval, would, at the time of the email exchange, give the Murdochs almost total control over pay and cable television in the U.K. and would provide new platforms for control of digital media and entertainment. The previous minister, Vince Cable, had indiscreetly leaked that he was planning to "wage war on Murdoch" and would provide obstacles to Murdoch's takeover of BSkyB. During April and May 2012, however, revelations leaked out that Jeremy Hunt and his office had repeatedly sent emails to James Murdoch and a Murdoch PR operative Frederic Michels assuring them that the BSkyB merger was on track, making it clear that the Cameron government was supporting the bid. Hunt's assistant, Adam Smith, had sent 542 text messages to Michels, gushing support for the BSkyB bid (Watson, 2012).

The Cameron government had obviously wanted the Murdoch cable merger to go through and had replaced Vince Cable with Jeremy Hunt as the government representative in charge of overseeing the prospective merger—on the very day that Hunt had emailed and phoned James Murdoch concerning his support for the deal! Hunt was called to explain himself at the Leveson Inquiry on May 31, which unfolded other details of his support for the Murdoch media empire. Yet Hunt insisted that he had done nothing illegal to assist the Murdochs, and Cameron allowed Hunt to keep his portfolio, despite copious demands for his resignation (Wintour, 2012).

Succeeding follow-up testimony by Andy Coulson and Rebekah Brooks at the Leveson Inquiry, nailing again their close connections to the Murdoch–Cameron nexus, was upstaged by separate new arrests for the duo. On May 15, Brooks and five others, including her husband and personal assistant, were arrested and told they would face charges of concealing documents, computers, and archive material from officers investigating the Murdoch scandals. And on May 30, 2012, Andy Coulson was again arrested, this time on charges of lying about phone hacking in a case before the Scottish High Court in December 2010, involving a Scottish politician, who claimed that Coulson's *NOTW* had intercepted voice-mail messages from his cell-phone account used in stories prejudicing him; while Coulson denied knowledge of phone hacking under oath at the time, subsequent evidence suggested he was lying.

Module 3 on relations between media and politicians in the Leveson Inquiry wrapped up with high-profile and high-drama testimony of major political leaders such as John Major, Tony Blair, Gordon Brown, and David Cameron, promising a week of high drama and spectacle. Rupert Murdoch had testified on April 25 that he had never asked any government official for any favors and that no major government figure had ever done anything he requested, although Gordon Brown and John Major were to challenge this claim. Tony Blair's testimony to the Inquiry on May 28 made clear he had decided to court and not to challenge Murdoch and his media, but his successor and political rival, Gordon Brown, took on Murdoch in his June 11 Leveson testimony. Brown vehemently denied Murdoch's claim that when Murdoch switched from Labour to Cameron and the Tories, who won the 2010 general election with Murdoch's support, he'd had a telephone call with Murdoch and threatened to "wage war" against Murdoch's businesses since Murdoch had turned against him in the election. Brown insisted that the conversation never took place and was a blatant lie, although Murdoch continued to defend his story. Brown also claimed that he had a contentious discussion with Murdoch about U.K. involvement in Afghanistan and claimed that Murdoch's media had "undermined" the U.K.'s effort in Afghanistan.

In his Leveson Inquiry testimony on June 12, former British Prime Minister John Major refuted Murdoch by recounting in detail how Murdoch had confronted Major on his desire to take the U.K. into the European Union and how Murdoch told Major that if he continued this direction, he would no longer support Major. Major refused to buckle in to Murdoch's imperious demands, and Murdoch switched to Labour, which won the next election in 2007; and under Tony Blair, the U.K. stayed out of the E.U., as Murdoch desired. Major also claimed that Murdoch's newspapers "have lowered the general quality of the British media" and described Murdoch's influence as "unattractive," surely one of the understatements of the era.

David Cameron's testimony on June 14, 2012, was full of further embarrassing revelations of his personal closeness to members of the Murdoch regime, the vast number of private and official meetings with Murdoch and other members of his clique. Yet Cameron insisted that he hadn't made any "deals" with Murdoch nor ever done any favors for Murdoch in exchange for his support, dismissing such claims as a "specious" and "unjustified" conspiracy theory. Further, Cameron also dismissed the idea that there had been what he called "a nod and a wink" covert arrangement with Mr. Murdoch, although he admitted courting Murdoch and seeking his support.

The next module in the Leveson Inquiry scheduled for July 2012 would involve searching for solutions to the problems discussed concerning the media and politics, including whether current regulatory schemes were adequate, or whether new regulation was needed. Before this inquiry got underway, however, the Murdoch media conglomerates dropped a bombshell that dramatized the seriousness of the Murdoch scandals and the need for radical changes within the Murdoch empire. Murdoch's U.S. flagship *Wall Street Journal* announced on June 26 that Murdoch was considering dividing his company into news and entertainment divisions, and great media fanfare followed his board meeting on June 27 with News Corporation executives who discussed the split. The board and stockholders had long been pushing such a division, so it was no surprise on Thursday morning, June 28, when the split of the Murdoch media empire was formally announced. Rupert Murdoch would serve as the chairman and chief executive of the media and entertainment company and would be chairman of the new publishing entity, while News Corp. Chief Operating Officer Chase Carey would be chairman and continue to run the entertainment business.

Stockholders were ecstatic that the highly profitable entertainment division was split off from the troubled news division, suffering from the inevitable decline of newspapers and the attack, shutdowns, and lawsuits on Murdoch's U.K. news properties. For Murdoch and his news corporation, however, this was a major blow as they could no longer use profits from the entertainment division to finance news operation, and declining news properties would weaken the Murdoch's already declining media and political power, further humiliating and weakening Murdoch, his family, and minions.

While the Leveson Inquiry continues to hold hearings and generate stories concerning malpractices and worse of the Murdoch media empire, I would like to draw some preliminary conclusions concerning the Murdoch media scandals, journalistic practices and ethics, and the crisis of democracy.

Preliminary Conclusions and Concluding Comments

> Sir, your newspapers for two decades have engaged in the degradation of the proper feelings of our people. What is vile they offer to gloating eyes, what is vindictive they applaud. You have done more harm to this country than any of its external enemies. (Shawcross, 1992, p. 58)[33]

By November 2011, the number of hacking victims in the Murdoch media empire scandal had been expanded to over 5,800, of which 638 had been contacted by the police (O'Carroll, 2011). These numbers suggest that Scotland Yard's phone-hacking investigation, Operation Weeting, running since January 2011 and staffed by 45 full-time detectives, is only at a beginning stage and will be active for months, perhaps years to come. In addition to Operation Weeting, British police are carrying out Operation Elveden to investigate illicit payments to police officers, and Operation Tuleta to investigate allegations of computer hacking, both of which have begun arresting suspects as I noted previously. U.S. Department of Justice investigations are also ongoing into whether the Murdoch corporation has violated the Foreign Corrupt Practices Act, which would include the Murdoch corporation's crimes in the U.K. These investigations are accompanied by the Leveson Inquiry that has been holding hearings on unethical behavior by the Murdoch media empire and other members of the U.K. press and produced a wealth of information on the malfeasance of the Murdoch and other British journalistic corporations.

Although official investigations of the Murdoch media scandal and ethical journalistic violations by the British press are continuing to unfold at the time that I am concluding this study in early May 2012, it is still possible to draw preliminary conclusions concerning crises in democracy, journalism, and the Murdoch empire as well as the legacy being shaped by the Murdoch media scandals. To begin, the extent of hacking of public and private citizens by the Murdoch media is truly shocking as is its bribing police and other authorities for stories and its slandering and spreading libelous falsehoods about individuals. Clearly, the Murdoch media empire is one of the most unethical media corporations in history, and its astounding violations of journalistic ethics and the law are currently under multiple investigations. Yet the failure in the U.K. of the Press Complaints Commission (PCC), which is supposed to regulate the media and respond to complaints by citizens of mistreatment by the media, suggests that stricter regulatory legislation is necessary, in the U.K. and in other countries where the Murdoch media have been running amok, to provide regulatory bodies and laws to safeguard the public from media abuse.

Further, the vulgarization and tabloidization of the media are among Murdoch's most noxious legacies. This sentiment is expressed in the passage from the 1946 novel *Lucinda Brayford* quoted by Murdoch's school tutor to express his sentiments about Murdoch as a journalist and cited as the epigram for this section. From his beginnings as a newspaper publisher in Australia in the 1950s, through his acquiring of media properties in the U.K., the U.S., and throughout the world—newspapers, broadcasting, and new media—Murdoch has engaged in sensationalist tabloid journalism of the lowest common denominator, subverting established journalistic standards, ethics, and traditions. Of course, the Murdoch media empire assault on journalistic news-gathering standards now has Murdoch and his family and minions involved in serious criminal investigations, so the courts, governments, and future publics will ultimately provide the most serious critique of Murdoch's journalistic practices over the past decades.

In addition, and perhaps most worrisome, is the excessive political power accrued by the Murdoch media empire, which has intensified crises of democracy in the U.K., the U.S., and other areas of the world where the Murdoch media have unduly influenced politics. Earlier in this chapter, it is noted that a robust democracy requires separation of powers between arenas of government and the media. While excessive state control of media in many countries has made democracy impossible or has severely undermined it, in the United States, as I have argued since the 1980s, corporate media have been biased in favor of conservative political parties like the Republicans and have advanced their corporate interests, thus undermining U.S. democracy (see Kellner,1990, 2005). In the U.K., by contrast, British democracy has been subverted by the vast power that the Murdoch corporation had amassed and the influence it used to shape British public opinion and state policy, as this study has argued.

During Rupert Murdoch's testimony to the Leveson Commission in April 2012, demonstrators outside of the proceedings wielded giant puppets of Murdoch as Puppet Master, dangling Tony Blair and David Cameron on his strings. Yet it appears that Murdoch's days as the most powerful media mogul in the U.K. are over as his media empire faces accelerating lawsuits and criminal investigations, government inquiries, and media investigative reporting that have been for months undermining his credibility and reputation, leading him to break up his media empire into news and information and entertainment divisions. Already Murdoch's media empire has paid out millions in lawsuits by hacking victims and faces scores of further lawsuits. A British government communication board, Ofcom, is "stepping up" its investigation whether Murdoch's news corporation is "fit and proper" to keep its broadcasting license, which could lead to revoking of the Murdoch empire's lucrative broadcasting licenses (Halliday, 2012b).

These U.K. investigations could have especially serious consequences for the Murdochs in the U.S. where there are investigations by the FBI, Department of Justice, and Senate into the Murdoch media scandals, which are prosecutable in the United States under the Foreign Corrupt Practices act since Murdoch's News International is headquartered in the U.S. Indeed, after Rupert Murdoch's Leveson Inquiry appearance, the *Guardian* reported that U.S. News Corporation stockholders are concerned over the ever-proliferating Murdoch corporation scandals and the possibilities that U.S. investigations could uncover similar scandals in the United States.[34] Further, on May 1, 2012, it was revealed that Senator Jay Rockefeller (D–W.V.) has written to Lord Justice Leveson to inquire whether it has uncovered evidence that News Corporation has broken American laws.

Hence, the possibility of the continuation of a Murdoch dynasty seems ever more unlikely. Rupert watchers like Michael Wolff note that for years, Murdoch has been obsessed with perpetuating a family dynasty and passing down his media empire to his family (Wolff, 2010, pp. 1ff, 351ff), which has created many family tensions and conflicts. But with James Murdoch having been expelled from the chairmanships of News International and Britain's leading satellite television network BSkyB, and with the board having oversight of London's two prestigious papers, the *Times* and *Sunday Times*, the heir apparent is heir no more. Murdoch's children, Lachlan and Elisabeth, who have had major media responsibilities in the past, have been sidelined, but most crucially, the Murdoch family name—once signifying wealth, power, and immense success —has become toxic, and as the criminal proceedings unfold, the family could be expelled from its empire.[35]

In conclusion, the Murdoch media empire scandals provide a singular example of how excessive control of media across the spectrum of press, broadcasting, and new media has given the Murdoch empire overwhelming political power and the ability to corrupt journalism, police, and governments as well as intensify crises of democracy. The Murdoch scandals show the danger of allowing media corporations to develop giant conglomerates and to amass tremendous power that can easily be abused. During the past decades in the U.S., the U.K., and globally, there have been tendencies toward allowing media corporations to buy competitors and develop mergers, producing gigantic media conglomerates in a deregulatory political environment.[36] The Murdoch scandals show the dangers to democracy in allowing powerful media conglomerates to emerge and to use their power without regulatory constraint to promote their own corporate interests and the interests and ideology of the political party that shares their corporate agenda, thus producing a crisis of democracy.

The current investigations into the scandals of the Murdoch media empire may well curtail the power of its corporations in specific countries and even globally, and the future of democracy in the U.K. and other sites of Murdoch power may be decided in the current investigations of Murdoch media scandals now ongoing. Hence, the ultimate resolution of the crimes and journalistic wrongdoing of the Murdoch media empire will have momentous consequences for the future of media and democracy in our time.

Notes

This text is extracted and expanded from my book, *Media Spectacle and Insurrection*, 2011*: From the Arab Uprisings to Occupy Everywhere!* (Kellner, 2012), which traces the major media spectacles of 2011 from the North African Arab Uprisings through the Occupy Movement. Thanks to Richard Keeble for sending me a PDF of his coedited book, *The Phone Hacking Scandal: Journalism on Trial*, on the Murdoch scandal and making useful comments on an earlier version of the study. A later version of this study appeared as "The Murdoch Media Empire and the Spectacle of Scandal," *International Journal of Communication*, Vol. 6 (2012): Feature 1169–1200 at http://ijoc.org/ojs/index.php/ijoc/article/view/1613/754), and I would like to thanks its editors, Larry Gross and Arlene Luck, for their constant support of my work over the years.

1. Questions were later raised concerning whether it was indeed Mulcaire, the Murdoch-employed private investigator who admittedly hacked Milly Dowler's email, who had also deleted the emails, as evidence suggested that messages had been deleted from Milly's cell phone before Mulcaire got on the case, and might have been deleted because the cell

phone was full, leading the British government to call for a specific investigation into this issue (see Leigh, 2011).

2. Davies and Hill's (2011) article, "Missing Milly Dowler's voicemail was hacked by *News of the World*," revealed how the Dowler family lawyer described the Dowlers' anguish at the revelation, stating: "It is distress heaped upon tragedy to learn that the *News of the World* had no humanity at such a terrible time. The fact that they were prepared to act in such a heinous way that could have jeopardized the police investigation and give them false hope is despicable."
3. The daily unfoldings of the Murdoch scandals were registered and archived on a daily blog by the *Guardian*; see, for example, the "Live blog" coverage at http://www.guardian.co.uk/media/blog/2011/aug/16/phone-hacking-scandal-live. The *Guardian* continued its intensive coverage and blogs on the Murdoch scandal through the winter of 2011 and into 2012.
4. On the scale of Murdoch's media empire, see Wolff (2010). The first critical account of Murdoch's growing media and political influence and its nefarious effects on journalism and democracy is found in Thomas Kiernan's *Citizen Murdoch* (1986). For a detailed account of the rise of the Murdoch media empire up until 1992, see Shawcross (1992). Chenoweth (2001) provides a much more in-depth and revealing analysis of Murdoch's questionable financial transactions, the constant crises of his media empire as it relentlessly expanded, and how Murdoch responded to various stages of new media changes in media ownership patterns and technological revolutions of the era to increase the size and influence of his media empire. Chenoweth also provides detailed accounts of how Murdoch's practices have flirted with illegality and criminality for decades. See also Watson & Hickman (2012), who provide detailed critique of Murdoch's media empire and its close connections with U.K. governments.
5. See Rupert Murdoch profile in *Forbes* at http://www.forbes.com/profile/rupert-murdoch
6. On the history and development of Murdoch's tabloid aesthetic and politics, see Chippindale & Horrie (1999) and Chenoweth (2001). On the Fox News aesthetics and politics, see Amann & Breuer (2007). In this study, I am focusing on the U.K. Murdoch scandal, where investigations of Murdoch's media empire unfolded as a media spectacle, beginning in summer 2011. Murdoch's American media empire involves other sets of scandals, and it is hoped that government, our legal system, journalists, and scholars will investigate and uncover the slimy underbelly and crimes of Murdoch's global media empire, which is located in the United States.
7. On how the O.J. Simpson murder trial and Bill Clinton sex scandals became media spectacles that contributed to the tabloidization of news and information during the decade in which Murdoch established his Fox News channel, see Kellner (2003).
8. See the discussion in Kellner (1990), Chapters 2 and 3.
9. For how media deregulation in the 1980s undermined democracy and made the media more subservient to megacorporations and conservative politics, see Bagdikian (1990) and Schiller (1990). *Television and the Crisis of Democracy* (Kellner, 1990) documented the ways that television promoted the agenda of the Reagan administration, championed George H.W. Bush in the 1988 election, and was generally supportive of him during the first years of his presidency, showing corporate media bias in the United States toward

conservative Republican administrations, which advanced the corporate interests of the media conglomerates that controlled mainstream media in this country. In the U.K., as this study documents, the crisis of the media and democracy was due to excessive media power and political influence of the Murdoch media empire that arguably corrupted British democracy. For a series of studies of the corruption of journalism and democracy in the U.K. in the Murdoch scandals, see Keeble & Mair (2012).

10. On Coulson and the Murdoch relations, see Hopkins (2012) and other articles in *The Phone Hacking Scandal. Journalism on Trial*, (Keeble & Mair, 2012). Labour MP Tom Watson and journalist Martin Hickman (2012) have published an explosive book, *Dial M for Murdoch: News Corporation and the Corruption of Britain* that delves into the seamier sides of Coulson, the Murdoch empire, and the British government. Watson and Hickman recount, among other things, how Coulson had hired Jonathan Rees, a shady character running a private detective agency, who had served years in jail and whose partner was found murdered after having a drink in a pub with Rees. Despite Rees's jail-time and sleazy record, Coulson rehired Rees to do "investigations" for Murdoch's *NOTW*, until Rees was formally charged with the murder of his detective agency partner, Daniel Morgan, although he was eventually acquitted (for details of the astonishing saga of Coulson, Rees, and the criminal underworld, see Watson & Hickman 2012, especially pp. 107–10, 167–181).
11. For an illuminating portrait of Rebekah Brooks, see Andrews (2011). Wolff presents some amusing accounts of the once Rebekah Wade's wilder and crazier sides that endeared her to the old rogue Rupert (Wolff, 2010, pp. 210ff).
12. It later came out that Dick Fedorcio, London Metropolitan Police P.R. chief and one of the most powerful people in the British police establishment, had hired Wallis to do public-relations work for the London police over more qualified firms that had bid for the job. In the Leveson Inquiry, it was also revealed that Fedorcio's own son was hired by Murdoch's tabloid the *Sun* around this time, before getting a job with the London police, further revealing the corruption of the London police establishment. Fedorcio, on extended leave while under investigation by the Independent Police Complaints Commission looking into his award of the P.R. contract to Wallis and other actions, had apparently gone so far as to allow a *NOTW* crime reporter, Lucy Panton, to use his office computer in police headquarters and his email to send in a story concerning London police; see O'Carroll (2012a). On Fedorcio's testimony in the Leveson Inquiry, see O'Carroll & Baird (2012). On March 29, Fedorcio resigned as the scandal mounted; see Laville (2012).
13. See Chippindale & Horrie (1999), who note that "by the time the Elton John saga was over he [i.e., Wallis] had collected so many writs [i.e., documents with threats of legal action from law firms] that the 'Wallis Collection' had become a stock office joke" (pp. 310–311).
14. On the role of Murdoch's media in supporting Thatcher and attacking Labour, see Chippindale & Horrie (1999). Recently, it was revealed that Murdoch had a secret meeting with Thatcher before the 1979 election in which he told her of his resolve to bust unions, introduce new technologies, and reduce the work force at his media enterprises. Murdoch also, according to minutes of the meeting, discussed his resolve to take over the *Times of London* and other papers and his approval of Thatcher's conservative policies. Murdoch

was able to take over the *Times* and other affiliated papers, and the Thatcher government supported his activities. Both sides had long denied that any meetings had taken place between the Iron Lady and Murdoch before the election, but memos released from Thatcher's government records detailed the meeting with Murdoch. See Travis (2012). This article also has the text summary of the Murdoch-Thatcher meeting.

15. See Chippindale & Horrie (1999) who tell how Murdoch and his media initially supported John Major in the 1992 general election and viciously attacked the Labour Party, which was mounting a spirited campaign against the Tories, crowing at the end of the election on a front page that "IT WAS THE SUN WOT WON IT" (pp. 432–434, 438). Chippindale & Horrie then recount how Murdoch and his media turned fiercely critical of John Major and his allies, had a well-known meeting with Tony Blair in 1995, and turned to support Blair in the 1997 election; Blair won and his government allowed Murdoch to expand his media empire, to avoid meaningful regulation, and to have access to government and Blair personally, disclosing the tremendous political power that Murdoch had accrued (438ff).
16. See Wolff (2010). Wolff's interviews on the Keith Olbermann *Counterdown!* TV show from July 8 to 18, 2011, discuss the connections among Coulson, the Murdoch media, and Cameron, and the embarrassment of Cameron and the Conservatives when it was revealed that Coulson was a major figure in the *NOTW* hacking scandals. Over the years, Olbermann pursued Murdoch, and especially his Fox News network, with intense critical passion. Thus, it was with sadness that I turned on my telly to watch Olbermann on March 30 and found out that his show was no longer airing, having been replaced by a new show with Eliot Spitzer; after a quick look at the Internet, I discovered that earlier in the day Olbermann had been fired by Current TV (Al Gore's left-liberal alternative to Fox), and that Olbermann was threatening to sue, marking a sad moment for progressive media in the United States; see Stelter (2012).
17. The term "legitimation crisis" was introduced by Jürgen Habermas (1975) in his book *Legitimation Crisis*. Habermas distinguished, on an abstract level, among "legitimation crises," "rationality crises," and "economic crises." In his book *The Fiscal Crisis of the State* (1973), James O'Connor used the term "legitimation crisis" to explain part of what he saw as a crisis of the state in the United States during the 1970s. Following these analyses, I am suggesting that the term "legitimation crisis" can be concretized through analysis of specific societies, such as U.S. society in the 1960s and 1970s when Habermas developed his analyses and contemporary British society, which Murdochgate is propelling into a legitimation crisis.
18. The charges that Murdoch company former employees questioned James Murdoch's parliamentary testimony and that the law firm of Harbottle and Lewis questioned both father and son's testimony was extensively discussed in the *Guardian* from August 10 to 16 and on the BBC; it was summarized in Lyall (2011).
19. See Sabbagh (2012). It was later revealed that *NOTW* editor Rebekah Brooks had received a £1.7 million payoff after she was forced to resign when the scandal erupted; she was subsequently arrested and forced to testify before the British Parliament. See Boffey (2011).

20. The Murdoch corporation employees who contradicted James Murdoch's testimony were Colin Myler, the former editor of the tabloid *NOTW*, and Tom Crone, the former News International legal manager. See Becker & Van Natta (2011).
21. On the history and development of Murdoch's tabloid aesthetic and politics, see Chippindale & Horrie (1999) and Chenoweth (2001). On the Fox News aesthetics and politics, see Amann & Breuer (2007). In this study, I am focusing on the U.K. Murdoch scandal, where revelations and investigations of his media empire began in summer 2011. Murdoch's American media empire involves other sets of scandals, and it is hoped that government, our legal system, journalists, and scholars will investigate and uncover the slimy underbelly and crimes of Murdoch's global media empire.
22. For complete audio, video, and transcripts of the Leveson Inquiry, see http://www.levesoninquiry.org.uk/hearings. There have also been daily blogs on the hearings in *the Guardian*, which has also published many articles on the Leveson Inquiry and continues to follow the Inquiry and the Murdoch media scandals with close attention into 2012. In 2012, *Guardian* reporter Nick Davies, who had earlier broken hacking stories concerning the Murdoch media empire and who broke the Milly Dowler story that helped generate the media spectacle over the corporation's crimes, was given the Paul Foot Award for his investigative journalism; see Sabbagh (2012). Shortly thereafter, it was announced that *Guardian* senior editor Alan Rusbridger was awarded the prestigious Harvard Kennedy Government School journalism prize; see Pilkington (2012a).
23. For a highly entertaining history of Murdoch's beloved British tabloid the *Sun*, see Chippindale & Horrie (1999).
24. Akers added "The cases we are investigating are not ones involving the odd drink, or meal, to police officers or other public officials. Instead, these are cases in which arrests have been made involving the delivery of regular, frequent and sometimes significant sums of money to small numbers of public officials by journalists" (Lyall, 2012, #14).
25. James White, Michael Seamark, & Rob Cooper (2012) note: "James Murdoch should lose his BSkyB job after quitting as boss of his dad's scandal-hit British newspaper empire, MP demands."
26. In a disgraceful performance, NBC's Brian Williams had a long interview with Cameron and failed to ask him any questions about his connections with the Murdoch scandals. In portions of the interview—broadcast on *NBC Nightly News* on March 14 and an extended interview segment on *Rock Center with Brian Williams* later in the evening, the NBC anchor asked Cameron his opinions of Hollywood representations of British royalty and politicians, as well as his personal feelings about Margaret Thatcher, Cameron's beloved inspiration, rather than probe the prime minister's connections with some of the major British media/political scandals of the era, confirming again the collapse of the news standards of U.S. TV network news organizations. On March 27, PBS' *Frontline* partially redeemed the honor of American television news broadcasting with an episode on "Murdoch's Scandals" that for the first time systematically laid out the extent of the wrongdoing, corruption of journalism, and crimes of the Murdoch media empire for U.S. audiences. Video of the episode is available online at http://video.pbs.org/video/2204235161. Further, a segment on Jon Stewart's *Daily Show* also nailed Cameron on his U.S. visit. Explaining how David Cameron used his son-in-law's plane to call on

Murdoch vacationing on his yacht, Stewart noted with incredulity, "In the States, we're not even allowed to give congress people T-shirts and hats, and our country's corrupt as shit!" (cited in Hyde, 2012).

27. For more on the BBC *Panorama* program and the global nature of the mushrooming Murdoch cable code-hacking scandal, see Pilkington, 2012b.
28. For the first day of Murdoch's Leveson Inquiry testimony, see Halliday & Plunkett, 2012a.
29. These events suggest that a war is now raging between Myler and Crone on the one side and the Murdoch family mafia centered on Rupert, James, and their henchmen—a war that could be both entertaining and instructive, albeit destructive for those concerned. Earlier in the week, a story circulated about Myler claiming that he had commanded the *NOTW* staff to collect all the dirt they could on all British politicians, as if a Murdoch newspaper were J. Edgar Hoover (Pilkington & Rushe, 2012a).
30. Murdoch's Day Two testimony was collected on the *Guardian* blog (Halliday & Plunkett, 2012a; Halliday & Plunkett, 2012b) and generated a global firestorm of news stories.
31. The Full Report by the House of Commons Culture, Media and Sport Committee, News International and Phone-hacking. Eleventh Report of Session 2010–2012. Volume 1 is available at http://www.publications.parliament.uk/pa/cm201012/cmselect/cmcumeds/903/903i.pdf
32. The same day it was announced that Cameron and other major figures in his coalition would receive advance access to Leveson inquiry witness statements (O'Carroll, 2012d).
33. When asked to comment on Rupert Murdoch and journalism in 1991, Sir James Darling, who had been Murdoch's headmaster at Geelong Grammar in Australia and helped get him into Oxford, quoted from *Lucinda Brayford*, the 1946 novel by Martin Boyd, to express his negative sentiments toward his former pupil, providing an apt commentary on Murdoch's newspapers and their baleful effects.
34. See Rushe & Treanor (2012). Michael Moore predicts that such government and criminal investigations will unfold in the United States (see Child, 2012).
35. During the annual U.S. Press Club roasting of political and media celebrities on April 30, 2012, broadcast live on CNN, host Jimmy Kimmel's roasting of Murdoch and Fox News was especially pungent, showing how a name associated with a great political and media family and feared for its possibilities of retaliation is now the butt of celebrity roasts and late-night comics' jokes, as well as riveting British government hearings and criminal proceedings. Similarly, in the U.K., the media roasted the Murdochs after their Leveson Inquiry testimony, with Peter Preston (2012) concluding:

    > Some absolutely lousy things happened at the *News of the World*, and inside News International, during the last 10 years (at least). Management, perhaps because the ageing boss over the water couldn't cope any longer, was murky, going on vestigial. Trusted servants betrayed that trust. A re-energised Yard is finally on that case. The power of Rupert—real or alleged—is broken. He's a blot and a chump. His prospects of handing over to his kids are gone. Full BSkyB ownership is beyond News Corp.'s grasp now. The back door to Downing Street is closed forever. (#9)

36. In the U.K., there are already conclusions that the Murdoch media scandals show that strict regulation of media ownership and practice is needed (Enders & Goodall, 2012).

References

Amann, J. M., & Breuer, T. (2007). *Fair and balanced, my ass! An unbridled look at the bizarre reality of Fox News*. New York: Nation Books.

Andrews, S. (2012, February). Untangling Rebekah Brooks. *Vanity Fair*, 102–107, 141–145.

Bagdikian, B. (1990). *The media monopoly* (3rd ed.). Boston, MA: Beacon Press.

BBC. (2012, February 11). Eight people held over payments inquiry. BBC. Available at http://www.bbc.co.uk/news/uk-16996275

Becker, J., & Somaiya, R. (2011, August 2). Latest arrest highlights a tabloid's cash payments. *New York Times*. Available at http://www.nytimes.com/2011/08/03/world/europe/03hacking.html?_r=1&pagewanted=print

Becker, J., & Van Natta, D. (2011, July 21). Ex-executives dispute testimony of Murdoch son. *New York Times*. Available at http://www.nytimes.com/2011/07/22/world/europe/22murdoch.html?_r=1&pagewanted=print

Bernstein, C. (2011, July 11). Murdoch's Watergate? *Newsweek*. Available at http://www.thedailybeast.com/newsweek/2011/07/10/murdoch-s-watergate.html

Boffey, D. (2011, November 5). Murdoch gave loyal lieutenant Rebekah Brooks £1.7m payoff, car and office. News International chairman may face questions in Commons over generous severance deal despite phone-hacking scandal. *Guardian*. Available at http://www.guardian.co.uk/media/2011/nov/05/murdoch-phone-hacking-rebekah-brooks

Bowers, S., & Rusche, D. (2012, May 1). Phone-hacking report: What is 'wilful blindness'? MPs make pointed allegation with accusation of 'wilful blindness,' a term that carries weight in U.S. anti-corruption legislation. *Guardian*. Available at http://www.guardian.co.uk/media/2012/may/01/phone-hacking-report-wilful-blindness?intcmp=239

Burns, J. (2012, April 25). Murdoch, center stage, plays powerless broker. *New York Times*. Available at http://www.nytimes.com/2012/04/26/world/europe/rupert-murdoch-testimony-leveson-inquiry.html?pagewanted=all

Chenoweth, N. (2001). *Virtual Murdoch. Reality wars on the information highway*. London: Secker & Warburg.

Chenoweth, N. (2012, March 28). Murdoch's inside job. *The Australian Financial Review*. Available at http://afr.com/p/business/marketing_media/murdoch_inside_job_sZrtO3tNzsy2TD1Z3TpNvJ

Child, B. (2012, April 23). Michael Moore predicts phone-hacking scandal will spread to Fox News. Documentary film-maker has 'gut feeling' investigations will reveal phone hacking at Murdoch subsidiary Fox News. *Guardian*. Available at http://www.guardian.co.uk/film/2012/apr/23/michael-moore-phone-hacking-fox-news

Chippindale, P., & Horrie, C. (1999). *Stick it up your punter! The uncut story of the* Sun *newspaper* (2nd ed.). London: Simon & Schuster.

Chozick, A. (2012, March 4). News Corp. staving off a scandal. *New York Times*. Available at http://www.nytimes.com/2012/03/05/business/media/a-disconnect-from-news-corps-scandal.html?pagewanted=all

Davies, N. (2012, January 29). Mysteries of Data Pool 3 give Rupert Murdoch a whole new headache. The arrest of four *Sun* journalists threatens to open a fresh phase of the scandal surrounding News International. *Guardian*. Available at http://www.guardian.co.uk/media/2012/jan/29/data-pool-3-sun-arrests-murdoch

Davies, N., & Hill, A. (2011, July 4). Missing Milly Dowler's voicemail was hacked by *News of the World*. *Guardian*. Available at http://www.guardian.co.uk/uk/2011/jul/04/milly-dowler-voicemail-hacked-news-of-world

Deans, J. (2012, February 28). Bryant: Phone hacking may be worst corporate corruption case for 250 years. Chris Bryant tells MPs Scotland Yard had been suborned and effectively become a subsidiary of News International. *Guardian*. Available at http://www.guardian.co.uk/media/2012/feb/28/chris-bryant-phone-hacking

Deans, J., & Plunkett, J. (2012, May 1). Phone hacking: Select committee report unveiled. *Guardian*. Available at http://www.guardian.co.uk/media/blog/2012/may/01/select-committee-report-james-rupert-murdoch

Enders, C., & Goodall, C. (2012, April 30). News Corp case shows a cap on media ownership is the way forward. The lessons from the Leveson inquiry are clear: The hold on our media of proprietors like Murdoch must be restricted. *Guardian*. Available at http://www.guardian.co.uk/commentisfree/2012/apr/30/cap-media-ownership-lessons-leveson

Guardian (editorial). (2012, April 27). Leveson inquiry: When the probe becomes the excuse. The trail of destruction which the Murdochs have wrought in court this week is getting closer to Downing Street. *Guardian*. Available at http://www.guardian.co.uk/commentisfree/2012/apr/27/leveson-inquiry-murdochs-downing-street

Habermas, J. (1975). *Legitimation crisis*. Boston, MA: Beacon Press.

Halliday, J. (2012a, March 28). Australian minister wants News Corp hacking claims investigated. Communications minister wants police to look into accusations News Corp software firm NDS engaged in 'dirty tricks.' *Guardian*. Available at http://www.guardian.co.uk/media/2012/mar/28/australian-minister-news-corp

———. (2012b, April 26). Ofcom studies phone-hacking evidence in BSkyB 'fit and proper' probe. Media watchdog steps up its investigation into News Corp's stake and requests court documents. *Guardian*. Available at http://www.guardian.co.uk/media/2012/apr/26/ofcom-phone-hacking-bskyb?newsfeed=true

Halliday, J., & Plunkett, J. (2012a, April 25). Leveson inquiry: Rupert Murdoch appears, day one. *Guardian*. Available at http://www.guardian.co.uk/media/2012/apr/25/rupert-murdoch-live-blog

———. (2012b, April 26). Leveson inquiry: Rupert Murdoch appears, day two. *Guardian*. Available at: http://www.guardian.co.uk/media/blog/2012/apr/26/rupert-murdoch-live-blog

Hill, A. (2011, September 6). Phone hacking: James Murdoch faces second grilling by MPs. *Guardian*. Available at http://www.guardian.co.uk/media/2011/sep/06/phone-hacking-james-murdoch-parliament

Hope, C. (2012, March 7). Horsegate: Deal to lend Raisa discussed at lunch between Lord Blair and Rebekah Brooks. A deal to lend a retired police horse to former tabloid editor Rebekah Brooks was agreed over lunch with the head of the Scotland Yard, it has been claimed. *Telegraph*. Available at http://www.telegraph.co.uk/news/uknews/phone-hacking/9128660/Horsegate-Deal-to-lend-Raisa-discussed-at-lunch-between-Lord-Blair-and-Rebekah-Brooks.html

Hopkins, H. L. (2012). Nobody likes a rotten apple, but someone picks them. In R. L. Keeble & J. Mair (Eds.), *The Phone Hacking Scandal. Journalism on Trial*, pp. 9–15. Suffolk, U.K.: Abramis.

Hyde, M. (2012, April 27). Lord O'Donnell is expected to state his views when he appears in front of the inquiry himself. Rupert Murdoch may be a monster but David Cameron and co are far worse. *Guardian*. Available at http://www.guardian.co.uk/commentisfree/2012/apr/27/rupert-murdoch-monster-david-cameron-worse

Keeble, R. L., & Mair, J. (Eds.). (2012). *The phone hacking scandal. Journalism on trial.* Suffolk, U.K.: Abramis.

Kellner, D. (1990). *Television and the crisis of democracy*. Boulder, CO: Westview Press.

————. (2003). *Media spectacle*. London & New York: Routledge.

————. (2005). *Media spectacle and the crisis of democracy*. Boulder, CO: Paradigm Press.

————. (2012). *Media spectacle and insurrection, 2011: From the Arab uprisings to Occupy everywhere!* London & New York: Continuum/Bloomsbury.

Kiernan, T. (1986). *Citizen Murdoch*. New York: Dodd, Mead.

Laville, S. (2012, March 20). Met's PR chief Dick Fedorcio resigns after force begins disciplinary action. IPCC inquiry found Dick Fedorcio should face gross misconduct charge for awarding contract to former NoW executive Neil Wallis. *Guardian*. Available at http://www.guardian.co.uk/uk/2012/mar/29/dick-fedorcio-resigns-metropolitan-police?intcmp=239

Leigh, D. (2011, December 11). Leveson launches spin-off inquiry into hacking of Milly Dowler's voicemail. Judge signals that fresh statements will be taken from police about latest developments. *Guardian*. Available at http://www.guardian.co.uk/media/2011/dec/12/leveson-inquiry-milly-dowler-voicemail?newsfeed=true

———. (2012, January 17). Times reporter hacked into police blogger's email account. Newspaper article revealing identity of anonymous blogger Nightjack was based on material obtained from Hotmail account. *Guardian*. Available at http://www.guardian.co.uk/media/2012/jan/17/times-reporter-hacked-nightjack-email

Lyall, S.. (2011, August 16). Letter counters hacking avowals from News Corp. *New York Times*. Available at http://www.nytimes.com/2011/08/17/world/europe/17hacking.html?_r=1

———. (2012, February 27). A fresh blot on Murdoch's *Sun*. *New York Times*. Available at http://www.nytimes.com/2012/02/28/world/europe/murdoch-hacking-inquiry-expands-to-uk-officials.html?pagewanted=all

Lyall, S., & Somaiya, R. (2012, April 4). British broadcaster with Murdoch link admits to hacking. *New York Times*. Available at http://www.nytimes.com/2012/04/06/world/europe/murdochs-sky-news-channel-discloses-email-hacking.html?pagewanted=all

O'Carroll, L. (2011, November 9). Phone hacking: Police have told fewer than one in eight potential victims. Some 638 of 5,800 possible victims have been contacted by Met, highlighting how far the investigation has still to run. *Guardian.* Available at http://www.guardian.co.uk/media/2011/nov/09/phone-hacking-police-potential-victims

———. (2012a, March 13). News of the World reporter wrote police story in Scotland Yard office. Dick Fedorcio reveals at Leveson inquiry that former *NoW* crime editor Lucy Panton used his e-mail to file story about Ali Dizaei. *Guardian.* Available at http://www.guardian.co.uk/media/2012/mar/13/news-of-world-scotland-yard-office

———. (2012b, April 26). Rupert Murdoch told a 'shameful lie' to Leveson, claims ex-*NoW* legal manager. Tom Crone denies he was responsible for phone-hacking cover-up and did not stop journalists telling bosses. *Guardian.* Available at http://www.guardian.co.uk/media/2012/apr/26/rupert-murdoch-shameful-lie-leveson?newsfeed=true

———. (2012c, May 4). Government applies for advance access to Leveson written inquiry evidence. Move could give David Cameron and other ministers chance to read statements from Andy Coulson and Rebekah Brooks. *Guardian.* Available at http://www.guardian.co.uk/media/2012/may/04/leveson-inquiry-rebekahwade

———. (2012d, May 4). David Cameron wins advance access to Leveson inquiry witness statements. Prime minister, Nick Clegg, Jeremy Hunt and four ministers will give evidence in person after being given core participant status. *Guardian.* Available at http://www.guardian.co.uk/media/2012/may/04/david-cameron-leveson-inquiry-wins

O'Carroll, L., & Baird, D. (2012, March 14). Leveson inquiry: Dick Fedorcio, Sara Cheesley appear. *Guardian.* Available at http://www.guardian.co.uk/media/2012/mar/13/leveson-inquiry-dick-fedorcio-sara-cheesley-live

O'Carroll, L., Halliday, J., & Baird, D. (2012, March 15). Leveson inquiry: Jeff Edwards, Sandra Laville, Jon Ungoed-Thomas appear. *Guardian.* Available at http://www.guardian.co.uk/media/2012/mar/14/leveson-inquiry-jeff-edwards-sandra-laville-live

O'Connor, J. (1973). *The fiscal crisis of the state.* New York: St. Martin's Press.

Pilkington, E. (2012a, March 6). Alan Rusbridger wins journalism award in U.S. *Guardian*'s editor is first non-American journalist to be given Goldsmith career award for excellence in journalism. *Guardian.* Available at http://www.guardian.co.uk/ media/2012/mar/07 /alan-rusbridger-journalism-award?newsfeed=true

———. (2012b, March 28). News Corp. faces new rash of hacking allegations on a global scale. Murdoch's media empire denies fresh wave of claims that his firms undermined rivals through code cracking and piracy. *Guardian.* Available at http://www.guardian.co.uk/media/2012/mar/28/news-corporation-nds-panorama-frontline

Pilkington, E., & Carroll, L. (2012, May 1) Murdoch facing new challenge as US senator contacts Leveson over hacking. Jay Rockefeller writes to British judge in bid to find out whether News Corporation has broken American laws. *Guardian.* Available at http://www.guardian.co.uk/media/2012/may/02/murdoch-phone-hacking-us-senator

Pilkington, E., & Rushe, D. (2012a, April 23). NY *Daily News* editor Colin Myler under scrutiny over *NoW* allegations. Allegations made that Myler, when *News of the World* editor, told reporters to dig for dirt on MPs investigating phone hacking. *Guardian.* Available at http://www.guardian.co.uk/media/2012/apr/23/colin-myler-news-of-the-world-scrutiny

———. (2012b, May 1). Rupert Murdoch's Fox broadcast licences targeted by U.S. ethics group. FCC called on to revoke licences in wake of British parliamentary report as phone hacking scandal widens abroad. *Guardian.* Available at http://www.guardian.co.uk/media/2012/may/01/rupert-murdoch-fox-licences-us?newsfeed=true

Preston, P. (2012, April 28). As Rupert Murdoch leaves the stage, trouble waits in the wings. Murdoch's appearance before Leveson was merely a sideshow—the real problem is now what the lord justice is going to do about Jeremy Hunt. Available at http://www.guardian.co.uk/media/2012/apr/28/rupert-murdoch-leveson-inquiry

Putnam, D. (2012, April 28). News Corporation has sought to undermine elected governments. Rupert Murdoch is a man driven not so much by market forces as a deep desire to optimise his empire's power and influence. *Guardian.* Available at http://www.guardian.co.uk/commentisfree/2012/apr/28/news-corporation-governments?newsfeed=true

Rayner, G. (2012, April 26). Rupert Murdoch: There was a cover-up at the *News of the World.* Rupert Murdoch has admitted that 'a clever lawyer' at the *News of the World* was involved in a cover-up over phone hacking. *Telegraph.* Available at http://www.telegraph.co.uk/news/uknews/leveson-inquiry/9228382/Rupert-Murdoch-There-was-a-cover-up-at-the-News-of-the-World.html

Rolle, D. (2012, May 4). The economics of free speech. *Huffington Post U.K.* Available at http://www.huffingtonpost.co.uk/daniel-rolle/the-economics-of-freespe_b_1127132.html

Rushe, D., & Treanor, J. (2012, April 26). News Corp. shareholders 'troubled' by Murdochs' Leveson testimony. U.S. shareholders worry testimony raises new questions and poses threats to other areas of company's media empire. *Guardian.* Available at http://www.guardian.co.uk/media/2012/apr/26/news-corp-shareholders-murdoch-leveson?newsfeed=true

Sabbagh, D. (2011, August 23). Andy Coulson's payout: A problem for the Tories? News International's severance payments to the former communications director raises several questions. *Guardian.* Available at http://www.guardian.co.uk/media/2011/aug/23/andy-coulson-payments-news-international

———. (2012, February 26). Nick Davies wins Paul Foot award for hacking exposé. Guardian reporter praised for long investigation into tabloid phone hacking. *Guardian.* Available at http://www.guardian.co.uk/media/2012/feb/28/nick-davies-hacking-investigation-award

Sabbagh, D., & Hill, A. (2011, January 19). How News Group hid the phone-hacking scandal. Judge criticises Murdoch empire as it agrees aggravated damages for 37 victims *of News of the World. Guardian.* Available at http://www.guardian.co.uk/media/2012/jan/19/news-group-phone-hacking-scandal

Sabbagh, D., & O'Carroll, L. (2012, February 13). Rupert Murdoch hit by feud over *Sun* arrests. Trevor Kavanagh, associate editor and former political editor, gives voice to the anger emanating from the *Sun*'s newsroom. *Guardian.* Available at http://www.guardian.co.uk/media/2012/feb/13/rupert-murdoch-sun-trevor-kavanagh

Schiller, H. (1990). *Culture, Inc.* New York: Oxford University Press.

Shawcross, W. (1992). *Murdoch.* New York: Simon & Schuster.

Stelter, B. (2012, March 30). Current TV dismisses Keith Olbermann. *New York Times*. Available at http://mediadecoder.blogs.nytimes.com/2012/03/30/current-tv-dismisses-keith-olbermann

Travis, A. (2012, March 16). Murdoch did meet Thatcher before *Times* takeover, memo reveals. The media mogul requested a meeting at Chequers to personally lobby the PM, and explicitly briefed her on his bid—something long denied by both sides. *Guardian*. Available at http://www.guardian.co.uk/media/2012/mar/17/rupert-murdoch-margaret-thatcher

Watson, T. (2012, May 31). Watching Hunt at Leveson revealed the depths of politicians' debasement. Jeremy Hunt's ministerial career is surely over. But after today's Leveson sitting, the scent now leads to George Osborne. *Guardian*. Available at http://www.guardian.co.uk/commentisfree/2012/may/31/jeremy-hunt-leveson-politicians-debasement

Watson, T., & Hickman, M. (2012). *Dial M for Murdoch: News Corporation and the corruption of Britain.* New York: Blue Rider Press.

White, J., Seamark, M., & Cooper, R. (2012, March 1). James Murdoch should lose his BSkyB job after quitting as boss of his dad's scandal-hit British newspaper empire, MP demands. *MailOnline*. Available at http://www.dailymail.co.uk/news/article-2108198/James-Murdoch-quits-News-International-boss-keeps-new-job-New-York.html#ixzz1oAjxuMWf

Wintour, P. (2012, May 31). Jeremy Hunt's evidence reveals hidden depth of sympathies for Murdoch. Culture secretary had difficulty at Leveson inquiry setting aside sympathies and showing he could handle BSkyB bid fairly. *Guardian*. Available at http://www.guardian.co.uk/politics/2012/may/31/jeremy-hunt-leveson-struggles-achieve-goals

Wolff, M. (2010). *The man who owns the news: Inside the secret world of Rupert Murdoch.* New York: Broadway Books.

6 Media and Ethics: The Public Sphere, Truth Telling, and Practice of Freedom

Ali Kashani

DO MEDIA HAVE an ethical responsibility toward the public? The obvious answer is yes, but what conditions will render media to recognize an ethical responsibility toward the public? Thus, it's worth considering the following concepts: the public sphere, truth telling, and the practice of freedom.

Aristotle describes humans as political animals (*zoon politikón*).[1] He also notes that humans are rational and social animals. This assertion by Aristotle implies that humans as rational and political beings practice politics in a social space. The emphasis on the social aspect of human life indicates that the practice of politics takes place in a public space, in the form of enquiry, discussion, and debate. In turn, the ideal notion of the public space as a social forum, a place of public discourse and debate requires practices of freedom, truth telling, and democracy. In 1784, the editor of *Berlinische Monatsschrift*, a monthly periodical in Berlin posed the following question to his readers: "What Is Enlightenment?" (*Was Ist Aufklärung?*). Immanuel Kant, as a philosopher and public intellectual, replied to the question in an essay entitled, "An Answer to the Question: What Is Enlightenment?" (*Beantwortung der Frage: Was Ist Aufklärung?*). In this article, Kant notes, "the motto of enlightenment is therefore: *Sapere aude!* Have courage to use your own understanding."[2] Furthermore, he suggests that freedom is necessary for enlightenment, in particular, freedom to make public use of reason. He emphasizes that the public use of reason must always be free. By public use of reason, Kant means that every individual without coercion must be able to address the public concerning social and political issues of the day in the public space, such as social forums, publications, and media, without restriction and censorship, which implies freedom of thought and speech.

In the 21st century, editors of major newspapers and journals do not pose such difficult questions to their readers; nevertheless media still play a crucial role in the public sphere and the social and political discourse. Thus, it is important to examine the relation between media, the public sphere, truth telling, and practices of freedom. Vitality of the public sphere depends on media's ethical responsibility for truth telling and practices of freedom in any democratic society that values these core ideas as necessary for the possibility of critique and dissent. Jürgen Habermas argues that mass media must maintain their freedom and independence from political and social pressure, and be receptive to the public's concerns and proposals, take up issues and contributions impartially, augment criticism, and confront the political process by articulating demands (Habermas, 1992/1998, p. 378).

What is the "public sphere" (*öffentlichkeit*), what is its role, and why is it important? To answer these questions, it is crucial to examine briefly Habermas's idea of the public sphere in *The Structural Transformation of the Public Sphere: An Inquiry into a Category of Bourgeois Society* (1962/1989).[3] He argues that the public sphere was developed as a social space in 18th-century Europe, in cafes, salons, and social clubs, where bourgeoisie discussed private interests, public interests, social, political, and economic issues using the media to express their ideas and interests without fearing censorship. In turn, these critical views in the public sphere would enter into the media and into political debate in the state and parliament (Habermas, 1962/1989). Habermas was criticized for calling it the bourgeois public sphere. His critics claimed that it was not the bourgeoisie but rather the elite who had access to the public sphere. To some extent, this criticism might be valid today, because deregulated capitalist economy dominates media and the public sphere. Nevertheless, it would seem that the idea of the public sphere and its relation to media and practice of democracy remains as relevant today as it was in 18th-century Europe. Habermas elucidates the concept of the public sphere in the context of the 21st century this way:

> [T]he public sphere is a warning system with sensors that, though unspecialized, are sensitive throughout society. From the perspective of democratic theory, the public sphere must, in addition, amplify the pressure of problems, that is, not only detect and identify problems but also convincingly and influentially thematize them, furnish them with possible solutions, and dramatize them in such a way that they are taken up and dealt with by parliamentary complexes. Besides the "signal" function there must be an effective problematization.[4]

For Habermas, the public sphere is part of his larger political theory and project of enlightenment, which is necessary for a democratic political life, which includes rational communication, truth, ethics, freedom, and use of reason in the public sphere, without distortion, fear, and constraint from political and social power. Thus, according to this view, the decline of a critical public sphere can be a threat to a democratic political life. Since media play a critical role in social and political life, it can be argued that media without freedom and critical edge are only a business enterprise for profit, not serving the public good. It would seem that the public sphere could provide a platform for critique and dissent, in which media are pressed to truth telling and ethical responsibility by the public's demand for media's freedom and independence, because mass media are the media of the public sphere to disseminate information and influence public opinion.

Therefore, how public opinion is shaped is crucial for a democratic political life, in which citizens have rights and ethical obligations to be engaged in everyday life ethics and politics rather than being passive consumers without any rights and obligations and what Michel Foucault called "docile bodies."[5]

Furthermore, the public sphere is a social association and collectivity, which is not a formal institution but rather a network for communicating information and points of views (Habermas, 1992/1998, p. 360). This view of the public sphere to some extent resembles the way in which cyberspace and the social media function as a virtual public sphere, where associations are informal and loosely based, and through a network of communications opinions are expressed and ideas exchanged that can produce public opinion on social and political issues, which in turn can be debated in media and the political discourse formally. In some cases it may lead to social and political movements; consider the Arab Spring, Tunisia, Egypt, and the Occupy Movement. The question is can the public sphere in actual and virtual form keep media independent and free to practice truth telling? In a market economy with a profit-making agenda, there is tension between the informal public sphere, and the formal institution of media, which has an ethical responsibility toward the public. It would seem the public sphere in virtual and actual form must press media to recognize an ethical responsibility toward the public and to serve the public's interest. However, this seems a formidable task and a struggle for the public sphere as a free and open social-space with transformational power to assert itself against other powers, including state and economic powers.

Therefore, the idea of truth telling becomes crucial with regard to the public sphere and media; it must be noted that truth telling implies knowing the undisputable truth. Consider WikiLeaks for pressing media to practice truth telling. Truth telling in this sense involves criticism, courage, risk taking, and ethical responsibility. As Foucault points out, it's important to pay attention to truth telling as a practice and to know who is able to tell the truth, and why we should tell the truth. Foucault says this is at the root of what we could call the critical tradition in the West (Foucault, 1983).[6] In his lectures on *The Government of Self and Others* (1982–1984)[7] at the Collège de France, Foucault discusses the Greek idea of free speech or frankness in telling the truth (*parrhesia*). In German, *parrhesia* is translated as *Freimüthigkeit*, and in English as free speech. Foucault notes five distinct elements in truth telling (*parrhesia*), which includes frankness, truth, risk taking, criticism, and ethical responsibility or duty. Frankness refers to the idea of speaking to the public and saying everything, giving a complete account with precise and direct words. It takes courage to know the truth and to communicate it to the public. It involves risk taking because speaking the truth is about justice and exposing injustice, which can cause harm to the truth teller. Thus, truth telling demands ethical responsibility and the courage to speak the truth in spite of some risk. Consequently, the practice of truth telling is not merely about demonstrating the truth but also about exercising criticism. It's a form of criticism that comes from the minority position with less power toward the majority with a powerful position. In this sense, when the truth teller reveals a truth that imperils the majority, she risks her right to speak freely. Lastly, truth telling is considered an ethical responsibility toward the public as a free and voluntary practice of frankness and criticism, to practice freedom and choose truth over falsehood or silence, and to choose risk instead of security, self-interest, and ethical indifference (Foucault, 2011a, 2011b). Certainly, Julian Assange, the founder of WikiLeaks, took some risk by divulging state and corporate secrets.

This fifth-century Greek idea of truth telling (*parrhesia*) is critical for a democratic political life as well as ethical responsibility for citizens who must defend freedom of speech and the right to practice democracy. Therefore, truth telling is necessary for public speech, which takes place among citizens in the public sphere, what the Greeks referred to as *agora*, a gathering place, assembly, or marketplace, where citizens gathered to give speeches and opinions freely. It's clear that this Greek idea of truth telling, which includes frankness, courage, risk taking, and critical stance, must be a guideline and an ethical responsibility for citizens as well as mass media. As users of cyber technology and social media, citizens can demand from media a critical edge, truth, and freedom to defend the practice of democracy. Ultimately, ethics demand that media are critical and report the truth to the public, taking risks if necessary, because to practice freedom implies having the courage to tell the truth.

The question is: what is freedom, and what is its role in general and in the context of media? Freedom as a metaphysical notion seems to be a vague ideal; thus freedom without any concrete material understanding remains an ideal metaphysical notion. To address the question of what is freedom, it's worth considering freedom as an ethical and political activity, as a practice in concrete material terms, which implies that for freedom to have a concrete sense, it must be practiced in all aspects of everyday life. For instance, the practice of freedom is necessary in a democratic political life; without it, democracy cannot be materialized. Thus, in order to have an ethical responsibility, to tell the truth, to be critical and raise questions, the practice of freedom is required, which implies freedom is necessary for media in order to have an ethical responsibility toward the public. While it would be difficult for media to be completely free in a capitalist economy, it is possible for citizens to press media to assume its ethical responsibility and exercise and maintain a degree of freedom. In other words, freedom is a practice and an ongoing power struggle that involves resisting restrictions and limitations. Thus, when media practice freedom by telling the truth, they take an ethical and political stance; but when they remain silent, they side with falsification of truth and restrict its freedom. As Foucault puts it:

> When an individual or social group succeeds in blocking a field of power relations, immobilizing them and preventing any reversibility of movement by economic, political, or military means, one is faced with what may be called a state of domination. In such a state, it is certain that practices of freedom do not exist or exist only unilaterally or are extremely constrained and limited (Foucault, 1997).

If media are dominated by economic forces or hyper-security and military influences, they no longer practice freedom. Instead, they are dominated by market-driven economic and special-interest forces. Habermas calls this "the colonization of the lifeworld by the system"[8] since media and the public sphere are part of the lifeworld, citizens must decolonize and liberate everyday life, the public sphere, and media from economic and special-interest forces by resistance and struggle for freedom. Thus, freedom demands responsibility for the community and obligation for truth telling in everyday life. As Foucault notes:

> One must respond to every law established by the world, or by the powers of the world, by violating it, systematically breaking the law and, in effect, overthrowing the reign of the one who created the world….So we can say that there was an immediate and founding correlation between conduct and counter-conduct.[9]

Foucault's assertion is a reminder that in order to decolonize everyday life and resist domination by economic and state powers, there needs to be an act of "counter-conduct" to shift relations of power in society from passive consumers to active citizens, who defend society by demanding freedom of speech and truth telling in the public sphere and media. This is evident in WikiLeaks action of "counter-conduct" by disclosing secret state and corporate information to the public and therefore interrupting the rules and power relations. Similarly, the Occupy Movement, with its actual and virtual public discourse, asserts itself as a counter-conduct to media dominated by market and state forces. Counter-conduct simply means using the tools and rules that were intended for a specific conduct for other means and conducts, therefore interrupting the rules and power relations. To this end, it is crucial to note that the ethics of everyday life is intertwined with politics of everyday life, which demands active citizenship and practice of freedom as a way of life. The ethics of everyday life involves active participation in politics of everyday life by truth telling in the public sphere in virtual and actual form; being engaged in the political discourse through various means of communication in the public sphere; and by interrupting the rules and norms of a global capitalist economy that colonizes all aspects of everyday life in terms of individual and collective practices, which citizens are engaged in on a global scale. Furthermore, it is important to have ethical concern for social and political issues; however, this ethical concern must move into the everyday life practices in concrete social and political terms. In other words, ethical concern must be a social and political everyday life practice that transforms and becomes "transformational ethics" or to put it vigorously "radical ethics." The idea of radical ethics focuses on what people practice in social and political contexts, which forms social relations and informs and produces ethical practices. The best possible place to demonstrate radical ethics is in the public sphere and media by practices of counter-conduct that reshape power relations where citizens become media by representing truth, not a distorted and falsified notion of truth. Ultimately, the ethics of everyday life demands courage and recognition that the public sphere, truth telling, and practices of freedom must be defended in order to institute a democratic media that is for the people by the people.

Notes

1. See Aristotle's Politics in, *The Complete Works of Aristotle, Vol. 2*, edited by Jonathan Barnes (Princeton, N.J.: Princeton University Press, 1995).
2. See *Kant's Political Writings*, Immanuel Kant, translated by H. B. Nisbet, edited by Hans Reiss (Cambridge, U.K.: Cambridge University Press, 1989), p. 54. Kant's article was originally published in *Berlinische Monatsschrift* in November 1784; two months earlier, Moses Mendelssohn had replied to the same question, but Kant had not read Mendelssohn's article.
3. See Jürgen Habermas's *The Structural Transformation of the Public Sphere: An Inquiry into a Category of Bourgeois Society*, translation by Thomas Burger (Cambridge, MA: MIT Press, 1989), originally published in German as *Strukturwandel der Öffentlichkeit: Untersuchungen zu einer Kategorie der bürgerlichen Gesellschaft* (Hermann Luchterhand Verlag, Darmstadt und Neuwied, 1962).
4. See Jürgen Habermas's *Between Facts and Norms, Contributions to a Discourse Theory of Law and Democracy*, translated by William Rehg (Cambridge, MA: MIT Press, 1998, p. 359). Originally published in German as *Faktizität und Geltung, Beiträge zur Diskurstheorie des Rechts und des demokratischen Rechtsstaats* (Frankfurt am Main: Suhrkamp Verlag , 1992).
5. See Michel Foucault's *Discipline and Punish: The Birth of the Prison*, translated by Alan Sheridan. New York: Vintage Books, 1995; see especially the section, "Docile Bodies," pp.135–169.
6. See Michel Foucault's lectures on "Discourse and Truth" (1983), at the University of California at Berkeley, University of California, text and audio archives. Also, see lectures by Foucault in *Fearless Speech*, edited by Joseph Pearson (Semiotext(e), 2001).
7. See Michel Foucault's lectures at the Collège de France, *The Government of Self and Others* (1982–1983), translated by Graham Burchell (New York: Palgrave Macmillan, 2011), and *The Courage of Truth: The Government of Self and Others II* (1983–1984), translated by Graham Burchell (New York: Palgrave Macmillan, 2011).
8. See Jürgen Habermas's *The Theory of Communicative Action, Vol. 1 & 2*, translated by Thomas McCarthy (Beacon Press, 1984, 1987), originally published in German as *Theorie des Kommunikativen,* Band 1 & 2, (Frankfurt am Main: Suhrkamp Verlag, 1981). The concept of "lifeworld" in German (*Lebenswelt*) was originally developed by Edmund Husserl (1895–1938), which Habermas further develops and relates to the sociological notion of everyday life. Colonization of lifeworld in some respect relates to the idea of distorted communication and limiting freedom of discussion and communication by instrumental use of rationality in capitalist economy.

References

Aristotle. (1995). *The complete works of Aristotle, Vol. 2* (Jonathan Barnes, ed.). Princeton, N.J.: Princeton University Press.

Foucault, M. (1983). Lectures on "Discourse and Truth" in the fall of 1983, at the University of California at Berkeley, University of California [Text and audio archives]. Available at http://www.lib.berkeley.edu/MRC/foucault/parrhesia.html

Foucault, M. (1995). *Discipline and punish: The birth of the prison* (Alan Sheridan, trans.). New York: Vintage Books.

Foucault, M. (1997). *Ethics: Subjectivity and truth (Essential Works of Foucault, 1954–1984, Vol. I)* (Paul Rabinow, ed.; Robert Hurley, trans.). New York: New Press.

Foucault, M. (2001). *Fearless speech* (Joseph Pearson, ed.). Los Angeles, CA: Semiotext(e).

Foucault, M. (2007). *Security, territory, population: Lectures at the Collège of France, 1977–1978* (Graham Burchell, trans.). New York: Palgrave Macmillan.

Foucault, M. (2011a). *The government of self and others: Lectures at the Collège of France, 1982–1983* (Graham Burchell, trans.). New York: Palgrave Macmillan.

Foucault, M. (2011b). *The courage of the truth (The government of self and others II): Lectures at the Collège of France, 1983–1984* (Graham Burchell, trans.). New York: Palgrave Macmillan, 2011.

Habermas, J. (1962/1989). *The structural transformation of the public sphere: An inquiry into a category of bourgeois society* (Thomas Burger, trans.). Cambridge, MA: MIT Press.

Habermas, J. (1984). *The theory of communicative action, Vol. 1* (Thomas McCarthy, trans.). Boston, MA: Beacon Press.

Habermas, J. (1987). *The theory of communicative action, Vol.* 2 (Thomas McCarthy, trans.). Boston, MA: Beacon Press.

Habermas, J. (1992/1998). *Between facts and norms: Contributions to a discourse theory of law and democracy* (William Rehg, trans.). Cambridge, MA: MIT Press.

Kant, I. (1970). *Kant's political writings* (H. B. Nisbet, trans.; Hans Reiss, ed.). Cambridge, U.K.: Cambridge University Press, 1970.

7 Alienation in the Age of Spectacle Culture

Benjamin Frymer

IN ORDER TO make sense of some of the most prominent features of our contemporary media landscape, it is important to trace the theoretical pathway accounting for the uniquely abstract character of the alienation pervading modern societies. From modern to postmodern theory, there has been an attempt to grasp the advent of modernity in terms of historically novel forms of abstract life that generate a society of objects, symbols, codes, images, discourses, and ideals that come to have power over the very human beings who create them. The inversion of subject and object characterized by whole societies saturated with multiple modes of abstraction has been analyzed in many vastly different ways but typically is framed in terms of human beings becoming estranged from their own human qualities and possibilities. Whether a part of the existential, Marxist, feminist, or sociological traditions, these critiques come together to illuminate alienation as a historically contingent form of cultural and economic domination in which human capacities are undermined by the objectified modes of life that have become today's media-saturated societies.

Yet at the beginning of the 21st century, the term "alienation" has been used in so many ways to describe so many different psychological, existential, ontological, theological, social, political, and economic conditions that it has ceased to have any real meaning at all. In everyday use, the term has most typically been depoliticized to such an extent that it refers to the everyday personal speech or behavior that insults, angers, or offends others, thus pushing them away from the offender. Yet within the critical traditions that emerged in the modern period and that lead to Debord, alienation marked a particular form of inverted and distorted human existence within modern cultural and economic conditions. More specifically, the critical conception of alienation came to mean the historically contingent domination of the individual by social, economic, and cultural forces transforming the human subject into an object separated from his or her own humanity, other people, and larger social life. Beyond this, entire social formations were characterized as alienated if, as in modern capitalism, their mode of organization cohered around the subordination of human subjects to the world of objects and transformed human complexity, reality, and diversity into monolithic abstractions (Ollman, 1971; Horton, 1964; Schacht, 1970; Lowith, 1982).

In their efforts to understand the series of momentous forces undermining traditional societies and bringing about the advent of modernity in the

West, the group of philosophers and social theorists now referred to as "modern" thinkers wrote about the dawn of the individual in an age of abstraction. Even though such philosophical giants as Kierkegaard and Nietzsche along with such founders of social and political theory as Marx, Durkheim, Simmel, Weber, and Tonnies placed their emphases on very different spheres of social life, their seminal work in analyzing the birth of modernity shares common ground. At least to some extent, their work all explores new, modern relationships between self and society. These relationships are perceived to be radically different than pre-modern forms of integration through religion, tradition, and authoritarian economic and political orders because the very conception and life of the individual emerge out of modern transformations. However, while the modern age gives birth to the individual, it also paradoxically undermines its possibilities by subjecting human life to a constellation of abstract, objectified conditions such as symbolic exchange in the capitalist market, bureaucracy, the production of multiple media forms, and discursive normalization in modern institutions.

As modern individuals begin to confront these abstract modes of social life, the central problem for the individual shifts from the pre-modern one of authoritarian domination to the quintessentially modern one of alienation. No longer subject to the tyranny and brute power of authoritarian rule, the individual is, on the one hand liberated from naked control and the suppression of self. Yet this very liberation threatens to turn into its dialectical negation as the new-found self confronts modern abstract forms of control with the potential to separate individuals from themselves and social life. From the birth of modern philosophy and sociology through the critical traditions of Western Marxism, this new relationship between self and society, one which threatens to become characterized by specifically modern forms of dehumanization and fragmentation, becomes the central dilemma of contemporary life. This paradox of modernity and the fate of the individual is one that infused 18th- and 19th-century debates over the use of reason—between Enlightenment proponents of reason's promises and its critics, such as Kierkegaard and Nietzsche.

In his writings on the nefarious influence of the modern press (i.e., media), which "gives rise to the abstraction's "phantom, 'the public,' which is the real leveler" (1978, p. 93), Kierkegaard develops one of the first modern critiques of mass conformity to mediated abstractions, in writing that anticipates much of the Western Marxist tradition. He argues that the modern press has gradually generated what he terms a "phantom public" (Best & Kellner, 1997), a massive abstraction that not only shapes public opinion but also overwhelms the subjectivity of individuals. The modern individual has great difficulty living an authentic life in the face of the phantom public's pressure to conform to the mass. In fact, massification undermines the very possibility of authentic human selfhood, which is based on individual subjective truth, not reason (abstract systems) or society. The activity and thought of concrete, particular human beings are melted down into the objectified sameness of mass public opinion. The result is a society full of passive objects that together constitute a fictional public "made up of unsubstantial individuals" and that "cannot even have so much as a single representative, because it is itself an abstraction" (Kierkegaard, 1978, p. 91).

According to Best and Kellner (1997), Kierkegaard's recognition of the induced passivity of modern subjects by unreal social artifacts and media spectacle anticipates the post-modern analyses of Debord and Baudrillard. For Kierkegaard, not only is "the public" an unreal abstraction, it is also one that simultaneously creates a simulation of a real community of individuals. This community can't be located anywhere in space or time yet nevertheless exists in the public consciousness. As Best and Kellner note, "The press, therefore, not only helps to create the masses, it simulates the fictive "public" as a real referent to mask the fact that the individuated community it addresses doesn't exist (p. 46). Again, they note that, "Crucially, the press for Kierkegaard creates an age of 'publicity' that devalues action and manufactures an illusory pseudo-world, which Baudrillard would later call a 'hyperreality'....'The public likes to transform all actuality into a theater' (Kierkegaard, 1978, 136)" (p. 48). Best and Kellner conclude, "Thus, for Kierkegaard modern society is an abstraction, a nonentity, a fiction, a mass of individuals without connection to one another or to the religious Idea. In language that could come straight from Baudrillard, who characterizes the public by terms such as 'black hole' or 'opaque nebula' (Baudrillard, 1983: 3), Kierkegaard describes the social as 'an evasion, a dissipation, an illusion' (1978: 6)" (p. 48).

It is to a substantial extent this type of transformed relationship between self and modern society, and the fate of the individual in new conditions, that also became the preoccupation of modern social thought. One of the major dilemmas for this new field of study concerned the attempt to preserve the self and its freedom in the face of the very abstract forces that had made it possible. In other words, modern thinkers such as Rousseau, Marx, Simmel, Durkheim, and Du Bois observed that the very forces that give rise to the self threatened to estrange it from its potential development in society.

The artificiality of modern Western culture, its objectification, or anomic collapse of meaning (Durkheim), all in their own way complement Marx's analysis of alienation within the capitalist mode of production. Although Marx did not write about culture extensively like the other classical theorists, his concern with human estrangement in capitalist society has obvious implications for understanding modern media culture and connects his work with other analysts of modern society. For Marx, both alienation and commodity fetishism are hallmarks of capitalist society and describe an inverted form of species-being in which human beings become dominated by the objects they produce when working in capitalist relations of production.

In the master work of his later years, *Capital* (1967), Marx extends his earlier analysis of alienation to a thoroughgoing critique of the capitalist mode of production. His seminal critique of political economy proceeds through unraveling the answer to the central riddle of capitalist society—the true nature of the commodity. For Marx, commodification is another way to analyze the inverted subject-object world of capitalist society in which abstract exchange value takes precedence over concrete material use value and economic (market) relations come to dominate the whole of human and social life. The production and exchange of these commodity-objects, an abstract historical artifact of capitalist ownership, thus become the basis and purpose of capitalist life itself, subordinating real material needs to its workings and the benefits of the capitalist class.

As with the alienation of concrete labor in commodity production, Marx argues that the larger fetishism of commodities, through the inversion of exchange value over use value, operates according to the abstract, formal logic of the capitalist mode of production. Just as alienated labor constitutes the subordination of real human qualities and capacities to the objects they produce, exchange value transforms the different qualitative values and uses of unique products into quantitative rates of equivalent market value. Again, the concrete, here in the sense of specific use values that different products supply, is transformed into the abstract, in the form of exchange value. Thus the commodity form is analyzed by Marx as the major abstraction dominating human life in capitalist society to such an extent that only objects are endowed with value. In this inverted world, human qualities are transferred to commodities and the characteristics of objects are transferred to human beings. Marx's analysis of commodity fetishism uncovers the true source of capitalist value in the autonomous power the economy obtains over human life. With this autonomy, abstractions dominate the relationships and exchanges that once took place in local, concrete human communities, and human beings are governed by the appearances of economic categories and objects rather than governing themselves. These economic forms appear to have a reality independent of the real human beings who have created them in history.

Marx's critique of commodity fetishism in *Capital* proved to be of seminal importance for the Hungarian thinker Georg Lukacs, and it was not until his publication of *History and Class Consciousness* in 1923 that the next major analysis of capitalist abstraction would be conducted. Lukacs had no access to Marx's early writings on alienation yet nevertheless managed to extract Marx's concern with estrangement from his reading of *Capital.* In *History and Class Consciousness*, Lukacs transforms Marx's concept of commodity fetishism into his own theory of reification by integrating Weber's theory of Western rationalization into Marx's philosophy of praxis (Feenberg, 1986).

As with Marx, Lukacs aims to uncover the inversion of ideological appearance over reality in capitalist societies through rigorous examination of the very cultural logic of capitalist life. However, Lukacs generalizes Marx's conception of fetishism beyond the economic system, using Weber to analyze this cultural logic and its ideological effects in every institution of modern society. In his massive body of work, Weber had argued that formal or instrumental rationality had assumed dominance over substantive rationality, leading to irrational modes of life in which continual calculation regarding efficiency overrode consideration of the ends of human actions. From science, to law, to religion, instrumental reason had transformed quality, substance, and purpose into quantity, and technical calculations for controlling society and nature.

Lukacs argues that contemporary capitalist societies are pervaded by a similar type of formal rationality that dominates human beings to such an extent that they lose the ability to grasp the material and historical basis of their society's dominant cultural and institutional categories. His amalgamation of Weber's rationalization thesis and Marx's analysis of commodity fetishism comes together in a critical analysis of the "reification" of capitalist society. For Lukacs, reification refers to a political-economic, scientific, and cultural phenomenon whereby relationships between historical subjects are mystified by formal rationality into the abstract appearance of those between ahistorical objects. While the capitalist economic system is ultimately the basis of this formal rationality, the reified world comes to have a relatively autonomous hold over social life, including the economy. In fact, for Lukacs "What is customarily called the economy is nothing but the system of forms of objectivity of real life" (1971, pp. 152). With the development of reification he argued that not only autonomous individual reason but also the possibility of working-class consciousness was structurally blocked without the mediation of critical theory. However by opposing the reified world of formal rationality with a critical dialectical reason, Marxism could explode the realm of objectified appearances and transcend the gap between subject and object in revolution.

Lukacs of course was one of the primary influences on the Frankfurt School's critical theory of modern society. In the face of fascism and the post-war spread of capitalist ideology, Adorno, Horkheimer (with Adorno in *Dialectic of Enlightenment* [1972]), and Marcuse modified Lukacs into "end of reason" arguments that, if it wasn't proclaimed already, sounded the death-knell of the Enlightenment project. Marcuse's *One-Dimensional Man* (1964) is a particularly powerful examination of reason's perversion into capitalist ideology, and Marcuse's analysis of alienation in its many forms deserves of an entire chapter in and of itself.

It was Debord though who, following Lukacs, most seriously took up Marx's original analysis of capitalism in terms of the abstract power of the capitalist economy over everyday life. Debord's analysis of the society of the spectacle must be contrasted to common sense notions of spectacles and alienation. Although the term "spectacle" has taken on a vulgar meaning in everyday American media culture, Debord's work cannot be assimilated to this limited sense of a dramatic event that captures public attention. Nor can his thesis simply be considered another sociological theory of the power of the mass media to shape audiences and social understandings. Instead, it must be situated within the radical artistic, political, and social movements out of which it came in the 1960s.

As with Lukacs, Debord perceived the key to Marx's work in the concept of commodity fetishism. He places the following statement from Lukacs at the beginning of a section entitled "The Commodity as Spectacle":

> The commodity can only be understood in its undistorted essence when it becomes the universal category of society as a whole. Only in this context does the reification produced by commodity relations assume decisive importance both for the objective evolution of society and for the stance adopted by men towards it. Only then does the commodity become crucial for the subjugation of men's consciousness to the forms in which this reification finds expression....As labor is progressively rationalized and mechanized man's lack of will is reinforced by the way in which his activity becomes less active and more and more contemplative (Debord, 1995, p. 25).

Just as Lukacs sought to deepen Marx's analysis of the commodity form in his theory of reification, Debord argues that "the spectacle" is an extension of commodity fetishism to every realm of capitalist life. Jappe's (1999) reading of Debord through Marx, Lukacs, and the Hegelian-Marxist problematic of alienation illuminates the centrality of Marx's conceptions of the commodity-form and commodity fetishism in Debord's analysis:

> Debord's use of the terms 'image' and 'spectacle' should be understood as an extension of Marx's idea of the commodity-form. All these concepts reduce the multiplicity of the real to a unique, abstract, and equal form. And indeed the image and the spectacle occupy the same position in Debord's thought as the commodity and its derivatives do in Marx's. The first sentence of *The Society of the Spectacle* is a detournement of the first sentence of *Capital*: 'The whole life of those societies in which modern conditions of production prevail presents itself as an immense accumulation of *spectacles*.' Likewise, Debord substitutes the word 'spectacle' for the word 'capital' in another sentence borrowed from Marx: 'The spectacle is not a collection of images; rather it is a social relationship between people that is mediated by images' (SS, 4). According to Marx, money accumulated beyond a certain threshold is transformed into capital; according to Debord, capital accumulated beyond a certain threshold is transformed into images (SS, 34). The spectacle is the equivalent not merely of goods, as is money, but also of all possible forms of activity, the reason being, precisely, that 'whatever society as a whole can be and do' has been commodified (SS, 49). The 'essentially tautological' character of the spectacle (SS, 13) perfectly echoes the tautological and self-referential character of abstract labor, of which the only goal is to increase the mass of objectified dead labor and which in effect treats the production of use-values merely as a means of reaching that goal. The spectacle is conceived of by Debord as a visualization of the abstract link that exchange establishes between individuals, just as, for Marx, money was the materialization of that link. And images in their turn assume the material form and exert a real influence on society: this is why Debord insists that 'ideological entities have never been mere fictions' (SS, 212). (Jappe, 1999, p. 19)

The society of the spectacle then does not refer to one dominated by media displays of sex and violence or the mass communication of television and advertising although these are considered aspects of spectacular life. The mass media are, rather, the spectacle society's "most stultifying superficial manifestation" (Debord, 1995, p. 19). They represent a new deployment of power and a capitalist system that has perfected power in the realm of representation. Debord argues that "the spectacle" is the latest instantiation of an entire social structure inverted by commodity fetishism. The pervasive landscape of images and symbols in advanced capitalist life is the contemporary form of abstract power holding humanity in chains.

Debord begins his major work with a famous passage from Feuerbach's *The Essence of Christianity* (1957) stating that "for the present age...illusion only is sacred, truth profane." The passage indicates both Debord's position in the Hegelian-Marxist alienation tradition and his attempt to transcend it through a critical theory of a new capitalist formation that alienates its subjects in abstract life, becoming "lost in media." For Debord, advanced capitalist societies devalue and impoverish human life and powers through the projection of life, not into god, but into the spectacle. The society of the spectacle is a contemplative society in which real life and activity are separated from individuals and only occur in the external, manufactured world of abstractions. As in religious belief, the meaning and purpose of life are provided *for* human beings by power, by external forces of non-life.

Moving beyond Erich Fromm's similar argument in *The Sane Society* (1955), Debord's analysis of this phase of abstract life rests on a conception of alienation that involves the transformation of "having" into "appearing":

> An earlier stage in the economy's domination of social life entailed an obvious downgrading of *being* into *having* that left its stamp on all human endeavor. The present stage, in which social life is completely taken over by the accumulated products of the economy, entails a generalized shift from *having* to appearing: all effective "having" must now derive both its immediate prestige and its ultimate raison d'être from appearances. At the same time all individual reality, being directly dependent on social power and completely shaped by that power, has assumed a social character. Indeed, it is only inasmuch as individual reality *is not* that it is allowed to appear. (Debord, 1995, p. 16)

In advanced capitalist societies, whole populations have been reduced to passive spectators of manufactured appearances that come to be regarded as reality. Their passivity in the face of these spectacles means that "direct experience and the determination of events by individuals themselves are replaced by passive contemplation of images (which have, moreover, been chosen by other people)" (Jappe, 1999, p. 6). Human beings in the grasp of the spectacle forfeit their own active participation in life to the passive consumption of capital's vision of what life is supposed to be.

Debord's theory of alienation as induced passivity is asserted in the very first sections of his work. *The Society of the Spectacle* begins (paralleling Marx's *Capital*):

> The whole life of those societies in which modern conditions of production prevail presents itself as an immense accumulation of *spectacles*. All that once was directly lived has become mere representation.... Images detached from every aspect of life merge into a common stream, and the former unity of life is lost forever. Apprehended in a *partial* way, reality unfolds in a new generality as a pseudo-world apart, solely as an object of contemplation. The tendency toward the specialization of images-of-the-world finds its highest expression in the world of the autonomous image, where deceit deceives itself. The spectacle in its generality is a concrete inversion of life, and, as such, the autonomous movement of non-life. (Debord, 1995, p. 12).

The "autonomous movement of non-life" is one of Debord's most felicitous phrases in characterizing the domination of everyday life by abstractions that remove human beings from the stream of their own lives. The activity and movement of human beings are devalued in the contemplation of images of a spectacular pseudo-reality.

Marx uncovered the ground of alienation in the form of material *separations* in the capitalist mode of production; for Marx, in terms of those between the laborer and the process and end of production. Debord argues that separation is the "alpha and omega of the spectacle" (p. 20). The society of the spectacle is based on multiple, interrelated forms of separation. However, given that social power itself has always entailed separation in the form of the state, economy, or status privileges that set up social hierarchy and division, it is not general separation itself that is the hallmark of a spectacle society. Rather, it is the split between the realm of representation of real life and real life itself, a form of separation that divides human beings from life activity and from each other in the denial of real community. Debord explicates this by stating:

> The spectacle divides the world into two parts, one of which is held up as self-representation to the world, and is superior to the world. The spectacle is simply the

> common language that bridges this division. Spectators are linked only by a one-way relationship to the very center that maintains their isolation from one another. The spectacle thus unites what is separate, but it unites it only *in its separateness*. (p. 22)

Therefore, the material separations of capitalist society produce a form of power that leads to a penultimate division between the material ground of everyday life and the representational world over and above this life. The pseudo-world of the spectacle is not only a form of separation itself but divides modern subjects from one another, each of whom stands isolated in their private contemplation. Above all then, Debord's theory is an analysis of the extension and deepening of human and social alienation in everyday modern life.

Debord's question is one that is at the heart of post-modern and post-structuralist cultural theory—a body or work that places contemporary developments such as mass communications technology, the proliferation of signs and discourse, the fragmentation of identity, mass-mediated constructions of reality and self, and the breakdown of coherent metanarratives within the context of a critique of Enlightenment rationality and the historical shift to a purportedly new phase of capitalism. Post-structuralist thinkers such as Derrida, Foucault, and Baudrillard are divided in their response to the crisis of reason and the ostensible eclipse of modernity, but each in their own way places the breakdown of the unified rational subject at the forefront of their philosophical and social analysis. The post-modern subject that emerges from their work is fragmented by the multiplicity of discursive projects, media simulacra, and power/knowledge formations that call into question the progressive character of Enlightenment rationality and even the possibility of grounded individual identity.

Critical theorists of post-modern culture, such as Debord, Jameson, Kellner, Agger, and Ashley, take a different approach to the question of post-modernity, continuing to work within the problematic of Western Marxism in their interrogation of capitalist social relations and cultural products. By combining the Western Marxist analysis of reification and commodification, the post-structuralist interrogation of knowledge/power formations, and the new critical sociology of post-modernity, this new school of cultural studies makes visible new forms of post-modern alienation. With significant changes in capitalist production and consumption transforming the organization of society and subjectivity, critical theories of post-modernity speak to the new dialectic of domination and resistance in a globalized, digitized, high-speed information society where capital, images, and commercialized culture all flow freely across time and space. As the post-modern individual becomes subjected to a barrage of images and sped-up information flow, what are the consequences for identity, the self, learning, and education?

References

Adorno, T., & Max Horkheimer (1972). *Dialectic of enlightenment.* New York: Herder & Herder.

Baudrillard, J. (1983). *Simulations.* New York: Semiotext(e).

Best, S., & Kellner, D. (1997). *The postmodern turn.* New York: Routledge.

Debord G. (1995). *The society of the spectacle.* New York: Zone Books.

Feenberg, A. (1986). *Lukacs, Marx, and the sources of critical theory.* New York: Oxford University Press.

Feuerbach, L. (1957). *The essence of Christianity.* New York: Harper & Row.

Fromm, E. (1955). *The sane society.* New York: Rinehart & Company.

Horton, J. (1964). The dehumanization of anomie and alienation: A problem in the ideology of sociology. *The British Journal of Sociology, XV*(4), 283–300.

Jappe, A. (1999). *Guy Debord.* Berkeley: University of California Press.

Kierkegaard, S. (1978). *Two ages: The age of revolution and the present age.* Princeton, N.J.: Princeton University Press.

Lowith, K. (1982). *Max Weber and Karl Marx.* London, U.K.: Routledge.

Lukacs, G. (1971). *History and class consciousness.* London: Merlin Press.

Marcuse, H. (1964). *One-dimensional man.* Boston, MA: Beacon Press.

Marx, K. (1967). *Capital: Volume 1.* New York: International Publishers.

Ollman, B. (1971). *Alienation: Marx's conception of man in a capitalist society.* Cambridge, U.K.: Cambridge University Press.

Schacht, R. (1970). *Alienation.* Garden City, NY: Doubleday.

8 Neoliberal Media's Commodification of Occupy Wall Street and Radical Social Movements

Brian Klocke

NEOLIBERAL globalization, by enforcing the application of market logic to social life, expands the commodification of all spheres of society (Birchfield, 1999). It is a process that turns labor, products, services, exotic financial instruments, media consumers, social networking, and even protesters into products of capital accumulation for wealthy transnational corporations, while cloaking capitalism's inherent systemic exploitation through dramatic media narratives and spectacles.

Corporate mainstream media portray the Arab Spring and Occupy Wall Street movements as coming out of nowhere, as a rupture with history, or rather as a rupture with "the end of history"—an ideological belief in Western triumphalism through the advancement of global capitalism, which neoliberals erroneously equate with democracy. Republicans and Democrats, neoconservatives and neoliberals alike have celebrated this idea that communism has been defeated, capitalism has won, and there are no alternatives. It is encapsulated in Fukuyama's 1989 end-of-history thesis:

> The triumph of the West, of the Western *idea*, is evident first of all in the total exhaustion of viable systematic alternatives to Western liberalism.... What we may be witnessing is not just the end of the Cold War, or the passing of a particular period of postwar history, but the end of history as such: that is, the end point of mankind's ideological evolution and the universalization of Western liberal democracy as the final form of human government (#3–#4).

And it is enshrined in George W. Bush's 2002 National Security Strategy document:

> The great struggles of the twentieth century between liberty and totalitarianism ended with a decisive victory for the forces of freedom—and a single sustainable model for national success: freedom, democracy, and free enterprise.... These values of freedom are right and true for every person, in every society...the United States will use this moment of opportunity to extend the benefits of freedom across the globe. We will actively work to bring the hope of democracy, development, free markets, and free trade to every corner of the world (introductory letter, #1).

These passages from Fukuyama and Bush show how ideologies[1] such as neoliberalism come to be seen as natural (an outcome of "evolution"), as universal ("true for every person, in every society"), and complete ("decisive victory"; "the final form of human government").

Herbert Schiller and many other media scholars have shown how transnational news corporations are agents of ideological socialization that serve to stabilize capitalist systems by providing "in their imagery and messagery, the beliefs and perspectives that create and reinforce their audiences' attachments to the way things are in the system overall" (1979, p. 30). The Occupy Wall Street (OWS) movement challenges the assumptions of neoliberal globalization as a "desirable and inevitable" form of governing social life, as implied by the Declaration of the Occupation of New York City below.

> As we gather together in solidarity to express a feeling of mass injustice, we must not lose sight of what brought us together. We write so that all people who feel wronged by the corporate forces of the world can know that we are your allies….a democratic government derives its just power from the people, but corporations do not seek consent to extract wealth from the people and the Earth; and that no true democracy is attainable when the process is determined by economic power (New York City General Assembly, 2011, #1–#2).

The recovery from the Great Recession has occurred for large corporations and the financial elite but has still not happened for a majority of U.S. residents and many are righteously angry about this inequity. An October 2011 *Time* magazine poll (Brohinsky, 2011) showed that 79 percent of Americans agree that the gap between the rich and poor in the U.S. is too large. All this has provided a political opportunity for the OWS "brand" and other global protest movements to garner some national Western media attention, including being named as "Person of the Year" for 2011 by *Time* magazine.

While the exact timing and trajectory of social movements are rarely predictable, the surprising thing about OWS is not that it has begun, but that it didn't begin sooner, given the levels of socioeconomic inequality that have been increasing in the States and overseas since the 1970s. *Time*'s construction of "The Protester" as their 2011 "Person of the Year," like much corporate mainstream media, encourages audiences to be spectators of politics and consumers of entertaining social dramas rather than participants in deliberative discourses of democracy and movements for social justice.

"Over the past few decades," indicates scholar Daniel Hallin, media have become one of "the most important social institutions which have been subject to 'enclosure' by the logic of the market in the Age of Neoliberalism" (Hallin, 2008, p. 43).

The Rise of Global Infotainment Commodities

The incorporation of media into the structure of the market was facilitated by the 1996 Telecommunications Act (McChesney & Schiller, 2003), creating an accelerated "shift to neoliberal orthodoxy—which relaxed or eliminated barriers to commercial exploitation of media, foreign investment in the communication system and concentrated ownership" (p. iii). These changes in media ownership were accompanied with other structural, cultural, and content changes of news media work as well. Massive layoffs in newsroom staffs were initiated to increase corporate profits. By 2005, editors and executives of media corporations were telling the Project for Excellence in Journalism (PEJ) that the "battle at the top" between those arguing for the public good and those arguing for more profit, had been won by the accountants (Pew Research Center, 2006, p. 4). By 2010, newsrooms had been reduced by 30 percent in just a decade (Rosentiel & Mitchell, 2011). As a result, the PEJ reports there were "more outlets covering fewer stories" (Pew Research Center's PEJ, 2006, p. 3) in similar ways with a limited list of sources and shorter news stories across media platforms. As media provided fewer follow ups of story issues, news became more transitory, disjointed, and event driven (Iyengar, 1991). In this transformation, "people" and events "rather than issues" become "the pivot of the text in the articles" (Peri, 2004, p. 45), in what scholars call "soft" news or "infotainment"—a focus on trivial and entertaining information.

As media have become more global, they have shifted towards stories and images of dramatic spectacles. Following the mode and genre of television, news media have begun to "privilege an informal communicative style with its emphasis on personalities, style, storytelling skills and spectacles" (Thussu, 2008, p. 3). News is increasingly oriented towards a visual rhetoric that "places a premium on images over words, emotions over rationality, speed over reflection, distraction over deliberation, slogans over arguments, the glance over the gaze, appearance over truth, the present over the past" (DeLuca & Peeples, 2002, p. 133). Strong images and emotions are more easily transferable to a global media market than is text, which not only needs to be translated but explained in a cross-cultural context to be fully understood. Thus, the lowest common denominators of social conflict and violence, love and betrayal, car crashes and crime scenes are more profitable in a packaged news commodity than discussions of policy issues. The trend of presenting news as dramatic spectacle comes, as political scientist Daya Thussu says, "at the expense of news about political, civic and public affairs" (2008, p. 8). It also comes at the expense of deliberation about systemic issues of social inequality and what to do about it. *Time*'s selection of "the protester" as "person of the year" provides a useful example to understand the impact of neoliberalism on news coverage of social unrest.

Analyzing *Time*'s Story of "The Protester"

The news production process includes decisions on how to package news products in ways that will gather the greatest proportion of their targeted audience(s) in order to attract the most lucrative advertising contracts. In this context, the corporate media, including social media like Facebook, are selling other corporations the "product" of marketing access to particular consumer audience demographics. Media's development of infotainment commodities, as described above, has led to a more evocative image-centric and dramatic presentation of news.

At first glance, *Time* magazine's person-of-the-year cover image focuses, not on a mass movement of people demonstrating, but on a close-up illustration of a single female protester, wearing a hat and a scarf so that only her forehead, darkened eyebrows, and eyes are showing, accented, along with her face scarf, in thick red and black highlights, which seem to signal potential danger or violence. Upon close inspection, one begins to see a pattern of a few sprinkled protesters, faded into the background like wallpaper. They are yelling and marching, but their message is not clear, as only two signs are featured with the words cut short, their full messages in English concealed. What's illustrated as important then, are not the collective messages of a social movement but the actions of individuals. Even more faded and difficult to make out are maps of Egypt, Iran, and Los Angeles, and other individual protesters on and through the body of the one enlarged protester. This stylistic cover illustration, like the story within, tries to simultaneously and slickly represent an individualistic, iconic image of protesting, and a single, universal story of protesters—one that is timeless, yet unexpected and new. It is a drama detached from its historical, political, and social mooring.[2]

Time's editor, Rick Stengel, in introducing the special issue, identifies a single individual as the starting point and cause of all the revolutions of the Arab Spring:

> No one could have known that when a Tunisian fruit vendor set himself on fire in a public square in a town barely on a map, he would spark protests that would bring down dictators in Tunisia, Egypt and Libya and rattle regimes in Syria, Yemen and Bahrain. (2011, p. 53)

This constructs a narrative that all the uprisings are due not only to one event but to the actions of one person. This singular story fits into the American myth of rugged individualism and of remarkable individuals as the shapers of history. When explaining why "The Protester" was chosen for the cover of the special issue, Stengel emphasized the embodiment of the "idea that individual action can bring collective, colossal change." But while this narrative construction of a snapshot in time is dramatic and easy to digest, it also leaves out—like much of *Time*'s story—the historical context of social and economic conditions that give rise to protests.

Mohamed Bouazizi was not the first (Ryan, 2011) nor the last (Bakri, 2012) Tunisian to have set himself on fire, and the mass demonstrations that followed also arose out of the background of high unemployment and rising food prices, which had caused massive protests before, in 2008, in Tunisia, Egypt, and elsewhere. In late 2010 to early 2011, the U.N.'s Food and Agricultural Organization reported that world food prices surged to record highs (FAO, 2011), due largely to neoliberal financial speculation of food commodities and the impact of climate change—fueled by industrialized oil-dependent economies—on food production.

Stengel simultaneously celebrates Bouazizi as the historical rupture and spark of the revolutions, and as unlikely, depicting Tunisia as "a place where you can't imagine anything like that beginning" (Rose, 2011, transcript). In contrast, he sees "America" as being "conceived in protest," which he describes as the "source code for democracy—and evidence for the lack of it" (Stengel, 2011, p. 53). This implication of American exceptionalism is reminiscent of President Reagan's 1997 declaration (as cited in Ives, 2007) that "America is a shining city upon a hill whose beacon light guides freedom-loving people everywhere." The sentiment is subtly echoed in

Andersen's cover story, which quotes from Fukuyama's end-of-history essay and states that "America's great…contribution to fomenting freedom abroad was enabling it technologically, as an epiphenomenon of globalization" (Andersen, 2011, p. 89). Stengel and Andersen seem to exhibit a liberal version of what Edward Said identified as Orientalism, by highlighting "American 'greatness,'" while pointing to "the perils of 'other' revolutions (the American revolution being considered unique and unrepeatable anywhere else in the world)" (Said, 1993, p. 8). In the end of his introduction, Stengel celebrates the revolutions in Egypt and elsewhere "for steering the planet on a more democratic" trajectory "for the 21st century" but warns that it is a "sometimes more dangerous path" (p. 53).

While Stengel and Andersen provide a grand and dramatic narrative of protests and individual protesters, they offer almost no deliberation about economic inequality, poverty, and systemic global economic crises, nor the role of Western neoliberalism in exacerbating or causing these crises. Additionally, echoing what media scholars call the protest paradigm (McLeod & Detenber, 1999), Andersen belittles an entire decade of protests of the 1990s as "pointless emotional sideshows" (p. 58). Disingenuously, he calls the 1999 "Battle in Seattle" "ineffectual and irrelevant" (p. 58). The Seattle demonstrations sparked successive demonstrations around the world against neoliberal globalization in subsequent years, leading to the largest collective demonstrations against war in history in 2003, before the invasion of Iraq even started.

Social movement scholars see the Seattle demonstrations as a watershed moment of the Global Justice Movement, whose main goal is the struggle against neoliberal globalization (Pleyers, 2010). The GJM grew exponentially through 2005 (ibid.) and not only was effective in shifting the policy debate but is credited with affecting massive debt cancellation for the global south (Engler, 2009), defeating the Free Trade Agreement of the Americas, inspiring the World Social Forum, and creating the Independent Media Center (Korten, 2009), which has been replicated in multiple cities and countries on every continent.[3] Sociologist and cofounder of Focus on the Global South, Walden Bello, argues that the movement against neoliberal globalization has been so successful (Bello, 2009b) that it has started the process of deglobalization (Bello, 2009a), despite establishment leaders continuing the orthodoxy of neoliberal ideology. The free-trade advocacy magazine *The Economist*, citing Bello, mournfully conceded that "the integration of the world economy is in retreat on almost every front" (2009, p. 59).

Although different movements, the GJM is a forerunner of the OWS movement, and they both have overlapping concerns and approaches to not only believing (as the World Social Forum motto says) another world is possible but acting to bring it into being. Social movements "develop their effects to a great extent through their reception by the media" (Brand & Wissen, 2005, p. 9), and media develop revenue through their reproduction of continuous spectacles (Couldry, 2008), from pop stars to political scandals to social movement protests, by gathering and focusing the attention of multiple audiences. A detailed analysis of the news coverage of OWS by print media's industry leader, *The New York Times*, provided below, will show how neoliberal media commodify radical social movements in ways that are mostly contradictory to deliberation of ideas about systemic inequality and structural solutions for democratic social change.

The New York Times's Coverage of Occupy Wall Street

U.S. mainstream news coverage of the OWS movement was minimal in its early days, mostly relegated to news blogs and Twitter feeds. The weekly *Time* magazine did not produce an article on OWS until the fifth week of protests. The leading national newspaper located in the city of the birthplace of OWS, *The New York Times*, did not print a news article about it until eight days into the protests. The executive director of the liberal-leaning National Public Radio justified its early non-coverage by stating, on day nine that, "The recent protests on Wall Street did not involve large numbers of people, prominent people, a great disruption or an especially clear objective" (Schumacher-Matos, 2011).

Yet, newspapers from Canada, England, New Zealand, Australia, China, and alternative media outlets in the U.S. had news stories within the first few days, often in ways that legitimized the movement. In contrast, U.S. corporate, mainstream media were slow to report, and much of their early coverage was dismissive, if not derogatory (Naureckas, 2011). It would be easy to point out myriad derisive commentary on OWS from Fox News hosts and guests as a November 2011 *New York Times* article did (Stelter, 2011b), but it is more important to examine how industry leaders like *The New York Times*, which has won more than 100 Pulitzer awards, may cover social movements in ways that could hinder or facilitate discussion of systemic social problems raised by social movements. It is likely obvious to most critics how Fox News is more entertainment than news; however, this obscures the point that all news discourse is performative (Broersma, 2010).

News is not merely a reflection of reality but constitutes particular representations of reality (Fishman, 1997; Schlesinger, 1978) and works, as news, by convincing readers "that its interpretation of the social world is legitimate" (Broersma, 2010, p. 24). All newsmaking is a socially constructed process of writers and editors selecting which events and issues will be produced as news (or ignored); interpreting the social context, meaning, and importance of those events and ideas; and weaving it all into a coherent story that highlights certain ideological value judgments (Solomon, 1998) and claims of reality over others. The remainder of this section will analyze how news articles and commentaries printed in *The New York Times* from September through December 2011, and an end-of-the-year photo essay ("The Year in Pictures"), framed and interpreted as well as capitalized on OWS.

The first public gathering of OWS was in Zuccotti Park in New York City on September 17, 2011. *The New York Times* printed its first news article on the ninth day of the OWS encampment in the Metro section. The report, "Gunning for Wall Street with Faulty Aim" (Bellafante, 2011a), reads less like news and more like an editorial that frames the movement in denigrating ways, very similar to how corporate mainstream media framed the massive 1999 GJM demonstrations in Seattle. Social movements scholar Jules Boykoff's research (2006), found that the corporate mainstream media, in its 1999 coverage, framed the demonstrations (in order of frequency), as being violent, disruptive, freakish, ignorant, and lacking focus. While *New York Times*'s Bellafante did not frame the protests as violent or disruptive, she did focus on bizarre appearances of individual protesters rather than on the objectives of the protest, describing OWS as a "carnival," having a collection of concerns that to her signaled a "lack of cohesion" (Bellafante, 2011a). Bellafante portrayed protesters as ignorant, claiming they wanted to simply "pantomime progressivism rather than practice it knowledgably," and as representing "an intellectual vacuum." The overall ideological value judgment of the article was, at best, that the demonstrations for social equality were ineffective, and at worst, that they were pointless.

The New York Times printed its second article on September 27, two days after a video went viral on the Internet. The video showed a New York City cop pepper-spraying four unthreatening women—corralled behind police netting—in the face at close range. Rather than providing a sympathetic understanding of the screams of pain and questioning of police tactics, audible in the video, the article narrates a sympathetic portrayal of the police, focusing on the challenges of policing protests and the potential of serious violence from demonstrators. Activists identified the officer, who worked in the counter-terrorism division at the time (Baker, 2011a), as NYPD Deputy Inspector Tony Bologna. Eventually, due to public outrage, an internal investigation found him in violation of departmental guidelines for use of pepper spray (Baker, 2011b). Two of the women pepper-sprayed filed a lawsuit in February 2012 (Ax, 2012). Bologna is also a defendant in a pending case against NYPD for unlawful arrest during the 2004 Republican National Convention (Bellafante, 2011b). The September 26 article by Goldstein (2011) casually mentions the "use of pepper spray on four women" and interprets the cause as the NYPD being trained to "fight terrorism," thus being "less nimble in dealing with" OWS demonstrators. He describes the protesters as "unorganized" and "uninformed" and reports that they represent to police "a visible example of lawlessness akin to that which had resulted in destruction and violence at other anticapitalist demonstrations, like…the World Trade Organization meeting in Seattle in 1999" (Goldstein, 2011, p. A17).

The Protest Paradigm

The first two *New York Times* articles, while not capturing the range of articles on OWS through December 2011, are representative of several common themes in *The New York Times*'s framing of OWS and corporate mainstream media's framing in general, not only of OWS, but also of most radical social movements. Collectively, the themes described above are typical ways that corporate mainstream media construct protest stories that marginalize social movements that "challenge the prevailing power structure" (McLeod & Hertog, 1992, p. 259), making up what scholars call the protest paradigm (Chan & Lee, 1984). Paradigms of news reporting are created out of institutional, organizational, and cultural structures and result in standardized story genres to pull from for different types of events. Journalists are socialized directly and indirectly into the norms, values, and standard practices of their profession and their particular news organization. This is partially reflected in a *New York Observer* senior editor's comments about OWS, which acknowledge that he and many reporters are trained to see "that protests are generally a non-news item" (Owens, 2011, #2). They become a news item when there is a dramatic spectacle. A *New York Observer* article about OWS quoted an unnamed New York daily reporter explaining that the spike in coverage after the pepper-spray incident happened because every media person loves conflict, and having "over-educated college students sitting around talking about things—[is] not a story. It's a story when those people clash with police" (Jeffries, 2011, # 9). *New York Times* reporter Brian Stelter (2011a) concurred that, "It was the mass arrests of protesters in New York that initially led to much of the protest coverage" (p. A22).

My content analysis found that 23.5 percent of *The New York Times* news and commentary articles primarily about OWS, from September through December 2011, focused on clashes with law enforcement, almost twice the amount during the same period that focused on the key grievance of OWS, income inequality (12.3 percent). Social movement research has shown (Boykoff, 2006) that demonstrators face a double bind, because to get covered by corporate mainstream media, they have to intensify their tactics and rhetoric, but when they do, the corporate mainstream media focus on confrontations with police rather than on the messages of the social movement. The dramatic spectacle of police pepper-spraying peaceful protesters is a familiar news genre, which draws in more supporters and detractors of protests as media audiences. Statistician and *New York Times* blogger Nate Silver (2011) analyzed articles about OWS from 4,000 newspapers, TV stations, and magazines, from September 17 through October 7, 2011. He found that coverage spiked dramatically upwards on three occasions when police clashed with protesters: the day after the OWS pepper-spray incident on September 24, three consecutive days after the mass arrests on the Brooklyn Bridge on October 1, and the day after additional clashes with police on October 5. Extending his analysis, I found, using Lexis Nexis (All News), which includes more types of media outlets (e.g., including blogs) and English-language non–U.S. media too, that there was also a spike in coverage on November 15, when the NYPD cleared OWS from Zuccotti Park, that was sustained through the day after the two-month anniversary of the protests on the November 17, when police arrested large numbers of OWS and other Occupy protesters around the country. *The New York Times* followed the same trajectory of coverage, with steady and precipitous declines starting the week of November 19.

Along with the volume of coverage, media's placement of OWS stories on front pages of print media and as lead stories of broadcast media, according to the Project for Excellence in Journalism, followed a similar path. PEJ's indexing (Pew Research Center's PEJ, 2011) gives evidence to another aspect of the protest paradigm—corporate mainstream media's reliance on official sources and perspectives of the powerful, such as national and local politicians and law-enforcement agencies. Leading coverage of OWS the week of October 10–16 peaked as Washington Democrats voiced some sympathy for OWS, including President Obama, and as Republican officials, including the House Majority leader, voiced discontent. The threat of closure of the OWS encampment in New York City, voiced by Mayor Bloomberg, and then reversed, was big news that week as well. OWS, the largest story of that week, consisted of 10 percent of the newshole (Pew Research Center's PEJ, 2011). Media headlines of OWS also peaked the week of November 14–20, totaling 13 percent of the newshole (Pew Research Center's PEJ, 2011). Stories of that week focused on NYPD clearing the OWS encampment at Zuccotti Park in the beginning hours of November 15, as well as other evictions in California and Oregon. Leading news stories also covered clashes with police around the country on the November 17 anniversary.

As police continued to clear out protesters from encampments in many other cities, media as a whole reduced the volume and prominence of coverage. The PEJ index showed that by the last week of November, OWS coverage made up only 3 percent of the newshole and not enough to register the next three consecutive weeks (Pew Research Center's PEJ, 2011). This pattern was mirrored in my research of the volume of *New York Times* coverage as well as with other national and international news outlets in the Lexis Nexis database. *The New York Times* steadily diminished its news and commentary from its high of 32 articles that were primarily about OWS, during the ninth week of the protests (November 12–18) to just three articles by the fifteenth week of protests (December 24–30). From this overview of the trajectory of the coverage, I now return to further analysis of the content of *The New York Times*'s coverage.

Commodification of a Memetic Brand

The Occupy meme, with its fast-rising popularity, became a media commodity, a timely and profitable news hook to connect to a wide variety of subjects, many that would have been covered regardless, and some that would have not. In several *New York Times* articles throughout October and November, the substantive connections to issues raised by OWS demonstrations and publications are hard to find; it's also not clear how the reporting serves the purpose of enhancing public understanding of OWS and the social and political context out of which it arose. However, when competition for Internet search-engine hits and youth audience eyeballs translate to advertising revenue, having a hot brand like OWS turns into revenue. And brands apparently need logos, as one article pointed out. "Every Movement Needs a Logo" is solely about logo ideas for OWS (Chwast, 2011), as well as songs. The article "At the Protests, the Message Lacks a Melody" called for a protest song that would become a hit, quoting Rage Against the Machine singer Tom Morello saying, "Every successful movement has a soundtrack." The article reinforced the protest paradigm by putting forth another claim that OWS lacks "a coherent message" (McKinley, 2011, p. C1). *New York Times*'s columnist Charles Blow also reinforced the paradigm in his article, "Occupy-Apalooza Strikes a Chord," by quoting a young woman who responded to his question of "What specifically are you protesting?" with "I don't know. It's just cool." He then tied into the "cool" theme by writing "If the Occupy Wall Street protests were a band, I'd say the closest corollary would probably be the legendary '90s grunge band Nirvana" (Blow, 2011b, p. A17), and this was not from the arts, culture or entertainment desks. But neither was the article "Masked Protector of Gotham Has His Eye on Wall Street Protesters" (Taylor, 2011a)—and the Batman connection is that the latest movie in the franchise is being filmed on Wall Street, a few blocks from the OWS encampment. Although they won't be filming OWS, and no disruptions are expected, the article "informs" us that the film "is expected to be one of the blockbusters of next summer" (Taylor, 2011a, p. A31). *The New York Times* wasn't the only media outlet capitalizing off of the OWS brand, as sometimes reality is stranger than fiction, even when it is TV. The show *Law & Order: SVU* (that's Special Victims Unit) set up a fake OWS encampment, complete with a protest library, kitchen, peace signs, and tents, in New York City's Foley Square.

How do I know? That's right; it was reported in *The New York Times* (Moynihan & Barron, 2011).

This pop-culture infotainment approach to news and trivialization of protest coverage is more readily found in tabloid weeklies than in the prestige press, but all of the newspaper industry has been facing losses in profit for successive years, and neoliberal forces affect more aspects of news to be commodified and follow the trends of pop culture. Nonetheless, news production processes have long included decisions on how to package news products in ways that will gather the greatest proportion of their targeted audience(s), in order to attract the most lucrative advertising contracts. In this context, the corporate media, including social media like Facebook, are selling other corporations the "product" of marketing access to particular consumer audience demographics, ideally younger audiences with much disposable income and more easily influenced by pop-culture trends.

While I have been focusing on negative critique, a sizeable (but smaller) amount of *The New York Times*'s coverage of OWS was affirming the movement's messages and provided some concrete context to them, albeit most of it was commentary rather than news reporting. For example, columnist Nicholas Kristof cited research by the Economic Policy Institute that shows "the top 1 percent of Americans possess a greater net worth than the entire bottom 90 percent" (Kristof, 2011b, p. SR11), and in another article, he reported that "according to the C.I.A.'s own ranking of countries by income inequality, the United States is more unequal a society than either Tunisia or Egypt" (Kristof, 2011a, p. SR11), which gives an interesting global context to the demonstrations. Another *New York Times* columnist, Paul Krugman, was even more adamantly affirming as to the legitimacy of OWS, arguing that "wealthy Americans who benefit hugely from a system rigged in their favor react with hysteria to anyone who points out just how rigged the system is," adding, "So who's really being un-American here? Not the protesters, who are simply trying to get their voices heard. No, the real extremists here are America's oligarchs, who want to suppress any criticism of the sources of their wealth" (Krugman, 2011b, p. A23). In another column, he declares, "We have a society in which money is increasingly concentrated in the hands of a few people, and in which that concentration of income and wealth threatens to make us a democracy in name only" (Krugman, 2011c, p. A31).

However, critical media studies scholars should not just be concerned with whether media portrayals are favorable, unfavorable, or "balanced" but should analyze how it facilitates or hinders serious democratic discussion of systemic social issues in ways that do not simply reconstruct hegemonic power relations but rather empower action for positive social change. Large national media outlets often have "press coverage of protest [that] evolves in contradictory ways" (Rauch et al., 2007, p. 142), and delegitimizing and legitimizing media discourses often co-vary, even within the same article. Douglas McLeod recently extended the protest paradigm to explain why a protest may get positive coverage, and here I am using part of it as a proxy, with some modifications (shown in brackets), to explain why the media coverage of OWS expanded in October: 1) "the [increasing] size and scope of the demonstrations made them hard[er] to ignore; 2) the [message] of the protest [resonated] with the interests of readers and [could be capitalized on by] the power structure; 3) the tactics of the protest were relatively peaceful [compared to documented police aggression] making it [more] difficult for the media to find fault" (McLeod, 2007, p. 191). Additionally, several credentialed reporters, including a freelance reporter for *The New York Times* (Baker & Moynihan, 2011), were arrested in police sweeps, which brought a new angle and self-interest in coverage. *The New York Times*'s Krugman confirmed the first factor: "the [OWS] protests not only continued but grew, eventually becoming too big to ignore" (2011a, p. A27). In October, OWS expanded to many cities and countries, highlighted by its "Global Day of Action" on October 15. The second factor was facilitated by the lingering impacts of the Great Recession and the resulting growing inequality. It was also pushed by the protesters and younger and more sympathetic journalists using social media and Internet streaming, within the context of a shift by corporate mainstream media to incorporate more digital and social media into its revenue streams and media production. In October, President Obama and other Democratic Party officials deciding, during an election campaign, to strategically make supportive statements regarding the concerns of OWS also gave the media more legitimacy in covering it. Finally, the third factor was facilitated by the viral spreading of pictures and videos of police brutality against non-threatening protesters, which, as I indicated previously, was confirmed by *The New York Times*'s Stelter. This created a spectacle that could be commodified by media outlets. *New York Times* journalist David Carr, in the paper's "Media Equation" column, explained that, "Reporters live for spectacle, and for more than two months Occupy Wall Street provided one," adding that protester clashes with police "gave the story an urgency" that "made for good television and print coverage" (Carr, 2011b, p. B1).

A shortcoming of the protest paradigm, and of other theories of media coverage of social movements, is that scholars often apply it by examining coverage as a static whole rather than looking at how coverage changes over time and interacts with the development of social movements or they fail to situate the analysis in the context of neoliberal hegemony. To help fill the gap and to explain why coverage of OWS declined in November and December 2011, I will apply the nuisance paradigm to *The New York Times*'s declining coverage of OWS and then discuss how coverage functioned to reproduce aspects of neoliberal hegemony.

The Public Nuisance Paradigm

The protest paradigm and the public nuisance paradigm are complementary theories. The former usually helps explain media coverage of individual protests, whereas the latter helps explain media formulation of a "negative view of protests in general through an emphasis on perceived bothersome effects of protests" (DiCicco, 2010, p. 136), such as disruption to normal activities of daily life, which often are an inherent tactic of protests, especially ones that engage in civil disobedience, like OWS. In addition to "bothersome," media following the public nuisance paradigm will also frame protests as an ineffective way to make real social change at best and as unpatriotic or dangerous at worst. In the Western context, the public nuisance paradigm acknowledges the right to protest while at the same time portraying it as causing more detriment than benefit. *The New York Times* coverage often blended protest paradigm frames and public nuisance frames in the same news story. For example, the article "When Occupying Becomes Irritating" spoke of interviewing perturbed business owners, mothers afraid for their children, and other annoyed residents, quoting one as saying, "It's been three weeks now. Enough is enough." It also quoted a business manager who said, "They are pests," with the reporter adding that the manager "closed his bathroom after it repeatedly flooded from protesters bathing there." The article ended with a quote from "a mother of two young daughters" declaring, "I do believe in the right to protest, but in other cities, the financial district is separate. Here, this is a neighborhood they're coming into. They're disrupting a lot of people's lives" (Buckley, 2011a, p. A15). Two photographs accompanied the article, one with the spectacle of piled trash by Zuccotti Park that a mother and child in tow were walking by, and the other with the spectacle of a line of supposed protesters at the bathroom at Burger King.

As the OWS encampment lasted into November, nearing its two-month anniversary, the frequency of articles highlighting the public nuisance aspects of OWS increased. Journalists reported concerns and complaints from not only residents but also official sources such as Mayor Bloomberg, health officials and politicians, including the New York State assembly speaker, a Democrat representing Manhattan, and even anonymous sources. Despite their expressed support, to varying degrees, of OWS, it was the concerns that news articles highlighted. The list of grievances *The New York Times* reported was similar to what media outlets in other states reported about their Occupy encampments: framing concerns in terms of public health and safety, sanitation issues, noise, and, ultimately, crime—signaling not only a nuisance but a dangerous threat. City officials, law enforcement, and others used the spectrum of these fears and concerns as justification, sometimes pretextual, for the eviction of activists from encampments in cities across the country. Specific mentions ranged from the specter of tuberculosis and a "virus which can lead to vomiting and diarrhea" (Flegenheimer, 2011, p. A26), to drug use (Walter, 2011), public urination (Taylor, 2011b), and drumming (Buckley & Moynihan, 2011), to violence and death: "They said they felt menaced by the protesters and sickened by unsanitary conditions in parts of the park. They feared that the violence and deaths that have occurred at other Occupy sites would unfold at Zuccotti, too" (Buckley, 2011b, p. A22).

The Department of Homeland Security, the FBI, and other federal agencies, local law enforcement, mayors, and a private company (Police Executive Research Forum), collaborated on strategies of evictions of dozens of Occupy camps in large cities throughout the United States (Ellis, 2011; Gaynor, 2011; Partnership for Civil Justice Fund, 2012). Most of the November raids of OWS encampments occurred late at night, out of sight of most news media, which then relied on official police narrative in reporting the news the following morning. *The New York Times* reported, that "stories of crimes and dangerous behavior, mostly anecdotal, have been used as fuel by those who say the protesters must go" (Buckley & Flegenheimer, 2011, p. A24). But it is precisely the corporate mainstream media, including news media such as *The New York Times* and *Time* magazine, among others, that focused audiences' attention on the spectacles of protest and encampments as "dangerous" public nuisances rather than on deliberation of issues of economic and social inequality and systemic failures of neoliberal capitalism being brought forward by OWS groups across the country. As encampments were cleared and OWS moved indoors to plan for spring, media coverage declined precipitously, as if that was the end of the three-act story, from setup, to confrontation, to resolution. On November 21, *New York Times* columnist David Carr acknowledged, that "when the spectacle disappears, reporters often fold up their tents as well" (2011b, p. B1).

"The Year in Pictures"

Like *Time* magazine, *The New York Times*, in a December issue, encapsulates each year into a dramatic story of the "most important moments." *The New York Times* product is called "The Year in Pictures," and in 2011, the newspaper allocated the largest number of photos to depicting the Arab Spring and the second greatest number to Occupy Wall Street. Also like *Time* magazine's "Protester of the Year," a fiction writer with a flair for the dramatic was selected to write a brief narrative. His written narrative of the selected pictures and their captions focus on OWS as a youthful (labeling them as "kids"[4]), dangerous, and directionless spectacle of anger. The introduction declared that, "Some protesters poured gasoline into bottles and lit the sky with fire," and that "The year 2011 was an evanescent spectacle of anger" (McCann, 2011, p. SR4). Confrontations with police (including burning fires, arrests, and a bleeding protester) or being a public nuisance were the focus of 10 of the 16 photos (62.5 percent), while only 2 of the 16 photos (12.5 percent) selected by *New York Times* editors had protest signs or banners that were readable. *The New York Times* summative pictorial essay, like its news coverage during the year, focused more on the spectacle and dangers of protest rather than on informing the public about the messages and concerns of this global movement, which seeks to be a "rebuke of neoliberal economics" (Blow, 2011a, p. A21).

Reproducing Neoliberal Hegemony

The protest and public nuisance paradigms in news coverage of OWS, combined with much of the argumentation in *New York Times* commentaries, served to reproduce cultural ideologies that undergird neoliberal hegemony. Three of the main ways this was accomplished were through: (1) comparisons with the Tea Party and calls for working through the political and policymaking systems (reform over revolution); (2) portraying the solution as occurring only through private pursuits and individual organizational leaders rather than public collective action; and (3) the assumption that there is no viable alternative to "free-market capitalism (i.e., neoliberalism).

Forced comparisons of OWS with the Tea Party (TP) were abundant, with more comparisons mentioning similarities and drawing connections than differences. *The New York Times*'s public editor even claimed that the TP is OWS' "ideological counterpart" (Brisbane, 2011, p. SR12), and columnist Frank Bruni said that "the ties that bind Occupy Wall Street and the Tea Party," make them "flowers of the same frustration" (Bruni, 2011, p. SR3). The reports that focused on differences usually placed them as dichotomous equivalents on the political spectrum (i.e., a Tea Party for the left). Most importantly, across types of reporting, the TP was frequently held up as a model of effective activism and a way to criticize OWS. For example, in the article "Hippies and Hipsters Exhale," a *New York Times* columnist chastised OWS for not having "a specific political agenda" like the TP does, declaring that "it would be a waste for them to push back only against corporate enemies and put forward no political heroes" (Blow, 2011a, p. A21), and another *New York Times* columnist, in an article titled "The Decadent Left," moralized that "many protesters seemed more interested in founding a kind of Paris Commune or Oneida Community in Zuccotti Park than in actually participating in public-policy debates" (Douthat, 2011b, p. SR12).

The New York Times's comparisons with the TP are faulty on many grounds. The TP is not simply a movement initiated by the grassroots, rather it is also an astroturf movement propelled and funded by national, conservative, neoliberal organizations (Good, 2009; Monbiot, 2010) that are financed by wealthy corporations and rich Republican and Libertarian individuals, such as the Koch brothers. The TP serves to bolster neoliberalism by advocating self-reliance and fiscal discipline, lobbying for the de-funding of social service programs, the deregulation of corporations and global trade, and increased funding for the military. As Brishen Rogers explains, "the rejection of neoliberal governmentality distinguishes Occupy from the Tea Partiers" (Rogers, 2012). All but one of *The New York Times* articles avoided the fact that OWS is precisely an attack on political, economic, and cultural neoliberalism globally, and as such, a more fitting comparison is the Global Justice Movement (GJM), and not the neoliberal-oriented TP.

The OWS movement is not as much about right versus left politics as *The New York Times* often framed it in its comparisons to the Tea Party but about ending corporate domination and resisting the application of market-based logic to all aspects of political, economic, and social life. The Occupy encampments, like the convergence centers of the GJM demonstrations before it, were about creating, as one protester put it, a "public sphere not mediated by commodities or mainstream political discourse" (Hoffman, 2011, p. A19). OWS' objection, like the GJM's, "is not that the rules are being broken," points out Rogers, but that "the problem is the game itself—the pursuit of market rationality—does not reflect or advance a valid good or ethic" (Rogers, 2012).

Many op-ed writers framed the causes and solutions of economic inequality to be a private matter of individual self-discipline for elites and consumers alike. Neoliberalist Thomas Friedman, after warning that another economic crisis would cause "the cry for justice" to "turn ugly," advised bankers and financial corporations to continue their bullish behavior in the market but cautioned them to "stop being pigs" (Friedman, 2011, p. SR11). But conservative columnist David Brooks complained that OWS was demonizing the 1 percent, arguing that many of the 99 percent were implicated in the economic crisis, such as all Americans who "have overconsumed and overborrowed." He indicated his support for "slash[ing] corporate taxes" and "aggressively us[ing] market forces" (Brooks, 2011, p. A27), in other words, more neoliberalism. Similarly, *New York Times* columnist Ross Douthat, blamed the "bloated public sector," and "Medicare costs" (2011a, p. SR11) for the current economic divide and called for a smaller government (i.e., cutting social services and deregulating the market) as the solution. Within the neoliberal project, argues political scientist Wendy Brown, citizens should "be the opposite of public-minded," instead, they should "become wholly responsible for their well-being and citizenship is reduced to success in this entrepreneurship" (Brown, 2005, pp. 43–44).

One of the well-known, now somewhat reformed, architects of neoliberalism, Jeffrey Sachs, in an op-ed, confounds progressivism with capitalist reform and proposes individual actions within the system of corporate capitalism to be the solution, such as "shareholder and consumer activism," and running for political office by using social media to lessen "the cost of political campaigning" (Sachs, 2011, p. SR6). Similarly, a self-identified conservative and libertarian, Tyler Cowen, writing in a *New York Times* op-ed titled "Whatever Happened to Discipline and Hard Work?", takes the neoliberal American exceptionalism approach even farther by praising American culture as cultivating an ethic of rags to riches, declaring that "the best approach for fighting poverty is often precisely not to make fighting poverty the highest priority." Cowen heartlessly argues for the "survival of the fittest" approach that underlies neoliberal ideology, as a way to justify excessive private wealth at the expense of the common public good. He calls for more economic inequality rather than less, which he believes will bring about a "tough, pro-discipline and pro-wealth cultural revolution" (Cowen, 2011, p. BU6).

In summary, *The New York Times*'s coverage, as well as other U.S. corporate mainstream media coverage, of OWS began late and largely delegitimized OWS, portraying it as not having a clear message or goals, as uninformed, ineffective, and carnivalesque. Its late September to early October articles framed marginalized protesters with use of the protest paradigm. As the movement gained size and expanded to other cities and countries, the volume and prominence of corporate mainstream media coverage expanded too. The protest paradigm frames continued, but commentary supportive of OWS also began to appear as OWS became part of the political discourse and debate of top national politicians, including President Obama and Republican leaders. *The New York Times* criticized other corporate mainstream media coverage more often than it was reflective of its own. It capitalized on the Occupy meme and participated in the trivialization of the Occupy "brand." Corporate mainstream media, including the Nobel Prize–winning *New York Times*, led readers to believe that "Occupy's relevance has seriously dwindled," elucidated Spencer Mandel, and "that this erosion is due to Occupy's own shortcomings—an inevitable outcome of its disjointed message and decentralized leadership" (Mandel, 2012).

Most of *The New York Times* commentary, in conjunction with broad strokes of the news coverage, functioned to reproduce the ideological hegemony of neoliberalism, in spite of OWS acting collectively in opposition to neoliberalism—which has reinforced the commodification of nearly all elements of private and public spheres of life. Most of the articles imply that not only is protesting an ineffective solution, and neoliberal reforms are all that is needed, but also that there is no alternative to global corporate capitalism (i.e., neoliberalism).

Constraints of Corporate Mainstream Media and Limits on Democracy

Corporate mainstream media seem ill equipped to develop new ways of understanding the social crises of capitalism and the radical social movements that arise in response to growing inequality or to engage the public in deliberation of systemic issues and social problems. However, it may be more of an inability or even refusal to risk a new approach. While *New York Times* reporters and columnists often claimed OWS had unclear goals or an incoherent message, it never reported in its newspaper about the OWS New York General Assembly's (NYGA) passage of an end to corporate personhood resolution and never discussed the issues raised in the NYGA passage of the Declaration of the Occupation of New York City. It did mention the Declaration but ironically only as a point of contention and dissension (Hoffman, 2011; Speri, 2011) among activists rather than as the consensual agreement that it was. Additionally, OWS published its own media to get its messages out to the world, which included the publishing of a professional-looking newspaper edited by people with professional experience, called the *Occupied Wall Street Journal. The New York Times* did mention the paper in an October 10 news article (Carr, 2011a) after two issues had already been published but provided no discussion of its content in that article nor in future articles or commentaries. Similarly, OWS published a quarterly journal called *Tidal: Occupy Theory, Occupy Strategy*, which received no mention in *The New York Times* print edition, despite it being about what OWS wants and how it plans to get it, a question that not just *The New York Times* but most corporate mainstream media claimed to be befuddled by.

The New York Times Company (NYTC) is a corporation that is obligated to its stockholders to increase its market value, and like most media corporations and newspapers in particular, it has been facing the pressures of neoliberal economics that encourage businesses to increase share value by cutting staff and other operating costs and to continually find new streams of revenue, which is what the NYTC has done. Its 2008 through 2011 annual reports (NYTC, 2008, 2009, 2010, 2011) show that every year since 2004 it has reduced the number of full-time employees (from 12,300 in 2004 to 7,273 in 2011) as it has increased its online revenue streams.

My point is not simply to identify market pressures on media, the professional socialization of journalists into news values, and the framing paradigms that journalists use in covering protests and social movements. But to shed light on how and why corporate mainstream media encourage audiences to be passive spectators of politics and consumers of entertaining social dramas rather than participants in democratic deliberation and active empowerment—through a critical analysis of coverage of social movements in general, in this age of neoliberal hegemony.

Although Occupy organizations continue in many towns and countries, media coverage beyond November severely waned. Since *Time*'s big splash with The Protester as Person of the Year, as of May 2012 the magazine has printed only one article each with OWS or Arab Spring as the main subject, signifying that their December issue was the definitive and final account of both Occupy Wall Street and the Arab Spring and that there is little more to discuss. The *Time* magazine and *New York Times* coverage and news in general, is not meant to provoke further deliberation of what could be done collectively about social inequality inherent within the system of capitalism, for that would make their corporate advertisers uneasy. Rather, it is meant to be a declarative statement of an unusual specimen, "The Protester" that serves to reconfirm the universalization of "western liberal democratic values" within corporate capitalist globalization (neoliberalism). *Time* and *The New York Times*, like other corporate mainstream media, mediate political spectacles for easy consumption (Edelman, 1988), for "a widening of the frame within which an event is viewed would change its meaning" and "create an account typically categorized as research rather than as news and often as dull rather than dramatic" (p. 102). Media corporations gain profit by delivering an entertained and depoliticized audience to advertisers, who do not expect programs to challenge mainstream values or encourage audiences to think deeply about social problems and public policy. Thus, as Allison Kilkenny (2011) argues, "the media assists in the commodification of movements by conditioning its audience to think of rebellions as brands.... Americans then 'participate' in the upheaval" as spectators, "just as they participate in *American Idol* or *Dancing with the Stars*." Thus, the experiences and ethics of everyday life become, as Douglas Kellner (2003) illuminates, "shaped and mediated by the spectacles of media culture and the consumer society." These mediated spectacles are then "tool[s] of pacification and depoliticization" (pp. 2–3), for hindering radical movements from becoming massive populist movements that would demand revolution rather than reform.

Research by Lewis, Wahl-Jorgensen, and Inthorn (2004) on broadcast news found that journalism allows citizens "to express basic *emotions* about the world," but little room "to express political opinions and offer solutions to problems" (p. 154). Neoliberal hegemony is never complete, and has always been contested, but it has come into dominance, in part by a declaration of the end of ideology, a claim that works if citizens believe there is no alternative. Jameson (2003) has defined this hegemonic moment of neoliberalism as a condition in which "it is easier to imagine the end of the world than to imagine the end of capitalism" (p. 76). Giroux also argues that the erosion of public space facilitates this, making it "more difficult to develop a democratic discourse for educating collective social agents capable of raising critical questions about the limits of a market-driven society" (2005, n.p.).

Another World Is Possible

Yet, along came OWS, imagining the end of neoliberal capitalism and reclaiming not only public space but what Giroux calls for, which is a public pedagogy, trying to "actualize a democratic notion of the social" (2011, n.p.), not simply through the occupation of a public space, but in how it "occupied that space"—by starting to build the foundations of a different culture, based on the needs of people over profit, and manifested in miniature with "the people's library," the Occupy kitchen, free emergency medical care, etc., at encampments. It also showed the world a more democratic way to make decisions and to account for the needs of a large group, with the human microphone and the hand signals for facilitating consensus at the general assemblies, as it demonstrated an alternative democratic culture.

In conclusion, the corporate mainstream media coverage continually shifted away from the vision and ideas of OWS and its purpose of demonstrating against inequality to clashes with police over physical space. Thus the corporate mainstream media coverage of OWS, in its totality functions, in effect, to depoliticize social movements in "established" as well as "developing" democracies, both through the reproduction of continuous spectacles and through the creation of anti-spectacles of un-seeing what is deemed to not be important or legitimate (Couldry, 2008). The multidecade intensification of "neoliberalism in the media sphere is not only a process of depoliticization" of protest, but to some extent of media as well, as they become "a commodified [infotainment] industry" that is in danger of erasing their democratic "function as institutions of the public sphere" (Hallin, 2008, p. 43). Whether new alternative social movements and new alternative and public media forms are able to build upon recent ongoing global resistance, remains to be determined, but without corporate media transforming itself at the same time, it will be a long struggle. Radical protests and social movements by definition are counter-cultural. Thus, they arise in opposition to existing power relations and seek not just to reform but also to build alternative institutions for systemic change. Indeed, another story and another world are possible. OWS, like the GJM before it, strives to model from the ground up, alternative, nonhierarchical ways of building community and institutions that democratically serve the needs of people over profit and implement a more just and sustainable world.

Notes

1. The author's definition of an ideology is a shared interpretive framework about how the world works that serves to regulate social practices of particular groups or institutions and their relations with other groups or institutions, in order to protect the collective interests of the originating group.
2. The cover illustration of a female poster was based on a photograph of Sarah Andersen, an Occupy Los Angeles participant, taken by an *L.A. Weekly* photographer at a protest at the Bank of America Plaza. See http://www.readersupportednews.org/opinion2/276-74/8985-focus-times-qperson-of-the-yearq-cover-the-photo-you-didnt-see and http://www.boulder weekly.com/article-7203-in-case-you-missed-i.html
3. See www.indymedia.org for list.
4. A Fordham University study found that the average age of OWS protesters was 33. See http://www.fordham.edu/images/academics/graduate_schools/gsas/elections_and_campai gn_/occupy%20wall%20street%20survey%20results%20102611.pdf

References

Andersen, K. (2011, December 14). The protester. *Time*, *178*(25), 56–89.

Ax, J. (2012, February 13). Occupy protesters sue New York City over pepper spray incident *Reuters.* Available at http://www.huffingtonpost.com/2012/02/13/occupy-protesters-sue-new-york-city-pepper-spray_n_1275138.html

Baker, A. (2011a, September 29). Officer's pepper-spraying of protesters is under investigation. *The New York Times*.

———. (2011b, Oct 19). Commander faces penalty over use of pepper spray. *New York Times*.

Baker, A., & Moynihan, C. (2011, October 2). More than 700 arrested as protesters try to cross Brooklyn Bridge. *The New York Times*, A18.

Bakri, N. (2012, January 20). Self-immolation is on the rise in the Arab world. *The New York Times*. Available at http://www.nytimes.com/2012/01/21/world/africa/self-immolation-on-the-rise-in-the-arab-world.html

Bellafante, G. (2011a, September 25). Gunning for Wall Street, with faulty aim. *The New York Times,* MB1. Available at http://www.nytimes.com/2011/09/25/nyregion/protesters-are-gunning-for-wall-street-with-faulty-aim.html

———. (2011b, October 25). Every action produces overreaction. *The New York Times,* MB1.

Bello, W. (2009a, September 5). The virtues of deglobalization. *Huffington Post*. Available at http://www.huffingtonpost.com/walden-bello/the-virtues-of-deglobaliz_b_277531.html

———. (2009b, November 25.). The meaning of Seattle. Truth only becomes true through action. *Yes Magazine*. Available at http://www.yesmagazine.org/new-economy/the-meaning-of-seattle-truth-only-becomes-true-through-action

Birchfield, V. (1999). Contesting the hegemony of market ideology. *Review of International Political Economy*, *6*(1), 27–54.

Blow, C. M. (2011a, October 1). Hippies and hipsters exhale. *The New York Times*, A21. Available at http://www.nytimes.com/2011/10/01/opinion/hippies-and-hipsters-exhale.html

———. (2011b, October 22). Occupy-apalooza strikes a chord. *The New York Times*, A17. Available at http://www.nytimes.com/2011/10/22/opinion/blow-occupy-apalooza-strikes-a-chord.html?gwh=D03536F64331B23BB5347C7EDDA59FCA

Boykoff, J. (2006). Framing dissent: Mass-media coverage of the global justice movement. *New Political Science*, *28*(2), 201–228.

Brand, U., & Wissen, M. (2005) Neoliberal globalization and the internationalization of protest: A European perspective. *Antipode*, *37*(1), 9–17.

Brisbane, A.S. (2011, November 13). Who is Occupy Wall Street? *The New York Times*, SR12.

Broersma, M. (2010). The unbearable limitations of journalism: On press critique and journalism's claim to truth. *International Gazette*, *72*(1), 21–33.

Brohinsky, S. (2011, October 11). As economic frustrations grow, protesters gain support. Majority of Americans have a favorable opinion of the Occupy Movement. Available at http://www.srbi.com/Economics_2011_Poll.html

Brooks, D. (2011, October 11). The milquetoast radicals. *The New York Times*, A27.

Brown, W. (2005). *Edgework: Critical essays on knowledge and politics,* Princeton, N.J.: Princeton University Press.

Bruni, F. (2011, October 30). Pizzas and Pessimism. *The New York Times*, SR3.

Buckley, C. (2011a, October 8). When occupying becomes irritating. *The New York Times*, A15. Available at http://www.nytimes.com/2011/10/08/nyregion/occupy-wall-street-begins-to-chafe-its-neighbors.html?pagewanted=all

———. (2011b, November 14). For annoyed neighbors, the beat drags on. *The New York Times*, A22. Available at http://www.nytimes.com/2011/11/14/nyregion/for-neighbors-of-zuccotti-park-and-ground-zero-beat-drags-on.html

Buckley, C., & Flegenheimer, M. (2011, November 9). At scene of Wall St. protest, rising concerns about crime. *The New York Times*, A24. Available at http://www.nytimes

.com/2011/11/09/nyregion/at-occupy-wall-street-protest-rising-concern-about-crime.html?_r=1& gwh=D2D10F18503AAC24223052E2435A4F2A

Buckley, C., & Moynihan, C. (2011, November 6). A protest reaches a crossroads. *The New York Times*, MB1. Available at http://www.nytimes.com/2011/11/06/nyregion/occupy-wall-street-protest-reaches-a-crossroads.html?pagewanted=all

Bush, G. W. (2002). *National security strategy of the United States of America.* Available at http://nssarchive.us/?page_id=32

Carr, D. (2011a, October 10). A protest's ink-stained fingers. *The New York Times*, B1. Available at http://www.nytimes.com/2011/10/10/business/media/wall-street-protesters-have-ink-stained-fingers-media-equation.html?pagewanted=all&gwh=6B18C0C6451144533E36 D86892D5D034

———. (2011b, November 21). For a movement, a question: What now? *The New York Times*, B1. Available at http://www.nytimes.com/2011/11/21/business/media/the-question-for-occupy-protest-is-what-now.html?gwh=8D3E89F86DD9E1CF81B21A6EDB952E5C

Chan, J. M., & Lee, C. C. (1984). The journalistic paradigm on civil protests: A case study of Hong Kong. In A. Arno & W. Dissanayake (eds), *The news media in national and international conflict*, pp.183–202. Boulder, CO: Westview Press.

Chwast, S. (2011, October 09). Every movement needs a logo. *The New York Times*, SR4. Available at http://www.nytimes.com/interactive/2011/10/08/opinion/20111009_OPINION_LOGOS.html?gwh=E8C685C290E72F7E346021189BA8440A

Couldry, N. (2008). Form and power in an age of continuous spectacle. In D. Hesmondhalgh & J. Toynbee (Eds.), *The media and social theory*, pp. 43–58. New York: Routledge.

Cowen, T. (2011, November 13). Whatever happened to discipline and hard work? *New York Times*, BU6.

DeLuca, K. M., & Peeples, J. (2002). From public sphere to public screen: Democracy, activism, and the "violence" of Seattle. *Critical Studies in Media Communication, 19*(2), 125–151.

DiCicco. C. T. (2010). The public nuisance paradigm: Changes in mass media coverage of political protests since the 1960s. *Journalism & Mass Communication Quarterly, 87*(1), 135–153.

Douthat, R. (2011a, October 30). What tax dollars can't buy. *The New York Times*, SR11.

———. (2011b, December 4). The decadent left. *The New York Times*, SR12.

Economist. (2009, February 19). Turning their backs on the world. *The Economist, 390*(8619), 59–61.

Edelman, M. (1988). *Constructing the political spectacle*. Chicago, IL: University of Chicago Press.

Ellis, R. (2011, November 15). Update: 'Occupy' crackdowns coordinated with federal law enforcement officials. *Examiner.com.* Available at http://www.examiner.com/article/update-occupy-crackdowns-coordinated-with-federal-law-enforcement-officials

Engler, M. (2009). The "Battle in Seattle" at ten. Available at http://www.democracyuprising.com/2009/11/the-battle-in-seattle-at-ten/

Fishman, M. (1997). News and nonevents: Making the visible invisible. In D. A. Berkowitz (Ed.), *Social meanings of news: A text-reader*, pp. 210–229. Thousand Oaks, CA: Sage.

Flegenheimer, M. (2011, November 11). A Petri dish of activism, and germs. *The New York*

Times, A26. Available at http://www.nytimes.com/2011/11/11/nyregion/for-occupy-wall-street-health-is-a-growing-concern.html

Food and Agricultural Organization of the United Nations. (2011, February 3). World food prices reach new historic peak: 3.4 percent surge in January—FAO updates food price index. *United Nations* press release. Available at http://www.fao.org/news/story/en/item/50519/icode/

Friedman, T. (2011, October 30). Did you hear the one about the bankers? *The New York Times*, SR11.

Fukuyama, F. (1989, Summer). The end of history? *The National Interest*, *16*, 3–18.

Gaynor, S. (2011, November 18). The cop group coordinating the Occupy crackdowns. *San Francisco Bay Guardian.* Available at http://www.sfbg.com/politics/2011/11/18/cop-group-coordinating-occupy-crackdowns

Giroux, H. A. (2005). Cultural studies in dark times: Public pedagogy and the challenge of neoliberalism. *Fast Capitalism*, *1*(2).

———. (2011, October 26). Occupy Wall Street's battle against American-style authoritarianism. *Truthout*. Available at http://truth-out.org/index.php?option=com_k2&view=item&id=4264:occupy-wall-streets-battle-against-americanstyle-authoritarianism

Goldstein, J. (2011, September 27). Demonstrations test police trained for bigger threats. *The New York Times*, A17.

Good, C. (2009, April 13). The Tea Party movement: Who's in charge? *The Atlantic*, Available at http://www.theatlantic.com/politics/archive/2009/04/the-tea-party-movement-whos-in-charge/13041/

Hallin, D. C. (2008). Neoliberalism, social movements and change in media systems in the late twentieth century. In D. Hesmondhalgh & J. Toynbee (Eds.), *The media and social theory*, pp. 43–58. New York: Routledge.

Hoffman, M. (2011, October 17). Protesters debate what demands, if any, to make. *The New York Times*, p. A19.

Ives, A. (2007). The importance of the idealist discourse in defence of American foreign policy initiatives: Beyond rhetoric towards a new form of imperialism. *Revue LISA/LISA e-journal*, *5*(3). Available at http://lisa.revues.org/1611?lang=fr

Iyengar. S. (1991). *Is anyone responsible? How television frames political issues*. Chicago, IL: University of Chicago Press.

Jameson, F. (2003, May/June). Future city. *New Left Review*, *21*, 65–79.

Jeffries, A. (2011, October 4). From blackout to circus: The evolution of media coverage at Occupy Wall Street. *New York Observer.* Available at http://observer.com/2011/10/from-blackout-to-circus-the-evolution-of-media-coverage-at-occupy-wall-street/2/

Kellner, D. (2003). *Media spectacle*. New York: Routledge.

Kilkenny, A. (2011, November 1). The commodification of Occupy Wall Street. *The Nation.* Available at http://www.thenation.com/blog/164300/commodification-occupy-wall-street

Korten, F. (2009, December 1). 7 ways the battle of Seattle changed the world: Ten years later, the protests of 1999 are still having an impact. *Yes Magazine*. Available at http://www.yesmagazine.org/people-power/7-ways-the-battle-of-seattle-changed-the-world

Kristof, N. D. (2011a, October 16). America's 'primal scream.' *The New York Times*, SR11. Available at http://www.nytimes.com/2011/10/16/opinion/sunday/kristof-americas-primal-scream.html?gwh=B79818700CBD5FAE9250A8AFB8AF9DA0

———. (2011b, November 20). Occupy the agenda. *The New York Times*, SR11. Available at http://www.nytimes.com/2011/11/20/opinion/sunday/kristof-occupy-the-agenda.html?gwh=B23856586F0C052F0527106DA961E8EF

Krugman, P. (2011a, October 7). Confronting the malefactors. *The New York Times*. A27. Available at http://www.nytimes.com/2011/10/07/opinion/krugman-confronting-the-male factors.html?gwh=9A7FA97F173759A0D3011B519BF98325

———. (2011b, October 10) Panic of the plutocrats. *The New York Times*. A23. Available at http://www.nytimes.com/2011/10/10/opinion/panic-of-the-plutocrats.html?gwh=7092663762825617C06C10B849085C75

———. (2011c, November 4) Oligarchy, American style. *The New York Times*. A31. Available at http://www.nytimes.com/2011/11/04/opinion/oligarchy-american-style.html?gwh=BF FAC999A4B6EE9004D2F0AD226828B0

Lewis, J., Wahl-Jorgensen, K., & Inthorn, S. (2004). Images of citizenship on television news: Constructing a passive public. *Journalism Studies*, *5*(2), 153–164.

Mandel, S. (2012, May 21). I spy an occupy: Obama's DHS surveils legit protesters. *WhoWhatWhy.com.* Available at http://whowhatwhy.com/2012/05/21/i-spy-an-occupy-obamas-dhs-surveils-legit-protesters/

McCann, C. (2011, December 25). Occupy Wall Street. *The New York Times*, SR4.

McChesney, R., & Schiller, D. (2003, October). The political economy of international communications: Foundations for the emerging global debate about media ownership and regulation. *United Nations Research Institute for Social Development*, Technology, Business and Society Programme, Paper Number 11.

McKinley, J. C., Jr. (2011, October 19). At the protests, the message lacks a melody. *The New York Times*, C1. Available at http://www.nytimes.com/2011/10/19/arts/music/occupy-wall-street-protest-lacks-an-anthem.html?_r=1&gwh=25864EBE09B714998A864A12D 1F6C2FD

McLeod, D. (2007). News coverage and social protest: How the media's protest paradigm exacerbates social conflict. *Journal of Dispute Resolution*, 1, 185–194.

McLeod, D. M., & Detenber, B. (1999). Framing effects of television news coverage of social protest. *Journal of Communication*, *49*(3), 3–23.

McLeod, D. M., & Hertog, J. K. (1992). The manufacture of public opinion by reporters: Informal cues for public perceptions of protest groups. *Discourse and Society*, *3*(3), 259–275.

Monbiot, G. (2010, October 26). The Tea Party movement: Deluded and inspired by billionaires. *The Guardian*, 31. Available at http://www.guardian.co.uk/commentis free/cifamerica/2010/oct/25/tea-party-koch-brothers

Moynihan, C., & Barron, J. (2011, December 10). 'Law & Order: SVU' imitation occupation draws real protesters, and city's ire, *The New York Times*, A19. Available at http://www.ny times.com/2011/12/10/nyregion/law-order-svu-imitation-occupation-draws-real-protest ers-and-citys-ire.html?gwh=4421340A2727C1A821980A91C5D1C94B

Naureckas, J. (2011, November). They are the 1 percent: Corporate media slow to wake up to Wall Street protests. *Fairness & Accuracy in Reporting.* Available at http://www.fair.org /index.php?page=4465

New York City General Assembly. (2011, September 29). Declaration of the occupation of New York City. *New York City General Assembly.* Available at http://www.nycga.net/ resources/declaration/

New York Times (2011) Newspaper media kit, Available at http://nytmarketing.whsites .net/mediakit/newspaper

New York Times Company. (2008). 2008 Annual Report. Available at http://www.nytco.com /pdf/annual_2008/2008NYTannual.pdf

———. (2009). 2009 Annual Report. Available at http://www.nytco.com/pdf/annual_2009 /2009NYTannual.pdf

———. (2010). 2010 Annual Report. Available at http://www.nytco.com/pdf/annual_2010 /2010NYTannual.pdf

———. (2011). 2011 Annual Report. Available at http://www.nytco.com/pdf/annual_2011 /2011NYTannual.pdf

Owens, S. (2011, October 25). As Occupy Wall Street evolves, news sites find it a great opportunity for web journalism. *Nieman Journalism Lab.* Available at http://www. niemanlab.org/2011/10/as-occupy-wall-street-evolves-news-sites-find-it-a-great-opportunity-for-web-journalism/

Partnership for Civil Justice Fund (PCJF). (2012, May 23). DHS releases more documents on Occupy to PCJF. Available at http://www.justiceonline.org/commentary/dhs-releases-more-documents.html

Peri, Y. (2004). *Telepopulism: Media and politics in Israel.* Palo Alto, CA: Stanford University Press.

Peters, J. W. (2011, March 17). *The Times* announces digital subscription plan. Available at http://www.nytimes.com/2011/03/18/business/media/18times.html?_r=1&pagewanted=al l.

Pew Research Center. (2006). State of the news media 2006. *Project for Excellence in Journalism.* Available at http://stateofthemedia.org/2006/

Pew Research Center's Project for Excellence in Journalism. (2011). Archive of PEJ news coverage indexes. Available at http://www.journalism.org/news_index/99

Pleyers, G. (2010, July 1). The Global Justice Movement. *Globality Studies*, 19. Available at http://globality.cc.stonybrook.edu/?p=146

Rauch, J., Chitrapu, S., Eastman, S. T., Evans, J. C., Paine, C., & Mwesige, P. (2007). From Seattle 1999 to New York 2004: A longitudinal analysis of journalistic framing of the movement for democratic globalization. *Social Movement Studies*, *6*(2), 131–145.

Rogers, B. (2012, March 2). Occupy Wall Street and neoliberal governmentality. *Concurring Opinions*. Available at http://www.concurringopinions.com/archives/2012/03/occupy-wall-street-and-neoliberal-governmentality.html#more-58736

Rose, C. (2011, December 14). *The Charlie Rose show* (TV talk show). Available at Lexis Nexis.

Rosentiel, T., & Mitchell, A. (2011). State of the news media 2011. *Project for Excellence in Journalism.* Available at http://stateofthemedia.org/overview-2011/

Ryan, Y. (2011, January 26). How Tunisia's revolution began. *Al Jazeera*. Available at http://www.aljazeera.com/indepth/features/2011/01/2011126121815985483.html

Sachs, J. D. (2011, November 13). The new progressive movement. *New York Times*, SR6.

Said, E. (1993). *Culture and imperialism*. New York: Knopf.

Schiller, H. (1979). Transnational media and national development. In K. Nordenstreng & H. Schiller (Eds.), *National sovereignty and international communication*. New York: Ablex.

Schlesinger, P. (1978). *Putting "reality" together: BBC News*. London, U.K.: Constable.

Schumacher-Matos, E. (2011, September 26). Newsworthy? Determining the importance of protests on Wall Street. *National Public Radio*. Available at http://www.npr.org/blogs/ombudsman/2011/09/26/140815394/newsworthy-determining-the-importance-of-protests-on-wall-street

Silver, N. (2011, October 7). Police clashes spur coverage of Wall Street protests. *The New York Times*. Available at http://fivethirtyeight.blogs.nytimes.com/2011/10/07/police-clashes-spur-coverage-of-wall-street-protests/

Solomon, N. (1998). Big media myths. In P. Phillips (Ed.), *Censored 1998: The news that didn't make the news*, pp. 157–158. New York: Seven Stories Press.

Speri, A. (2011, October 29). Struggling to make 'the 99%' more representative of reality. *The New York Times*, A22.

Stelter, B. (2011a, October 13). A news story is growing with 'Occupy' protests. *The New York Times*, A22. Available at http://www.nytimes.com/2011/10/13/us/occupy-wall-street-protests-a-growing-news-story.html

Stelter, B. (2011b, November 21). Protest puts coverage in spotlight. *The New York Times*, B1.

Stengel, R. (2011, December 14). Person of the year introduction. *Time*, *178*(25), 53.

Taylor, K. (2011a, October 21). Masked protector of Gotham has his eye on Wall Street protesters. *The New York Times*, A31. Available at http://www.nytimes.com/2011/10/21/nyregion/dark-knight-rises-to-film-near-occupy-wall-street-site.html?gwh=FE58BBDBC5F4C2F002790CA50934FF54

Taylor, K. (2011b, November 3). Mayor says protest hurts life in area around park. *The New York Times*, A28.

Thussu, D.K. (2008). *News as entertainment: The rise of global infotainment*. Thousand Oaks, CA: Sage.

Walter, S. (2011, November 13). Occupy Oakland and news media coexist uneasily. *The New York Times*, A29A. Available at http://www.nytimes.com/2011/11/13/us/occupy-oakland-and-news-media-coexist-uneasily.html

9 With No Responsibility: The Colbert Show

Jjenna Hupp Andrews

IN OCTOBER 2005, the first episode of *The Colbert Report* opened with Stephen Colbert seated at his C-shaped news desk, writing on a pad of paper, as is the convention of most nightly news anchors. At the time, no one could have predicted how *The Colbert Report* would change the world, or at least how we as viewers relate to and understand that world.

It is in this first episode that Colbert (in character) introduced the concept of "Truthiness," which became the manifesto for the program. Blurring the boundaries between beliefs and facts, truthiness is "truth that comes from the gut, not books" (Detmer, 2009, p. 131). Detmer explains *truthiness* as having "nothing to do with facts, evidence, reason, logic, or correspondence with the way things really are.... If you *believe* something strongly enough, even if that belief is merely based on wishful thinking, then it is true (or, rather, 'truthy')" (2009, p. 131). Truthiness elevates personal beliefs to the level of fact regardless of its validity and is presented in such a way as to assert that everyone believes or should believe it to be Truth. Colbert developed the concept of truthiness as a response to and critique of the ideologues that have come to dominate mainstream news media.

Through emulating mainstream news personalities, Colbert creates his truthy satire as a weapon, challenging the rhetoric and hypocrisy of the news media itself. What follows is an inquiry into the blurring of boundaries between "real" and "fake" news, where, as Jean Baudrillard (1994b) observed, the "fake" has become more real than the "real." Utilizing deadpan satire and provocative rhetorical techniques, Colbert challenges the elitist positioning of news media as "unbiased" by revealing the subjectively constructed and partisan nature of the "real" news. Colbert assumes the hyperreal position of (satirical) conservative news pundit to expose the simulacrum of "real" news personalities, which vividly illustrates that he is not the only news personality to employ truthiness.

Blurring Boundaries

The Colbert Report was conceived as a spin-off and "conservative" counterpart to *The Daily Show* where Colbert is at once a comedian, a political pundit, an actor, a social commentator, and an entertainer through his parody of ultra-conservative, over-the-top news personalities such as Fox News' Bill O'Reilly and Sean Hannity. Colbert has built his whole persona around this blurring of the boundaries between entertainment, news media, and sociopolitical reality; however, his blurring of boundaries is not altogether new in that Colbert takes his cues on how to create spectacle from "mainstream" news outlets such as Fox, CNN and MSNBC. Geoffrey Baym (2010) explains:

> …the boundaries that once shaped television news—between fact and opinion, public service and private profit, information and entertainment—are deeply obscured. Most news has become a product packaged to sell, its interests resting far more with attracting audiences and protecting corporate priorities than in the older mission of informing the citizenry and holding power accountable. As we have seen in the past decade on nearly every issue of public significance—from the invasion of Iraq in 2003, to the economic crisis of 2008, to the health care debate of 2009—when we have deeply needed critical information and reasoned debate, the most influential sources of television news instead provided a steady and often debilitating diet of distraction, distortion, spectacle, and spin. (Jones & Baym, 2010, p. 281)

Here Baym highlights how traditional media such as broadcast news have morphed into spectacle entertainment that caters primarily to corporate interests. What is significant in relation to Colbert and "soft news" or "fake news" in general is that they have become the trusted source of "critical information and reasoned debate" Baym calls for. He explains that *The Daily Show* and *The Colbert Report* both are "marked by border-crossing and hybridity" as they "interweave information with entertainment, politics with pop culture, and reasoned conversation with spectacle," but that this boundary blurring becomes their "critique of news and an interrogation of political power that rests on a firm belief in fact, accountability, and reason in public discourse" (Jones & Baym, 2010, p. 281).

Colbert's brand of spectacle, which blends satire, irony, and exaggeration into sociopolitical commentary/entertainment, has taken on an important role in American political-media culture. As political "news" sources, *The Daily Show* and *The Colbert Report* have become major sources from which many people under 30 get their news and understand American politics (Robinson, 2010, p. 219). When asked, viewers' common response is that despite being comedy, Stewart and Colbert's comedic "news" programs come across as being more "authentic" and "genuine, honest or real" than most other cable "real news" shows (Jones & Baym, 2010, p. 282). Colbert and Stewart create a counter to the mainstream media by highlighting the inconsistencies and errors being presented as fact and challenging news media agendas by opening up their positions to critique. This then directs the viewer's attention to what is not being said or what is being glossed over or ignored. Colbert takes the spectacle further by espousing the logical extremes of the world views that media and political personalities present as fact. He challenges the status quo of "real" news media through satire by utilizing the same techniques that the news personalities use to make ethical and moral issues into spectacle.

Spectacular Satire

In her essay "Truly Funny: Humor, Irony, and Satire as Moral Criticism," E.M. Dadlez (2011) defines satire as "the use of irony or sarcasm to expose or deride vice" where humor is the "vehicle for moral criticism" (p. 12). Lisa Colletta (2009) references Cuddon's dictionary of literary terms that describes satire as a "critique of what an author sees as 'dangerous religious, political, moral, or social standards'" (p. 859). Satire is a critique that uses "comedic devices" to make its point(s), and it is this use of humor that both gives it power and separates it from being merely "editorial" (Colletta, 2009, p. 860). Both Dadlez and Colletta stress that in comedy, laughter is the goal in and of itself; however in satire, laughter is used "as a weapon" and against a target "outside the work itself" and can "shock its audience out of complacency and sentimentality (which is [*sic*] often the companion of convention and hypocrisy)" (Colletta, 2009, pp. 859–860).

Colbert's use of irony and satire provides a site for ambiguity of meaning and interpretation, and yet the Colbert character performs no such indecisiveness. Colbert is always sure and steadfast in what he believes, no matter what the facts say. He speaks as a narrow-minded bigot and uses that persona to criticize and challenge the narrow-mindedness and bigotry that is prevalent in current news media (Dadlez, 2011, p. 17). He embodies the steadfast self-assuredness that is common among "serious" conservative news personalities to the point that he has become the "celebrity" of the kind that he ridicules (Burwell & Boler, 2008). This is in line with what postmodern parody is and how it functions. It is "generally a 'double coded' address, undercutting but also lending legitimacy to that which it parodies" (Hutcheon, 1989, p. 97). Colbert embodies what he parodies to the point where the viewer is left uncertain of his sincerity and actual political position.

The role of the audience is essential in the performance of satire, in that the audience must have the ability to recognize the performance as satire before they can discern the meaning and purpose of the performance. Linda

Hutcheon (1989) explains this relationship between interpretation and the way in which irony/ parody work in that they are complicated by their "social and interactive dimensions" (p. 104). Colletta (2009) describes this process:

> Injustice, vice, or polite cruelty have to be recognized as the object of the attack, and they need to be judged against a better moral standard. The satirist may use irony with vicious anger, but it always has a deeper meaning and a social signification beyond that of the humor. If the irony is missed, or the better moral standard is also ironically presented as just another construction, then satire is no longer an effective social critique and may even be misunderstood as an example of the very thing it sets out to critique. (p. 860)

Irony is expressed by the ironist but completed by the audience; it is a "complex social interaction" (Burwell & Boler, 2008). The meaning created is never totally controlled by the ironist/parodist nor is it totally predictable. In fact, it is being discovered that one's prior political beliefs affect how one then interprets political irony/parody (Burwell & Boler, 2008).

Colbert's brand of parody is deadpan satire, which is a type of satire that relies upon "a straight-faced approach to joke telling" (LaMarre, Landreville, & Beam, 2009, p. 217). Colbert, as an actor, rarely breaks character as he parodies conservative news personalities, which increases the ambiguity of his intentions and meanings. This extreme form of deadpan provides no external clues for the audience to determine if the information being presented is serious or not, which in turn increases the ambiguity of not only the information but also the source of that information. Unlike Jon Stewart, who on *The Daily Show* remains himself, giving physical and verbal cues to aid in interpreting the irony, Colbert presents his satire as serious and as truth (truthiness). The audience of *The Colbert Report* does not have the benefit of external cues to point towards the intended meaning. Priscilla Meddaugh (2010) describes Colbert's approach as "based on the textual interplay between the said and unsaid, a convergence of rhetorical situation and historical reality" yet with no external clues as to what is real and what is "fake" (p. 380). The audiences are left to their own devices to interpret and make meaning from what they are seeing and hearing, which means that they do not always "get the joke."

Colbert assumes that the audience understands that the performance is satire and yet in some cases the audience instead interprets it as his actual beliefs. The audience's judgments of the satire then become based on the perception of sincerity. LaMarre, Landreville, and Beam (2009) explain:

> …studies show that audiences struggle with deadpan and other forms of satire, which have been associated with miscues and errors among message recipients…. That is, when the audience judges the satirist to be sincere, then the statements the satirist makes are judged as representing the satirist's true beliefs. What results is a situation where the audience member misidentifies the satirist's beliefs and intentions. (p. 217)

This ambiguity of meaning then becomes a site for the viewers to make their own assumptions, not only concerning the meaning of what is being presented but about Colbert as well. This is illustrated by LaMarre, Landreville, and Beam (2009) study results that revealed that the viewer's political beliefs affect the interpretation of Colbert's satire. They explain that though both liberals and conservatives recognize that Colbert is performing comedy, the interpreted meanings are markedly different in that conservatives see liberals as the target of the jokes, and liberals, the opposite (p. 226). Many conservatives go even further, perceiving Colbert's political positions and ideology as matching their own, which means that for the viewers of *The Colbert Report*, Colbert is either a bigoted conservative or someone not afraid to speak the truth, depending on the viewer's political beliefs.

This ambiguity of meaning and ideological position is pivotal in Colbert's deadpan satire, in that it vividly demonstrates the constructed nature of the news and the subjective nature of viewer interpretation. Colbert convincingly assumes the role of serious news pundit, purposefully blurring the distinction between serious news and entertainment to reveal the absurdity of the current news media pretense. He reports on the "news" as it is presented through the "real" news media outlets, which in turn demonstrates how the "news" is not so much reported but rather created by the news media itself. The ambiguity of Colbert's performance is not concealed but rather presented front-and-center for all to see and interpret. It is exactly this transparency that gives Colbert his legitimacy and authenticity that viewers value and privilege over the veiled spectacle that is presented continuously on news media outlets.

News as Spectacle

The "fake" news programs are highly stylized and designed to entertain, and yet audiences perceive them as confronting the propaganda of mainstream media. Jones (Jones & Baym, 2010) explains that there is a perception that these programs are more "authentic" and more reliable than the "real" news where the "talk is dominated by partisan polemics, inside-the-beltway thinking, or angry and agonistic confrontations" (p. 282). The average viewer is seeing the spectacle of the news being played out across the "real" and the "fake" news programs and has discerned that the performances being presented are qualitatively different, even though they are using similar rhetorical techniques; the perceived difference lies in their rhetorical approach to spectacle.

"Fake" news and "real" news both employ rhetorical techniques to create spectacle intended to incite the emotions of their viewers; however, Peter Robinson (2010) observes that "fake" news is "endowed with political legitimacy and authority in a popular culture in which the meaning of performance and its relationship to reality is highly contested" (p. 219). *The Colbert Report* does not hide the fact that the program is a performance, unlike many news channels today where a "penchant for sensationalism, blatant promotions of entertainment programming thinly veiled as hard news stories, and the exaltation of bombastic talk-show hosts and infotainment pundits in the guise of traditional journalists" all work to conceal their performance and present it as serious news and political analysis (Robinson, 2010, p. 220). Colbert capitalizes on this "fuzziness" in contemporary news media. For example on the surface, it is often very difficult to see much difference between Colbert's satirical performance and the "serious" performance of Bill O'Reilly on his Fox program *The O'Reilly Factor*. Both structure their arguments by referencing anecdote instead of fact, by appealing to emotions over reason, and by using everyday language and syntax (Colletta, 2009, p. 862). These techniques enable them to incite an emotional response of truthiness. The difference lies in how the performance is presented. O'Reilly presents his performance not as a "performance" but as objective news analysis in a "No Spin Zone." Colbert, whose character is modeled on O'Reilly (among other conservatives), takes his performed opinions to the logical extremes and does not pretend to be objective. Colbert uses the "comic device of exaggeration" as a "rhetorical strategy of showing how an opponent's argument can lead to absurd conclusions if taken far enough," and that is understood by the viewer (Colletta, 2009, p. 861). We can, again, contrast this with O'Reilly (or Beck, or Hannity, or Limbaugh, etc.) who could also use exaggeration but present those exaggerations as fact.

On *The Colbert Report*, Colbert satirizes rhetorical techniques popularized on the Fox News program *The O'Reilly Factor* by "submitting every topic to the highly charged 'elitist thinker vs. common-sense American' debate" popularized by O'Reilly" (Colletta, 2009, p. 861). Colbert employs truthiness as a way to intensify this type of debate, revealing that opposition is not so clear-cut as the news personalities present. Robert Tally (2010) explains Colbert's technique is not to "oppose bullshit" but to promote it (p. 160). He explains further:

> [Colbert can] make sure everyone knows that it is bullshit, and insist that such bullshit is a core foundation of conservative political philosophy. Indeed, by portraying the very thing he is parodying, Colbert can more actively undermine the authority of his targets. (pp. 160–161)

Colbert revels in an "All Spin Zone" as a foil to the self-proclaimed "No Spin Zone" of Fox News. Colbert does not hide that he "makes up facts" to support his arguments, which in turn further highlights the hypocrisy of those news personalities who will not admit they do the same thing.

Whose Truthiness?

In the early 1990s, Jean Baudrillard (1994b) observed that there was a distinct lack of critical analysis of current events and resulting interpretations. In its place had emerged an emphasis on events of "no importance" presented as events of extreme importance, which resulted in what is now common practice of "selling-off of the event on the over-heated news market" (pp. 14–15). Baudrillard (1994b) explains:

> Simulation is precisely this irresistible unfolding, this sequencing of things as though they had meaning, when they are governed only by artificial *montage* and non-meaning. Putting the event up for auction by radical disinformation. Setting a price on the event, as against setting it in play, setting it in history. (p. 15)

This creation of importance from the relatively insignificant has become the status quo of mainstream news, which in turn illustrates the "strategy of power" where media mystify the masses and impose their own truth on those masses (Baudrillard & Maclean, 1985, p. 587). The role of mainstream news personalities has become the overemphasis of insignificant events in order to incite emotion and divert attention from issues/events that are in actuality more important to the health/survival of western society and potentially dangerous to their own prestige and power.

Colbert, on the other hand, does not hide that he is diverting attention away from what is important and consequently focuses viewer attention on the events that are being glossed over or ignored. For Colbert, media's power is Baudrillard's "territory of the ruse of the masses" where the masses can refuse truth and reality and opt for their own (Baudrillard & Maclean, 1985, p. 587). Colbert is "destabilizing the real and the true, all historical or political truth" by employing exaggeration and satire to challenge the unreal reality of news media and by not hiding the fact he is creating his own unreal reality (1985, p. 587). Baudrillard (1994b) explains that there is "no 'objective' difference" between the simulation/parody and the "real; both utilize the same gestures and the same signs exist as for the real" (p. 15). Using the same sensational techniques as the "real," Colbert's critique of the news media has become simulacra of the news media's simulacrum; even though it is (generally) understood as entertainment and "not real," *The Colbert Report* has become more real and authentic than the "Disney World" of the news media conglomerates. *The Colbert Report* has created the funhouse mirror that refracts the twisted reality of mainstream news personalities.

Satire provides Colbert an entryway into popular and news media while also remaining an outsider. Colbert has repeatedly demonstrated an ability to critique current sociopolitical events and the media coverage thereof as well as mobilizing his audience into action through his deadpan emulation of serious "real" news personalities. Both Colbert and Stewart have developed "fake" news into something that has transcended mere comedic social commentary and blurred the lines between what is "fake" and what is "real," which in turn has created a source for news that is perceived to be more real and authentic than the news personalities they emulate. Colbert's brand of satire has morphed into a simulacrum, which exposes the simulacra of the mainstream news giants for what they are: pure spectacle.

Note

The title is in reference to *The Colbert Report*: "The Word: With Great Power Comes No Responsibility" (Colbert, 2011).

References

Baudrillard, J. (1994a). *Simulacra and Simulations.* (S. F. Glaser, Trans.) New York: University of Michigan Press.

———. (1994b). *The Illusion of the End.* (C. Turner, Trans.) Stanford, CA: Stanford University Press.

Baudrillard, J., & Maclean, M. (1985). The Implosion of the Social in the Media. *New Literary History, 16*(3), 577–589.

Burwell, C., & Boler, M. (2008). Calling on the Colbert Nation: Fandom, politics and parody in an age of media covergence. *The Electronic Journal of Communication, 18*(2, 3, & 4).

Colbert, S. (2005, October 17). *Debut Episode*. Available at http://www.colbertnation.com/the-colbert-report-videos/180900/october-17-2005/intro---10-17-05

———. (2007, April 24). *60% Good News*. Retrieved from *The Colbert Nation*: http://www.colbertnation.com/the-colbert-report-videos/182879/april-24-2007/60--good-news

———. (2011 , August 1). *The Word - With Great Power Comes No Responsibility*. Available at http://www.colbertnation.com/the-colbert-report-videos/393610/august-01-2011/the-word---with-great-power-comes-no-responsibility

Colletta, L. (2009). Political satire and postmodern irony in the age of Stephen Colbert and Jon Stewart. *The Journal of Popular Culture, 42*(5), 856–874.

Dadlez, E. (2011, Spring). Truely funny: Humor, irony, and satire as moral criticism. *Journal of Aesthetic Education, 45*(1), 1–17.

Detmer, D. (2009). Philosophy in the age of truthiness. In A. A. Schiller (Ed.), *Stephen Colbert and philosophy: I am philosophy (and so can you!)* (pp. 131–142). Chicago: Open Court.

Hutcheon, L. (1989). The politics of parody. In *Politics of postmodernism* (pp. 93–117). New York: Routledge.

Jones, J. P., & Baym, G. (2010). A dialogue on satire news and the crisis of truth in postmodern political television. *Journal of Communication Inquiry, 34*(3), 278–294.

LaMarre, H. L., Landreville, K. D., & Beam, M. A. (2009). The irony of satire: Political ideology and the motivation to see what you want to see in *The Colbert Report. The International Journal of Press/Politics, 14*, 212–231.

Meddaugh, P. M. (2010, October). Bakhtin, Colbert, and the center of discourse: Is there no "truthiness" in humor? *Critical Studies in Media Communication, 27*(4), 376–390.

Robinson, P. M. (2010). Epilogue: Back to the future. In *The dance of the comedians: The people, the president, and the performance of political standup comedy in America* (pp. 215–227). Amherst: University of Massachusetts Press.

Sternbergh, A. (2006, October 16). Stephen Colbert has America by the ballots. *New York Magazine*, p. nymag.com.

Tally, R. T. (2010). I am the mainstream media (and so can you!). In A. Amarasingam (Ed.), *The Stewart/Colbert effect: Essays on the real impacts of fake news* (pp. 149–163). Jefferson: McFarland & Company, Inc., Publishers.

10 The Devil Is in the Details: Christian Messages Gliding Unseen Within *Deep Blue Sea*

Kimberly M. Radek

RENNY HARLIN's *Deep Blue Sea* (1999) is a modern horror movie, a *Jaws* meets *Jurassic Park*, in which scientists seeking for a cure for Alzheimer's genetically engineer super sharks, combining their prehistoric predator brain cells with those of humans. In an early scene, Janice Higgins, a research scientist (played by Jacqueline McKenzie), is giving a tour of the research facility to a corporate pharmaceutical investor, Russell Franklin (Samuel Jackson). As they both stare into the ocean, Higgins remarks, "Beneath its glassy surface, a world of gliding monsters" before saying to Franklin, "Pretty scary stuff, huh?" Franklin, of course, agrees, and it is certainly probable that the audience does, as well, since viewers could hardly have missed the opening scene, in which a genetically modified shark escapes its enclosure and destroys a boat in the apparent attempt to ingest the four humans and one teddy bear on board. Minutes later in the film, the chief scientist, Dr. Susan McCallister (Saffron Burrows), and the resident shark wrangler, Carter Blake (Thomas Jane), are talking. McCallister asks, "How's life underwater?" Blake responds, "Well, it's a lot less complicated than it is on the surface, that's for sure." Given the number of scenes with sharks behaving badly—or at least suspiciously intelligently and athletically—and the number of shots with closed form or entrapping shots, viewers might believe that the movie is all that it purports to be: meaningless violent fun with a moralistic message against tinkering with nature. An analysis of the film, however, reveals that there are ideological monsters stirring right below its surface, undetected by many viewers who choose to view the film as just entertaining escapism; in fact, *Deep Blue Sea* is a film that offers an intentionally conservative message as it seeks to reify patriarchal and Christian values, while denigrating scientific discovery.

Hollywood cinema is more than entertainment; it communicates serious messages about how to think and behave, and because most people are not looking for those messages, they become more powerful as they are absorbed by the public at a subconscious level. Indeed, a close look at this simple horror film demonstrates that it contains many implicit messages about gender and social politics, as well as science and religion, some of which are spoken, some only visual, and all of these messages coalesce with what Shirley

R. Steinberg and Joe L. Kincheloe call *Christotainment* (2009). One can see that *Deep Blue Sea*, in spite of its apparent liberality in featuring female and black actors in leading roles, is an example of a film designed to pander to fundamental Christian viewers through sympathetic cinematic techniques and plot turns. *Deep Blue Sea* recalls the phrase about being between "the devil and the deep blue sea" and thus, alludes to Christianity, which is certainly apropos as the film sells conservative ideology along with its adrenaline rush.

Many horror films feature animal experiments gone awry; in this case, sharks are being subjected to genetic engineering and begin to take exception to that treatment, rebelling against the people exploiting them. *Deep Blue Sea* is a typical horror film, designed to entertain its audience through scary scenarios and fantastical action. In spite of rather sluggish domestic earnings upon its theatrical release, the film did manage to make a modest profit of around $100 million worldwide, according to the website BoxOfficeMojo, an online movie database affiliate. Perhaps more importantly in terms of its cultural effects, its DVD release and its almost incessant rebroadcasting on various cable channels such as SyFy, G4, BET, and others, have given it a cult-classic status and allowed it to find new newer, younger audiences, as well as continuing its ability to generate revenue.

Because it is a horror film, its action is nearly nonstop; viewers are bombarded by dialogue and action, granting them the adrenaline rush that they seek when they turn to films in this genre. This also has the effect of exploiting viewers' emotional reactions. Psychologists have observed that people can often be influenced emotionally by observing emotions in others. In *Social Intelligence* (2006), Daniel Goleman discusses the ways that the brain works when perceiving information, particularly that of an emotional content. Our brains, he explains, are hard-wired to see and evaluate the emotions of other people quickly, as the messages pass through into the amygdale, which "provides no direct access to the centers for speech" (p. 15), making us susceptible to "catching" others' emotions. "Mirror neurons [in our brains]," Goleman says, "make emotions contagious, letting the feelings we witness flow through us, helping us get in synch and follow what's going on" (p. 42). Since horror films function, as Tony Kashani explains in *Deconstructing the Mystique* (2009), by "tap[ping] into our psyche and extract[ing] the awesome fears" (p. 159), we can see that most people will have similar automatic emotional responses to them.

This natural empathic response reaction in people has two consequences. First, it allows a group's emotions to converge very suddenly. Goleman reveals that a "mood can sweep through a group with great rapidity, a remarkable display of the parallel alignment of biological subsystems that puts everyone there in physiological synchrony" (2006, p. 48). This, he believes, can explain why mobs—or groups of sports fans—can often initiate violence, but he acknowledges that it can take place "at any great performance, where actors or musicians create a field effect, playing the audience's emotions like instruments" (p. 48). Second, this emotional synchronization occurs without people being aware of its happening. Because their feelings resonate, they become vulnerable to suggestion. Goleman cautions that "feelings that pass through a group can bias how all the group members process information and hence the decisions they make. This suggests that in coming to a decision together, any group would do well to attend not just to what's being said, but to the shared emotions in the room as well" (p. 49). Of course, it is unlikely that most people discuss the ideological issues advanced by horror films, as most probably, upon viewing the film, want to know whether others enjoyed it, noticed its special effects, or found any plot holes.

In the case of a horror or action film, viewers are repeatedly exposed to emotional incidents, reacting with the characters and each other, feeling their emotions align but never really thinking about how or why they are reacting in these ways. In horror films, this emotional response is exploited, as people are constantly in fear for the characters', and thus their own, lives. This churns up their feelings and decreases their ability to think rationally about what they are seeing, rendering them susceptible to bias, a significant happenstance since people are exposed to many ideas in addition to the fear that they focus or thrive upon during these films. In this way, audiences can be nearly brainwashed to empathize or agree with emotional conclusions or accept conservative ideology without even being aware that it has happened.

Steinberg, for instance, reveals one aspect of influence that may not be immediately noticeable to horror film fans: religiosity in the films. In her work on rapture films, she explains that there is a difference between Christianizing and Christonormativizing. "Christianity," she explains, "is invisibly dictated. Hegemony occurs between different individuals and groups who consent to what the culture should be. Christianizing is different from Christonormativizing. When attempts are made to proselytize and convert, the nature of missionary work is apparent—that is an attempt to Christianize.

However, when the dominant culture includes themes and messages expected to be acceptable by all citizens, the outcome is not mere missionary zeal (Steinberg & Kincheloe, 2009), it is Christonormativization" (Steinberg, 2010, pp. 45–46.). In other words, Christian values are being communicated at subconscious levels, making it more likely that people will passively accept them without consciously realizing that they are being asked to do so. Steinberg, in considering the rapture films, cites three assumptions inherent in "contemporary evangelical Christianity: moralistic platitudes, fearsome threats of the end of the world, and a savior who must be acknowledged and worshipped to achieve eternal life" (2010, p. 51). *Deep Blue Sea* Christonormativizes more subtly than the rapture films, but it reinforces that evangelical ideology just the same.

Deep Blue Sea clearly advances the idea of Christian faith as being superior and in opposition to science while also suggesting that traditional gender roles are sanctioned by God and nature. This film, like many horror films, has scientists "playing God," this time in the search for a cure for Alzheimer's disease. What is most notable in this film, as opposed to the earlier *Jurassic Park* (1993), for example, is that instead of an army of scientists and technicians under male leadership, there is a relatively small staff led by a female scientist. *Deep Blue Sea* falls, ideologically speaking, into a subcategory of films about disasters that, as Cynthia Belmont (2007) explains, "overtly connect the destructive power of nature with a disapproving view of women in positions of authority, [and thus they] portray the trouble with nature as being tied to the dissolution of traditional gender roles: as they foster a fear of and drive to conquer nature, they also feed cultural anxiety about women's empowerment and suggest that meekness and passivity are required of women if order is to be restored to a chaotic, unstable world" (p. 350). Combining that subordinate view of women with overt religious messaging, *Deep Blue Sea* projects a very conservative worldview, one that many might find laden with injustice.

As in many films since the 1970s, several of the women in the film appear to represent the modern, liberated and successful woman. Belmont notices that "*Deep Blue Sea*'s Dr. McCallister, in addition to being a scientist, is knowledgeable about Navy ships, can fly a biplane, and is filmed from below, starting with her big black boots, as she emerges, looking very potent, from a helicopter" (p. 362). However, she cautions, this superficial success will be undone in the case of many disaster films, recognizing that "although initially these heroines do not conform to traditional expectations for women, at the films' closures, they have been stripped of authority and reduced to helplessness, passiveness, joblessness, and silence/death, occupying traditional roles as victims and sex objects/male status symbols, and validating the lingering notion that what is 'natural' for women is to be family centered, to nurture through mothering, and to be cared for by men" (p. 362). Certainly, McCallister conforms to this pattern. Although she presents as powerful, even challenging the corporate board that provides her funding, she ultimately is forced to accept that her methods of research were wrong, despite her good intentions—so wrong, in fact, as to be evil—and her only chance of redemption lies in sacrificing herself for others.

On the scale of actions, McCallister runs afoul of patriarchy in a number of ways, but perhaps her biggest error, from a conservative Christian point of view, is that she hires a male scientist with a God complex, empowering him to usurp divine authority. Belmont catalogues the malevolent male bias that manifests in insults and violent imagery toward McCallister throughout the film, and such violence, while seemingly anti-Christian in nature, actually reinforces conservative Christian ideology. This approval of violence—not generally advocated against women—can also be seen in a number of venues of Christotainment, such as novels, films, and video games, where any enemy of the "true" Christian mindset is seen as being ripe for righteous elimination. As Steinberg explains, the authors of such texts, "want revenge against the hated intellectuals, scientists, liberal/leftists, homosexuals, secularists, abortionists, feminists, Muslims, mainline Christians, Jews, and other enemies who have, in the evangelicals' eyes, worked to destroy true Christians" (2010, p. 48). *In Deep Blue Sea*, McCallister represents evils against God, man, and nature, a role that destines her, given the patriarchal and religious ideology of the film—as well as the viewers' expectations—for destruction.

McCallister's fate seems to be determined in the film. Next to the sharks, she is the largest antagonist in the film, and her fate, which most viewers will see as being directly related to her personal decisions, will seem justified, even though her motives for conducting the research and defying the ethical standards of the industry seem more altruistic than those of Whitlock, her colleague, whose motives are self-aggrandizing. The way McCallister is filmed is not likely to make her sympathetic, either. In most shots, her face is devoid of any emotion except stubborn certainty, sometimes bordering upon pouting. Her end in the film, it must be said, occurs after she has found a likely cure for Alzheimer's, but ultimately, even though she has risked her life and those of others, it has all been for no purpose, as the sum of that data is accidentally destroyed in her attempt to escape from one of the sharks. The message most viewers will receive is that women should not be trusted with power over others, as they will certainly make the wrong decisions.

The ideological messaging can be seen even more readily through the male characters. Not only do they act to judge and condemn McCallister, but they represent closer emissaries of divine intention as well. Their stories also show why traditional patriarchy and faith are superior to any other governance or belief systems. It is important to note that the most educated, successful men die first in this film, falling to the power of corrupted science and being punished, apparently, by an outraged and very present God, thus supporting Steinberg's observations, as the film certainly communicates and elevates "the normative assumptions of Christianity" (2009, p. 138).

The first man to die at the facility is Dr. Jim Whitlock, a "brilliant" scientist who mistakes his role for a divine one. When Franklin first sees the altered sharks, he asks, "What in God's creation?" Whitlock replies, "No, not his. Ours." Such usurpation might be an incidental or unintentional moment of hubris, but, unfortunately for Whitlock, it is not his last. A little later, as the scientists discover that they have reanimated dead brain cells, Franklin once again begins to speak, saying, "I'll be damned…," when Whitlock cuts him off, saying that because of their discovery he will "not be damned." The filmmakers obviously saw this as too great an encroachment on the ability of God—in creating and damning—and so within moments, Whitlock is attacked by one of the sharks. In spite of his arrogance, his attack is portrayed almost heroically. He seems positioned poetically as a victim. He is dressed in grey scrubs, barely darker than the white tile floor that he is lying on, blood spilling from him almost giving him a wing. The positioning of other characters close to him suggests their concern. Significantly, however, rather than as would be the case if he were truly heroic according to the film's ideological positioning, he lies horizontally on the floor, rather than having a crucifixion's verticality, with his remaining arm at his side. Indeed, he could not be splayed upon a crucifix because of his missing arm, and his positioning near a drain suggests that Whitlock, as well as his beliefs, are disposable—are, in fact, garbage—a judgment made more authoritative by the bird's eye-view shot that simulates a divine perspective. His end is prolonged even further after this, as he is literally snatched from the jaws of rescue by the jaws of one of his creations, with a close-up shot revealing to viewers the horrible understanding that he is aware of his hopeless situation. That he is killed by his creations so gruesomely is not coincidental; it is a conservative message about the punishment that can ensue when one believes they know more than God.

Franklin's death also sheds light on the ideological underpinnings of the film. He, we learn, has once before survived a terrible tragedy, an avalanche, and has been mostly nonjudgmental of others, concerned about but not inclined to remove the shark wrangler, for instance, upon learning that he is a parolee. Franklin has much to commend him in the film's tally of ethics. He is determined that his company will be operated in accordance with laws and conventions regarding genetic experimentation. He recognizes that the sharks' behavior is unusual without needing to be told. He reveals that although all seven people survived the avalanche, only five survived to be rescued. He breaks the survivors' oath by revealing the two who died may have been murdered by the others. Almost as soon as he mentions breaking the oath and revealing that he had been complicit in either murder or a cover-up of murder, a shark, perhaps as an instrument of a classical or vengeful god or God, consumes him. Apparently forgiven for whatever role he played in two people's demises, he will not be forgiven for breaking his word. Justice, as construed in the film, is swift and final.

The two male characters who survive also have narratives that help support a conservative Christian ideology. Carter, the wrangler and parolee, takes on the role of the classical hero. He both admires and is hostile toward McCallister. His heroic nature is depicted throughout the film through the action as well the visuals. At the beginning of the film, when he saves four young people from one of the escaped sharks, the shots of that rescue give him a larger-than-life appearance. A low-angle shot depicts him, holding the weapon, as being invulnerable to the danger; he does not seem to be risking his life, as he holds so much control over the situation. In this shot, he is the supreme protector, as is necessary of an ideal patriarch, and is not opposed to using violence or weaponry to protect people from the altered sharks, and other turns of the narrative show Carter's superior athleticism and judgment, and, as such, viewers take from this that he is either closer to nature or God than many of the other characters. Certainly, the narrative and the visuals privilege him, the less-educated former criminal and righteous-in-his judgments white man over most of the other characters—and much like a television evangelist, meekness does not seem to be requisite for his heroism.

The other male survivor best demonstrates the immediacy and validity of seeing *Deep Blue Sea* as a fictionalized narrative promoting Christian theology; what viewers of the film may miss in their emotional responses to Preach's plotline is that every time he is faced with moral temptation, if he resists it, he is then rewarded by the film, and most often these moments of temptation are linked with exposure to the dangerous man-eating sharks. Preach (played by LL Cool J) is black and has the job of sustaining people's bodies: he is the facility's chef. He is called Preach by the others because he apparently was a preacher whose addiction to alcohol cost him his living and his family. He now ministers to people's bodies and souls at the facility, with only a bird named Bird as a companion most of the time. Significantly, he is on one of the lowest levels of the facility as befits his fallen status in life, and his fight for survival will be a quest to conquer temptation more than it is a test of his ability to evade the large finned predators.

As Preach climbs from the symbolic depths of hell, visually represented throughout the film, he will continue to reaffirm his faith. At the first impact of the shark-directed human missile, the facility is rocked and partially destroyed. Preach's first impulse is to turn to a bottle of wine, which has fallen from a shelf into his vicinity, and he begins his escape with bottle in hand. He finds himself in a seemingly endless corridor from which he does not escape until he throws the bottle down. Once he proceeds without the alcohol, he finds the stairs to begin his ascent but soon discovers that they are impassable, a high-angle shot emphasizing the difficulty of his task as well as his vulnerability. His second temptation occurs when the flood delivers a *Playboy* magazine to him. Almost as soon as he picks it up, a shark appears behind him, as a shadow closing in on him. Dropping the magazine, he is able to escape into his flooded kitchen. As he is attempting to rescue Bird, Bird flies up and is devoured by the shark; this certainly has some symbolic meaning, as birds often represent souls. Bird seems to have sacrificed himself for Preach, reinforcing the evangelical Christian belief that God created the animals for humans. Still being pursued by the shark, Preach then takes cover in his own oven, his only weapon a small emergency hatchet. Hiding in the oven, despairing over the loss of Bird, he is nearly cooked to death by the shark—an inappropriate reversal of the God-ordained natural order—but he is determined not to lose faith and takes strength from the Bible, saying, "I'm not Daniel when he faced the lion—so I appreciate the irony, Lord—cooked in his own oven—I've got other plans." Like David against Goliath, Preach uses his hatchet to break his way through his oven, freeing himself, then felling the shark with a lighter and the gas escaping from the oven. With faith as his guide, he then continues his escape.

Throughout his ordeal, he pauses in prayer, often grasping the crucifix hanging on the chain over his chest. Indeed, the cross appears so often in the film that one would have to be asleep to miss it. The power of the image of Preach's cross is contrasted well with another image in the film, the key that hangs around McCallister's neck, which locks the storage area where she keeps her research, and the message that perceptive viewers will glean is that Preach's token carries great power, while McCallister's faith in science over God is misplaced. Less astute viewers might miss these Christonormative messages altogether, merely absorbing them as natural and true amid their emotional fear responses.

The film then uses Preach to more overtly preach its religious messages. He is joined by the others, but he is clearly considered morally superior to them. This superiority is conveyed visually as he meets up with the rest of the survivors, who are still lower in the facility than he is. One of the survivors begins to despair, calling out "Give us a god-damn break!" Preach is there to advise that "He [meaning God] always answers—sometimes the answer you get isn't the answer you want." In this set of shots, the despairing survivor is captured in the red-golden light of some of the facility's fires, paralleling his location and experience, symbolically, to that of hell. Although very near in distance to the other survivor, Preach is nonetheless bathed in cool blue light, giving a very different interpretation about the states of their souls, as well as foreshadowing their different fates. Significantly, in these shots, Preach is positioned to the right, paralleling his position with his political alignment, while the survivor who took the Lord's name in vain is positioned to the left in the frame of his shot. During the rest of the journey to the surface, Preach observes traditional religious rituals, making his confession to a video camera, which allows him to seemingly directly address the viewers (as if we are the God to whom he confesses), convincing us of his sincerity, faith, sorrow, and true repentance. Given our mirror neurons, we feel as he does, and we believe that he has transformed into the one who can provide spiritual strength to his companions. He advises McCallister that the shark is evil, saying, as Belmont records, "It's the devil, you know" (p. 366) and that it is not worth risking her life to go back for the data, that too many have died already in the pursuit of this science. In one instance, he and Carter even embrace his crucifix together. Significantly, they are the only two to survive, and they vanquish the last shark together. Preach's faith becomes his weapon, quite literally, as Belmont notes that, as in other disaster films, this one, too "associate[s] natural disaster with evil/Satan, as in *Deep Blue Sea*, where the religious cook stabs a shark in the eye with his crucifix" (2007, p. 366). The holy weapon is enough to temporarily confound the shark, and Preach seems almost to rise from the dead, as he is released from the certain death that the shark's jaws promise. One of the film's last images is of Carter and Preach, lying together on what remains of the facility, awaiting rescue, conveying the message of male Christian superiority, the power of God over science, and the infallibility of Christian faith.

Although many might believe *Deep Blue Sea* to be a progressive text upon first seeing it, it clearly reinforces conservative values regarding patriarchal and Christian superiority. Although it depicts educated, professional women who have attained success in their careers and showcases two powerful African American male leads, one of whom is depicted as the CEO of a major corporation, the images and plot points undermine the notion of equality. The brotherhood conveyed in the film's last images is a powerful one. The emotions evoked by the film prior to its release were purportedly so powerful, in fact, that it has been reported that focus groups' reactions led to the film's ending being rewritten. TV Tropes reports that "test audiences so despised the female scientist heroine (to the point of loudly screaming "Die, bitch!" throughout the film), as well as the killing of LL Cool J's character, that the final ending was changed (Focus Group Ending, n.d.). If the report of these screening audiences' reaction is correct, then it is powerful evidence of Goleman's mirror neurons working to create an emotional response in the film, one that blames McAllister's character completely for the horror in spite of her good intentions and empathizes with Preach. The ending released in theaters and on DVD becomes a testament to the incredible strength of emotions over thought as well as to the strength of Christian ideology and patriarchy over the ideas of scientific discovery and sexual equality.

Deep Blue Sea demonstrates that media are not neutral, that they convey the political, religious, and social messages of their creators, that they all have an agenda. As Richard Rorty acknowledges, the power of media is vast and "the novel, the movie, and the TV program have, gradually but steadily, replaced the sermon and the treatise as the principal vehicles of moral change and progress" (1989, p. xvi). In its narrative, *Deep Blue Sea* certainly acts as a sermon, demonstrating that, as Goleman suggests, media might convey a sense of morality and justice that does not stand up to scrutiny of analysis, especially if time permitted one to think about the images or implications presented, as may be the case with McAllister in *Deep Blue Sea*. The difficulty lies in one's ability to immediately understand that one feels emotions as responses to situations but that one can control recognize, identify, and control those responses. Although people are susceptible to biases, they can work to identify and eradicate them. *Deep Blue Sea* provides evidence that sometimes entertaining films, like oceans, that seem superficially shallow, might have monstrous and dangerous hidden depths once they are explored.

References

Belmont, C. (2007). Ecofeminism and the natural disaster heroine. *Women's Studies,* 36, 349–372.

Box Office Mojo. (n.d.) Deep Blue Sea. *Box Office Mojo*. Available at http://boxofficemojo.com/movies/?id=deepbluesea.htm

Focus Group Ending. (n.d.). *TV Tropes*. Available at http://tvtropes.org/pmwiki/pmwiki.php/Main/FocusGroupEnding

Goleman, D. (2006). *Social intelligence: The new science of human relationships*. New York: Bantam Books.

Harlin, R. (Director). (1999). *Deep blue sea* [Motion picture]. U.S.: Warner Home Video.

Kashani, T. (2009). *Deconstructing the mystique: An interdisciplinary introduction to cinema.* Dubuque, IA: Kendall/Hunt.

Rorty, Richard. (1989). *Contingency, irony, and solidarity*. New York: Cambridge University Press.

Steinberg, S. R. (2010). Hollywood's missionary agenda: Christonormativity and audience baptism. In Frymer, B., Kashani, T., Nocella III, A. J., Van Heertum, R. (Eds.), *Hollywood's exploited: Public pedagogy, Corporate movies, and cultural crisis*. New York: Palgrave Macmillan.

Steinberg, S. R., & Kincheloe, J. L. (Eds.). (2009). *Christotainment: Selling Jesus through popular culture*. Boulder, CO: Westview Press.

11 Why *Harold and Kumar Go to White Castle*: The Representation of Otherness in Mainstream Teen Cinema

Ajay Gehlawat

WHEN I FIRST mentioned this topic to a friend, he replied: "Sounds interesting. But under no circumstances note that the name 'White Castle' is telling." Indeed, even as *New York Times* critic A.O. Scott noted in his review of *Harold and Kumar Go to White Castle* (2004), "in the future, a term paper will no doubt be written about the racial connotations of the name White Castle, about the way in which its elusiveness represents the mirage of assimilationist aspirations" (p. 2), by the time the film was released on DVD, such perspectives were already in evidence. In a Canadian review of recent "multi-ethnic" teen flicks, for instance, the White Castle restaurant in *Harold and Kumar* is described as "a potent metaphor," in which "'brown' and 'yellow' faces seeking this grail are now admitted, but American national mythology…is never challenged" (Janzen, 2007).

Without necessarily accepting this reading's conclusion, nor settling for Scott's conclusion regarding the title pair's ultimate motivation ("Dude, they're hungry"), and keeping my friend's warning in mind, I would like to suggest that the name "White Castle" operates as a cliché on multiple levels. In this "alternative," or "multi-ethnic" variation on both the Hollywood teen flick and stoner comedy genres, the "white," "assimilationist" goal is itself being parodied and reformulated (as generic storyline). *Harold and Kumar* is not the first film to play with such genre rules. Spike Lee's *Bamboozled* (2000) is another, earlier instance of such pastiche and parody being used to reformulate racial representations in 21st-century America.

Nevertheless, *Harold and Kumar* is unique in several ways. While the casting of older actors in the roles of teenagers—John Cho (Harold) was in his early 30s at the time of filming and Kal Penn (Kumar) in his late 20s—is a typical Hollywood strategy (think here of *The Breakfast Club* whose five central teenage characters' average age was 21), the casting of two Asian Americans as the central characters was not. The role of Asian American adolescents in Hollywood cinema has come a long way from the time of "Long Duk Dong" (Gedde Watanabe), the stereotypical Asian exchange student in *Sixteen Candles* (Hughes, 1984), whose arrival was always preceded by the sound of a gong. Now, with Harold and Kumar—and indeed its sequel, *Harold and Kumar Escape From Guantanamo Bay* (Hurwitz & Schlossberg, 2008)—one witnesses Asian Americans' assimilation into mainstream American culture (as represented by Hollywood). Yet the depiction of Asian American adolescents as fully immersed in mainstream American culture (and cinema) does not come without its problems (note the title of the sequel). On this note, my paper will focus on the use and, more specifically, the redeployment of cultural clichés in the original *Harold and Kumar*, by way of addressing the larger issue of how Asian American youth are currently incorporated by mainstream American cinema; in other words, why Harold and Kumar go to White Castle.

Much of the critical response to *Harold and Kumar* was surprisingly positive. The previously noted Canadian review described the film as engaging in "humour that exposes rather than propagates racial clichés and stereotypes" (Janzen, 2007). Grace Kao, director of Asian American studies at the University of Pennsylvania, described this "stoner comedy" in an interview with the *Chronicle of Higher Education*, as "a groundbreaking film" (quoted in Millman, 2007). In his *New York Times* review, Scott (2004) argued that the title duo "pretty much revolutionize the slacker-stoner-comedy genre," while the *New Yorker* review (Agger, 2004) warns not to "expect a revolution" and refers to the previous effort of the film's director as "the Brechtian drama *Dude, Where's My Car?*" Similarly, Stephen Holden, also writing in the *New York Times*, notes that the film "has one foot here and one foot there," the "here" being "a politically savvy universe where the title characters…puncture ethnic stereotypes," but the "there" being "the muck of perpetual puerility according to Hollywood." Though Holden's misidentification of Harold as "Chinese American" may be neither here nor there (he is in fact Korean American, both in the film and in real life), the critic ultimately finds the film's "balance between here and there still tilts overwhelmingly toward there."

Thus, while *Harold and Kumar* was generally applauded as "a multilayered goof on ethnic stereotypes" (Relic, 2005) or, indeed a film that "manhandl[es]…political correctness" (Agger, 2004), it is not "a radical movie" (Janzen, 2007). One should not "expect a revolution," as—the implication goes—this is hardly a "Brechtian" drama. But I would like to consider this film precisely as a drama in such a vein, engaging in such Brechtian strategies as interruption, astonishment, and what Brecht called "the gestic principle" (1965, p. 86). Furthermore, as with Brecht's epic theatre, the implied audience for such a film is, as Walter Benjamin notes, "a relaxed one" (1973, p.15). Indeed, one might speculate whether the implied audience of "the stoner comedy," *Harold and Kumar*, adopts the attitude Brecht most advocated, namely, that "of smoking-and-watching" (1965, p. 44).

To better understand how a Brechtian interpretation of *Harold and Kumar* can help us appreciate more fully its "multi-layered goof" and "manhandling" of ethnic stereotypes and political correctness (as well as its reformulations of multiple genre codes and conventions), let us first examine Brecht's dramaturgical theories in more detail.

In 1931, Brecht set out to describe how attempts to "renovate" the existing opera left the essential "culinary character" of that opera unchanged (Brecht, 1965, p. 33). Yet "new appetites" had to be reckoned with and a shift from a dramatic to an epic theatre became necessary. This new form would deviate from the Aristotelian nature of dramatic theatre, with its conceptions of mimesis, or imitation; identification (with one or more characters); and catharsis, or a dramatic purging of one's self through the unfolding drama. An epic theatre, along with eschewing these Aristotelian concepts, also deviated from an Aristotelian plot structure of beginning, middle, and end, inserting "astonishment…into the Aristotelian formula" in the place of empathy (Benjamin, 1973, p. 13).

This substitution was part and parcel with Brecht's larger aim of consistently interrupting the narrative by making events strange through a process of defamiliarizing their conditions (Benjamin, 1973, p. 18). The introduction of "a certain unreality, irrationality and lack of seriousness…at the right moment" would strike the audience "with a double meaning," simultaneously pleasurable and instructive, even if it "may not taste particularly agreeable" (Brecht, 1965, pp. 36–37). Thus this new style of drama "whose course need not be a straight one but may quite well be in curves or even in leaps," provides a new type of pleasure to a new type of audience—those "smoking and watching," whom "it is hopeless to try to 'carry away'" with a "few miserable scraps of imitation" (Brecht, 1965, pp. 45, 44).

Consider, then, the case of *Harold and Kumar*. The film, ostensibly about the title pair's quest for White Castle burgers, consistently detours and runs off course. After getting high and catching a White Castle commercial on their television, the duo decides to head for the nearest White Castle restaurant. Leaving their Hoboken apartment in Harold's car, the duo heads to New Brunswick, where Kumar claims there is a White Castle restaurant "right next to that multiplex." Upon hitting the road, the duo is immediately sidetracked, taking a wrong turn into Newark. They finally get to New Brunswick, only to discover that the White Castle has been replaced by a "Burger Shack." After the Burger Shack employee at the drive-thru window tells them there is a 24-hour White Castle restaurant in Cherry Hill, they return to the road.

At this point in the narrative, Kumar sees a sign for Princeton on the side of the highway:

> Kumar (hereafter "K"): Dude, we're getting off here.
>
> Harold (hereafter "H"): Why?
>
> K: Because we're gonna sweet talk Cindy Kim into finding us some weed.
>
> H: No!
>
> K: Why not? You talk to her on the phone all the time.
>
> H: She calls me! Then she rambles on about her East Asian students' club or whatever. Then I have to actually pretend I give a shit or she calls me Twinkie. No.
>
> K: A what?
>
> H: Twinkie. Yellow on the outside, white on the inside.
>
> K (laughing): Look, you Twinkie bitch, you were the one who threw our weed out the window, okay, so we're going to Princeton and it's your responsibility to make sure we're high as shit by the time we're eating those burgers.
>
> H: Forget it! End of discussion. I am not seeing Cindy Kim.

The camera then cuts to a close-up of an Asian girl's bespectacled face, as she says, "Harold, I'm so glad you showed up!" While Kumar roams the corridors of Princeton, trying to score some weed, Harold finds himself stuck at a meeting of Cindy Kim's aforementioned East Asian Club. The students, all ostensibly "East Asian," are neatly dressed and sit primly at attention in a small semi-circle around Harold. One of the particularly geeky Asian students, who identifies himself as "Kenneth Park, Class of 2004," with a giggle, raises his hand expectantly and waits for Harold to call on him before posing a question ("What's it like being a financial analyst?"). After a few more (career-related) questions, Cindy Kim interrupts, telling Harold, "We should be getting to the party. We can discuss all this stuff on the way there. It's just down the hall."

En route to the party, Harold and Cindy are stopped by Kumar who, in the meantime, having scored some weed and having met a pair of British Doublemint twins, gestures emphatically with his hands and body, scrunching up his face in a series of lascivious looks.

> K: Roldie, Roldie! You gotta come quick! They're these two filthy pussies just *aching* to get boned by us! [glances nervously from Harold to Cindy Kim, who folds her arms across her chest and assumes an air of disapproval.] I mean, there are these two very lovely pussies who would like to have a chat with you and I.
>
> Cindy Kim: Sorry! Harold's coming with us.
>
> K: No no, that's bullshit. He's coming with me, isn't that right, Roldie?
>
> H (weakly): Let's go to the party…
>
> K: No no no, fuck that [grabs a random student passing by, who turns out to be an Asian guy without the slightest resemblance to Harold.] Here [pointing to Asian guy], this is Harold's understudy, okay? He can do whatever you want. Roldie, let's go!

He grabs his friend by the sleeve and they run away. Later, smoking a joint in a deserted stairwell, Kumar says, "I can't believe you were gonna ditch me for the Joy Luck Club, dude. You know what their party's like?" Harold asks Kumar what he should have said. "Just say no!" Kumar replies, taking a hit and passing the joint to Harold. Suddenly a security guard passes by and, smelling something funny, calls out, "Hey, what's going on up there?" Once more the two are on the move, having yet again been interrupted (on their detour).

A musical montage of Harold and Kumar running from the security guards ensues, with the duo rushing into the girls' bathroom to hide in a toilet stall. When the British Doublemint twins unexpectedly arrive, however, and proceed to engage in a game of "Battleshits" from the stalls on either side of our duo, Harold and Kumar are forced to stagger out, with Kumar dropping his newly acquired weed in the toilet in the process. Upon emerging from the bathroom, Harold and Kumar are suddenly faced with the East Asian Club party scene. With numerous disco and colored lights flashing, and scores of young attractive women dancing to loud, hip-hop beats, Kenneth Park stands, now bare-chested and with spiked hair, on a stage in the middle of the party, holding a big plastic bag and shouting, "Who wants some Boodha?" Harold and Kumar stand astonished:

> H: Holy shit! Kenneth Park, Class of 2004!
>
> K: Dude, I'm thinking you really screwed up big by not coming to this party.
>
> H: *I* screwed up?

Just as two (ostensibly Asian) girls who want some pot brownies are flashing their breasts for Kenneth Park (and everyone else, including Harold and Kumar), the duo are again interrupted by the security guard. As they run away, the security guard gives chase and, passing the party scene and stopping to look at it, replete with Kenneth Park bare-chested and the two Asian girls holding up their tops, exposing their breasts, we witness yet again the moment of astonishment via the Princeton security guard. Hesitating, the guard again gives chase to Harold and Kumar, who escape once more from another detour.

Through the preceding sequence of events, we see how *Harold and Kumar*'s "curved" trajectory, introducing "unreality, irrationality and lack of seriousness" at certain moments, via interruptions, tableaux, and, in particular, Kumar's stepping out of character, creates a new form of drama, one less imitative (of some so-called reality) than gestural. In the process, what also becomes apparent is how the film engages in clichés— for instance, of college students of East Asian origin—only to deflate these stereotypes. Harold and Kumar, our pair of ostensibly hyphenated Asian-Americans, are repulsed by their (stereotypically portrayed) peers, only to be "dumbfounded" (perhaps along with viewers) upon being confronted with the Asian party tableau.

In these scenes or, for instance, when Kumar suddenly pulls out Harold's "understudy," the diegesis (world of the film story) as such is bracketed, held up to the viewer as precisely the artifice it is: not even someone stoned would confuse this with reality. Even if the first time the two Asian girls flash their breasts can be described as "titillating," that is, treating these women as sex objects (a strategy rather typical of the Hollywood teen flick with its generally testosterone-driven plot), the film immediately works to enacts a subversion of this sexist tableau. The second time the tableau is presented—from the security guard's perspective—the scene appears particularly strange, catching the moment just *after* they have flashed their breasts (rather than just before). Now, suddenly, the bare-chested Kenneth Park and the two Asian girls still standing with their tops up, seem displaced, and react accordingly, now blankly staring toward the security guard and lowering their tops, while one of the girls slaps Kenneth Park's outstretched hand, saying, "Hey!"

A similar form of "erotic sabotage" is enacted in the bathroom with the British Doublemint twins (Stam, 1985). Upon entering the bathroom (where Harold and Kumar are already hiding), the first "twin" says to the other, "Your breasts look beautiful." As they approach and face the mirror, the second girl replies, with British intonation intact, "I just want those cute little ping-pong breasts, that kinda go…bloop!" as she pulls down her shirt to reveal her cleavage in the mirror. At this point the scene, seen from Harold and Kumar's point of view, peeking over the toilet stall, is decidedly voyeuristic, an instance of what Laura Mulvey (1975) has described as the "male gaze" of the camera. The scene continues in its titillating direction, as Twin 1 says to Twin 2 (still admiring her breasts in the mirror), "Well, hurry up. I really want to go smoke weed with that dishy Indian guy." At this, Kumar's head pops up immediately above the toilet stall. Yet when Twin 2 replies, "It's gonna be a few minutes. I'm about to have the worst case of taco shits," the mood suddenly changes, even as Harold and Kumar, peering over their toilet stall, look at each other frowning. What had been set up as a scene to "deliver the goods," namely, to present a voyeuristic glimpse of women from the male point of view, turns out to be a stink bomb in disguise, as the women previously cast as objects of male desire engage in a flatulence contest (a.k.a. "Battleshits"), forcing the peeping toms out from their hiding place, simultaneously denying them and viewers the goods they may have been expecting or, indeed, led to believe they were getting.

In these ways, while the women in these scenes are decidedly being used as "sex objects," and Harold and Kumar (and particularly the latter) display a decidedly narrow-minded view of women, the underlying intention here is a Brechtian one, that is, a display of attitudes that is simultaneously presentation and interruption—a tableau of sexuality that perpetually leaves a strange aftertaste. Just as Harold and Kumar become unwitting tools in a larger operation to dismantle their desires, *Harold and Kumar* serves as the perpetually moving stage upon which "the contradictions of our society are acted out"

(Benjamin, 1973, p. 8). We are not, to paraphrase Brecht, meant to like what we see. Yet paradoxically, it is by frustrating pleasure or, indeed, by being displeasing, that *Harold and Kumar* affords pleasure. Much in the way of Buñuel's films, for instance, *That Obscure Object of Desire* (1977), in which the male protagonist is perpetually frustrated in his desires to sexually possess a woman, *Harold and Kumar*'s approach can be described as "bait-and-switch," promising the viewer one thing and delivering quite another.

The view this film presents of Asian American youth, via its title duo, in their crude sexual and scatological humor, casual drug use, and general disregard for what their parents (or the law) tell them, decidedly goes against the so-called normative view of this group in American culture, at least as depicted by Hollywood. Comparing *Harold and Kumar* to, for instance, the film Kumar initially invokes in describing the East Asians, *The Joy Luck Club* (Wang, 1993), these deviations become immediately clear. Though Kumar, too, humbly listens to his father's criticism of his wayward ways, it just as quickly goes out the other ear, in other words, his obeisance to his elder is purely a jest. Kumar deliberately sabotages his own medical school interview earlier in the film, which was the cause of his father's subsequent wrath. In the middle of the interview, Kumar picks up his cell phone and described to Harold in graphic terms his plans for their evening ("You need to chill the fuck out and prepare to get blazed"). Following the call, Kumar continues nonchalantly where he left off in answering the dean's question. The dean angrily cuts him off, stating, "You actually believe, after the way you've just behaved, that I would ever even *consider* recommending you for admission?" Kumar replies, "No. I'm gonna be honest with you. The only reason I'm even applying is so my dad'll keep paying for my apartment. I really don't have the desire to go to med school." The dean is incredulous: "But you have perfect MCAT scores!" Kumar gives him a puzzled look and says, "Just 'cause you're hung like a moose doesn't mean you gotta do porn!"

To paraphrase, Harold and Kumar demonstrate that just because they are Asian does not mean they have to adhere to the clichés of Asian Americans rampant in Hollywood teen flicks and, arguably, in American culture. It is precisely for this reason— for these deviations from the norm, both regarding Asian American clichés and the alternative, politically correct representations of this hyphenated experience (for instance, that of *The Joy Luck Club*)—that *Harold and Kumar* is not "a movie you can go see with your South Asian family" (Ahmad, 2004). Furthermore, *Harold and Kumar* not only challenges viewers' expectations regarding Asian American representations (in a Hollywood teen flick) but also the assumptions of the two title characters, no-nowhere more on display than in their open-mouthed reaction to the East Asian Club tableau.

Furthermore, in *consistently* straying off course, the film makes clear what may have been suspected from the get-go, namely, that the journey is more important than the destination. This series of structural deviations that, in many ways, becomes more of a narrative of interruptions than anything remotely resembling an Aristotelian plot, is crucial to note in light of the interpretation of the duo's quest as one for access to American cultural assimilation (in which the White Castle takes on metaphoric resonance). Here, along with a constant implosion of metaphors (e.g., those of "Asianness"), what we see is a shift from metaphor to metonymy, in which, for instance, the "green" hope of Gatsby's era has become the green of marijuana and, in which, similarly, the "White Castle" that our two Asian American leads seek is an actual White Castle restaurant in New Jersey.

The metonymic nature of the duo's journey across a hyper-real American landscape is also reflected in the DVD's chapter titles: "Home," "New Brunswick," "Princeton," "Rest Stop," "Detour," etc. In this sense, the "White Castle" of the film's title, to paraphrase Baudrillard (1983), becomes a perfect model of all of the film's "entangled orders of simulation" (p. 23). Just as Disneyland is comprised of various imaginary worlds, the New Jersey of *Harold and Kumar* is a simulation rather than a representation of American reality, in which "all its values are exalted…in miniature and comic strip form" (Baudrillard, 1983, p. 24). The title characters even come across a computer-generated cheetah that they subsequently get stoned and attempt to ride to their ostensible destination. (It takes them the wrong way, naturally, and they fall off.) Baudrillard defines the hyper-real as "the generation by models of a real without origin or reality" (p. 2). It is precisely in such a hyper-real context that White Castle becomes significant, as it functions in the capacity of what Baudrillard labels "a third-order simulation," working to conceal the fact that it is all of America itself, particularly as represented by Hollywood, which has become a 24-hour fast-food chain.

Yet given the story's consistent departures and deviations from its ostensible course, as well as the metonymic (as opposed to metaphoric) nature of these deviations, the White Castle ultimately becomes a strawman red herring, that is, an intentionally tenuous representation intended to deflect attention away from the hyper-real nature of this landscape, becoming overwhelmed by that which it is was attempting to conceal (that all of America is a White Castle restaurant). Another way of putting it: The film is aimless. Yet rather than dismissing this lack of telos as just another example of its trivial nature as a drama, this aimlessness should be seen as part and parcel with the film's larger aim, namely, to consistently decimate the reality principle it so tenuously maintains (both of the American cultural landscape and the Hollywood teen flick) and to revel in this decimation.

To engage in a cognitive mapping of the "ethnoscapes" of this hyper-real journey is to address the problem of identity(-formation) in a "deterritorialized context" (Appadurai, 1996, p. 37). Just as the film "substitute[es] signs of the real for the real itself" (Baudrillard, 1983, p. 2), it promotes racial and cultural clichés in the place of any actual identity politics. Or, another way of putting it could be: given the film's substitution of "the real" with hyper-real clichés, what type of cultural identity emerges or becomes possible?

What appears to be on display, paradoxically, in one of the first instances of two Asian American leads in a Hollywood film, is the joyful negation of the very notions of identity and ethnicity (Minh-Ha, 1991, p. 187). Eschewing any sense of a "double consciousness" (Du Bois, 1903/1996), it can be argued that while Harold and (particularly) Kumar are hyper-conscious of their cultural context (despite or due to being frequently high), they are entirely devoid of any sense of a racial consciousness. Indeed, as A.O. Scott notes in his review (2004), even when the duo is confronted with occasional racial taunts from caricaturized bigots on their journey, "Harold and Kumar tend to react by rolling their eyes" (p. 2).

It is precisely in this way that *Harold and Kumar* enacts a pastiche of identity in the place of any real sense of identity politics. Yet rather than this pastiche becoming "parody that has lost its sense of humor" (Jameson, 1988, p. 16), the pastiche of *Harold and Kumar* retains its distinctive sense and uses it to perform a hyper-mimicry of tropes associated with the process of assimilation. It might be useful at this juncture to employ Dean MacCannell's (1976) terminology recounting the tourist experience. MacCannell describes this experience as one engaging in "sight→marker→sight transformations" (p. 121). In this process, tourists replace recognition of a sight—London, for instance—with recognition of a symbolic marker, e.g., Big Ben. Thus in these instances sightseers do not in any empirical sense see the sight but rather its symbolic markers (MacCannell, 1976). In the case of *Harold and Kumar*, then, the White Castle marker serves as a semiotic substitution for the sight of consumption. To claim, however, that Harold and Kumar's hyper-real quest for White Castle burgers becomes a straightforward "endorsement" of consumerism becomes problematic. If one were to call *Harold and Kumar* an extended promotional advertisement for the White Castle chain, then one might argue that the advertisement is supplanted by its own representational strategies.

The hyper-real terrain of cultural identity is vividly captured in the film's presentation of "fantasyscapes" that fail to correspond to any social reality; rather, they seem to suggest a deconstruction of essentialized notions of "Otherness." Indeed, one might say that *Harold and Kumar* presents a "commercial postmodernism" that works to move beyond "oppressive binary categories" (Kaplan, 1988, p. 4). Yet just as the film's "promotional advertisement" for White Castle is overtaken by the hyper-real nature of this "film/ad," all of its characters' identities(cultural, racial) are also subsumed by the film's blatantly "commercial" aesthetic. More than gaining access to American mainstream culture through their hyphenated identities, Harold and Kumar are Americans because of their consumerist tendencies. Their hyphenation remains (they are forced to roll their eyes quite frequently), yet neither this status nor their consumerism completely supplants the other; the two, rather, are inextricably linked, thus making moot any reading in which the duo is depicted as attempting to gain access to this "grail" of America.

Harold and Kumar go to White Castle because the advertisement they saw on their television was for White Castle. Had it been one for Taco Bell, they might very well have starred in *Harold and Kumar Go to Taco Bell* ("It can happen this way, but it can also happen quite a different way"). But just as it would be erroneous to read too deeply, in such a case, into this hyphenated pair's "run for the border," their actual destination is chosen not to attain something they do not have access to (assimilation), but, in fact, precisely because of something they have both already had and are all too familiar with: American fast food. While one could argue that the implication here seems to be that Asian American actors can only become part of the mainstream by relinquishing their essential Otherness, one could point out that the film also liberates the on-screen representation of Asian Americans from the all-too-familiar, Aristotelian structure of the typical Asian American storyline (in Hollywood) and, furthermore, that it does so by paradoxically setting itself up as ostensibly being (on the metaphoric level) such a film.

To say, then, that the film engages in "false advertising" might be accurate only if one came to it expecting it to conform to said stereotypes or stereotypical plot structure. (We can surmise the radical effect *Harold and Kumar* would have on someone expecting a *Joy Luck Club* narrative.) We don't even need to go back so far as the 1990s to look for instances of the still-dominant alternatives: indeed, even as Harold and Kumar (that is, John Cho and Kal Penn) starred in *Harold and Kumar*, they also played more stereotypical roles, reminiscent of *Sixteen Candles*' Long Duk Dong, at the same time: Harold in the *American Pie* series (1999–2003) and Kumar in the *Van Wilder* films (2002–2006). It is precisely in relation to such a context that we can appreciate the radical innovations of *Harold and Kumar*: not only are both leads of this Hollywood teen flick Asian American, but as the lead actors noted in an open letter to the Asian American community at the time of the film's release:

> We don't have stereotypical accents, we don't passively tread through the story, we're not asexual or hypersexual, there are no martial arts scenes, one-dimensional cab scenes. We play a couple of all-American guys who happen to be of Indian and Korean descent.
>
> (Quoted in Ahmad, 2004).

To return to this paper's title question, one might reply by saying that the reason *Harold and Kumar Go to White Castle* is the same reason *Harold and Kumar Escape from Guantanamo Bay*; namely, because it is in their self-interest to do so. At the same time, given their ostensible racial identities (in the words of their FBI nemesis in the sequel, "North Korea and Al Qaeda") and the current American political climate (i.e., the reason they go to Guantanamo Bay), one might argue that such a "blithe" approach to ethnic difference becomes doubly powerful in that it provides a way to reveal the conditions and contradictions underpinning this cultural landscape to those "who do not think unless they have a reason to" (Benjamin, 1973, p. 4).

References

Agger, M. (2004, August 9). Review of *Harold and Kumar Go to White Castle*. *The New Yorker*. Available at http://www.newyorker.com/arts/reviews/film/harold_and_kumar_go_to_white_castle_leiner

Ahmad, N. (2004, September 1). Kal Penn goes to Hollywood. *Nirali Magazine*. Available at http://niralimagazine.com/2004/09/kal-penn-goes-to-hollywood/

Appadurai, A. (1996). *Modernity at large: Cultural dimensions of globalization.* Minneapolis, MN: University of Minnesota Press.

Baudrillard, J. (1983). *Simulations* (Paul Foss, Paul Patton, & Philip Beitchman, trans.). New York: Semiotext(e).

Benjamin, W. (1973). *Understanding Brecht.* (Anna Bostock, trans.). Bristol, U.K.: Western Printing Services Ltd.

Brecht, B. (1965). *Brecht on theatre.* (John Willett, trans.). London, U.K.: Methuen & Co. Ltd.

Buñuel, L. (Director). (1977)._*That Obscure Object of Desire* [Motion Picture]. France: Les Films Galaxie, Greenwich Film Productions, In-Cine Compania Industrial Cinematografica.

Du Bois, W. E. B. (1903/1996). *The souls of black folk.* New York: Penguin.

Holden, S. (2004, July 30). In search of a burger, demolishing stereotypes. *New York Times.* Available at http://www.nytimes.com/2004/07/30/movies/film-review-in-search-of-a-burger-demolishing-stereotypes.html

Hughes, J. (Director). (1984). *Sixteen Candles* [Motion Picture]. U.S.: Universal Studios.

Hurwitz, J., & Schlossberg, H. (Directors). (2008). *Harold and Kumar Escape From Guantanamo Bay.* U.S.: Kingsgate.

Jameson, F. (1988). Postmodernism and consumer society. In E. Ann Kaplan (Ed.), *Postmodernism and its discontents.* New York: Verso.

Janzen, E. (2007, January/February). Anti-racism Hollywood style. *Canadian Dimension, 41*, 60.

Kaplan, E. A. (1988). Introduction. In E. A. Kaplan (Ed.), *Postmodernism and its discontents.* New York: Verso.

Lee, S. (Director), (2000). *Bamboozled* [Motion Picture]. U.S.: New Line.

Leiner, D. (Director). (2004). *Harold and Kumar Go to White Castle* [Motion Picture]. U.S.: New Line.

MacCannell, D. (1976). *The tourist: A new theory of the leisure class.* New York: Schocken.

Millman, S. (2007, May 18). Penn to Penn. *Chronicle of Higher Education,* A7.

Minh-Ha, T. T. (1991). *When the moon waxes red: Representation, gender, and cultural politics.* New York: Routledge.

Mulvey, L. (1975). Visual pleasure and narrative cinema. *Screen, 16*(3), 6–18.

Relic, P. (2005, January 27). Review of *Harold and Kumar Go to White Castle. Rolling Stone.* 66.

Scott, A. O. (2004, July 25). *Harold and Kumar*: A dumb stoner comedy for a new American century. *New York Times.* Available at http://www.nytimes.com/2004/07/25/movies/hightimes.html

Stam, R. (1985). *Reflexivity in film and literature: From* Don Quixote *to Jean-Luc Godard.* Ann Arbor, MI: UMI Research Press.

Wang, W. (1993). *The Joy Luck Club* [Motion Picture]. U.S.: Buena Vista.

12 No-Win *Avatar*: Culture Clash in Pocahontas Revisited

M.A. Jaimes-Guerrero

THE MOVIE MECCA we call Hollywood has a reputation for its relativity in ethics that are reflected in its cinematic productions. In my view, *Avatar*, in which the dynamics of culture clash, race and class, ethnicity and identity, nation and religion, history and culture are central, is but a case in point of a "Hollywood-styled" movie that both relies on and feeds into American pop culture. This hyped-up "blockbuster" movie demonstrates the importance of investigating what the cultural critic bell hooks refers to as the "politics of race representation" in the context of her theory of "cultural criticism" in her seminal anthology, *Black Looks* (1992). In *Black Looks*, hooks explains that,

> Merging critical thinking in everyday life with knowledge learned in books and through study has been the union of theory and practice that has informed my intellectual cultural work. Passionately concerned with education for critical consciousness, I continually search for ways to think, teach, and write that excite and liberate the mind, that passion to live and act in a way that challenges systems of domination: racism, sexism, class elitism. (1992, p. 3)

Following hooks's logic, it pays dividends to examine politics of the medium (i.e., cinema). Media critic Tony Kashani corroborates the importance of studying the politics of film in *Deconstructing the Mystique* (2009):

> Film is a powerful medium of communication and influences us in many different ways. By way of deconstruction and Socratic questioning of a narrative in a typical Hollywood film, one can discover layers of mystification, indoctrination, and propaganda superficially that can be construed as pure entertainment. Deconstruction does not imply that meaning is relative. The last thing deconstruction wants to do is to undermine rationality. There is a lot more to a film than its song-and-dance number or the car chase scene. What is behind these images? The implicit is what deconstruction is after. One must always search for the implicit (i.e., "a lot more") to empower oneself. We must always have the bigger picture in mind….(p. 2)

Kashani then cites Jacques Derrida, as the father of deconstruction philosophy, explaining his "deconstruction of the law," which also requires the impulse for justice that improves the law (Kashini, 2009, p. 2), which lets us know that by analyzing films, we can hope not only to improve them but to use them to work toward improving society.

Avatar, the long-awaited and techno 3-D cinema, which was partly animated as a science fiction production, was expected to be a big winner at the Academy Awards and to endure as a testament to James Cameron as a visionary director. However, politics played a part in its winning second, rather than first, place. The reasons behind this outcome are several and may be considered along with the complaint from critics who were appalled at its appropriation of Native Americans and their respective indigenous cultures and beliefs worldwide. Media not only perpetuate stereotypes but also appropriates ideas and values with new and even opposite meanings. Of course, this could go both ways: Native peoples, generally speaking, could want recognition for *Avatar*'s conceptual ideas and themes and also want not to be identified with this movie in the first place. But this did not stop the critics, and among them Native American reviewers, from attacking the movie for its lack of cultural sensitivity. There is also the anti-U.S. sentiment, and that includes the anti-war and anti-Christian perception in the movie plot as a result of U.S imperialistic pursuits on an "alien" planet with indigenous "natives." Among these cinema review criticisms are those who call this movie a manipulating "160-minute cinematic thrill ride" (Gardiner, 2009) and a morality play on a "white guilt fantasy" (Newitz, 2009) in the setting of a clash of "race-cultures" (zoomzoom, 2009). Because the film's events take place in the year 2154, it has also been described as "a futuristic take on the conquest of [U.S.] America and the treatment of Native Americans" as the conquered.

The movie was partly filmed in the California redwoods and in the Brazilian tropical rainforest to simulate the visual beauty of a magical planet called Pandora. This film's visually seductive cinematography is stunning and took several years in the planning; the film had a generous $400 million budget, when production and promotion are tallied, and took in more than $200 million worldwide in its opening weekend at the box office, grossing $2.8 billion worldwide. This movie did win Oscars for Best Achievement in Art Direction, Best Achievement in Cinematography, and Best Achievement in Visual Effects, but it had to be content with Best Motion Picture and Best Director from only the Golden Globes. There were even expectations that it might launch another *Star Wars* series as a cinematic extravaganza, but that remains to be seen. It has already made money on commercial media products by way of books and toys, etc. Fans can feel good about this, too, as it has also been noted in the news that Cameron has given money and support from his profits to indigenous causes before or after the critics began to question the film's appropriation of Native American culture. However, it cannot be ignored that *Avatar* has a message that can be construed as having an anti-war and pro-environmental message.

The film's ideology can be exposed by brief character analyses. The main protagonist, named Jake Sully (starring the Aussie actor, Sam Worthington), is a likable but sad-sack soldier in the Marines, suffering from a depression brought on by the loss of his legs and also the presumed loss of his identical twin brother. Sully becomes a willing paraplegic guinea pig in a wheelchair for the military by taking his brother's place in this adventurous experiment—that is, until he goes rogue as an animated alpha mutant avatar for the catlike Blue People who have large yellow eyes; "avatar" here means the incarnation of one's alter ego. It could be said that Jake finds his "sea legs," liberating him from his disability. As hero, he represents the U.S. rebel who stands up against evil and does the right thing—an act made more poignant by the fact that he cannot stand. And while he certainly shows the power of a whistleblower, the fact that he, as a representative human White Man, is needed to save Pandora perhaps suggests that the Blue People cannot accomplish this feat on their own. Sully's antagonist in the movie, a gung-ho war-hawk senior-citizen military leader in this planetary operation, is the *Iron Man* personification of evil, recalling not only the Cameronian cyborg played by Arnold Schwarzenegger in *The Terminator* (1984), but both Robert Downey, Jr. and Jeff Bridges from *Iron Man* (Favreau, 2008); especially when he dons a robotic tank suit in his final battle with the hero among the Blue People, who are the "people of color and culture" on this planet. In Sully, military might, western materialism, conquest-oriented Christianity, techno-science, and environmental exploitation all unite against the hero, but there is a new twist to this "white man" as image savior, since he is actually a "mixed-blood" due to his pod-like neurological brain wiring. This is a pre–President Obama hero who some hopefully saw as a mixed-race avatar for change sans miscegenation.

Many of *Avatar*'s female characters serve as traditional tropes as well. The Latin actress Michelle Rodriguez plays an Earth bisexual soldier-pilot and ally to Sully, a relationship that leads to her demise in a secondary role, a role that she shares with several others who do not animate into the Na'vis. In spite of her nontraditional role as a fighter pilot, she calls her plane "Baby," perhaps suggesting that her career has taken the place of her more "natural" desire to nurture others and making her sacrificial death for Sully's life seem as though she is saving her own "race" in addition to the Pandorans. There is a Pocahontas-style princess, Neytiri (Zoe Saldana), the daughter of the Na'vi chief whom the hero woos. This scenario has a familiar ring to it from an age-old myth in Native/Cherokee American lore, in that the "white guy" (even though in this case he is a half–human and animated Na'vi avatar) wins the indigenous princess. In a previous piece, "Savage Erotica Exotica" (Jaimes-Guerrero, 1999), I mention that Rayna Green discusses the "Pocahontas Perplex" in Hollywood cinema, based on the mythological story of the real Pocahontas with Captain John Smith, from the "white male gaze" on the female images as psycho-cultural projections. In this version of the Madonna/Whore Complex, Native women are discriminated against by age, as either young pubescent girls imaged as a "Cherokee Princess" or older women as "Indian Squaws"; the latter word is a French term that has come to mean a "beast of burden." Therefore, there is a strong connection between early Eurocentric literature, such as romanticized novels and plays, that manifests this "savage erotic exoticism" into later media and movie images. Also the "white hero" is always winning the young Indian maiden as a reward, which is denigrating to the Indian male as a conquered "loser" in these xenophobic scenarios (Jaimes-Guerrero, 1999). Certainly, some of these patterns are reinforced in *Avatar*. Interestingly, in spite of her bravery and athleticism throughout the film, one of the last scenes of Neytiri is of her cradling Jake, as a mother cradles her infant in many iconic art works, linking her to the nurturing mother role she shares with the tree and the planet. One of the more interesting Earth characters, who does not get enough play, is a cosmic anthropologist and indigenous ally from Earth, played by Sigourney Weaver (of earlier *Alien* fame). She is the perceptive one who recognizes that these people are a part of a grander and amazing system within an indigenous worldview, where all things, including humans, are interconnected on a planet called Pandora. Upon her death, also dying violently for the Pandoran cause, she feels peace, believing that she, too, has become connected to the planet.

This movie even has a book to complement this animistic worldview in natural harmony, which includes amazing flying dragons as well as fauna and flora on hanging gardens floating in mid-air. The Blue People are even able to use their flashy tails to connect with other species and the ecosystem in this paradisiacal wonderland, with the center of their world being an iridescent Magic Tree that talks, as a mother lode to their ecosystem. In exciting scenes, the Na'vi fly colorful giant dragonfly-like creatures, reminiscent of the way the Plains Indian tribes (i.e., the Sioux/ Lakota, Pawnee, Comanche, Apache) and others took to riding the wild horses in "cowboy and Injun" times.

Granted, there were other dynamics effecting the negative reaction to *Avatar*, which include its candid depiction of U.S. military imperialism that takes place on a mythical planet. The film depicts an aggressive U.S. targeting a peaceful and colorfully mystical indigenous peoples—the term "indigenous" meaning they were born there, as their birthplace homeland—compared to the Earth invaders who are there to exploit their natural resources and threaten their homeland. Indigenous also means to live in a sustainable reciprocity with nature in one's homeland. This, of course, should sound familiar, as it closely parallels the history of the United States, where the arrival of European colonizers led to their accruing, using, and disposing of resources native to North America, even, certainly, the native people.

Kashani calls for interrogation in cinema criticism, which he writes is not unlike detective work. *Avatar* can be seen as being similar to Spike Lee's *Inside Man*, about which Kashani states, "One can argue that the entire film is one long interrogation of American [focused on U.S.] history, past, present, and future" (2009, p. 2). *Avatar*'s plot is not just about colonization; it is also xenophobic in the intended annihilation of these Blue People by the U.S. military, if they don't get with the program. Therefore, this can be seen as a planetary cultural clash between western materialists and nature-loving natives, among the "good, bad, and the evil" players. There is also the creation of the "avatar" as a heroic animated figure who is half Earthman mixed with an indigenous Blue Person and has super-human strengths that the military is using as a colonizing weapon. The cyber technology and luminescent peyote-induced colors are stimulating, especially with the super-sized cartoon characters as avatars. How this all works in scientific theory is complex, but it recalls the laboratory setting and molecular scrambling in the horror classic *The Fly*—albeit with less dire results in the *Avatar* plot. In this state-of-the-art sci-fi movie, in which human brains are wired to tie one's central nervous system to created archetypal avatars as animated half-human and half-Disney-like fluorescent blue characters, there is a sci-fi take on miscegenation with indigenous "aliens." But in point of fact, it is the U.S. soldiers and military leaders who are the aliens on this planet, which leads to a war finale when the indigenous Na'vi defend themselves against a military invasion of their homeland and sacred tree, while the Earth is no longer habitable to humans. The question becomes, then, who are the actual "savages" here compared to the wise and "civilized" and who are the "aliens" compared to "indigenous" people in this movie?

Other Hollywood movie sagas of this "native and alien" genre are called to mind, as the late 20th-century blockbusters, *Dances with Wolves* (starring and directed by Kevin Costner, 1990) and *The Last of the Mohicans* (starring Daniel Day-Lewis; Mann, 1992) in which the White Man leads the Indians to victory in war, also with mixed feelings from the critics who include Native American voices. There was also an earlier other–planetary sci-fi flick, *Enemy Mine* (Petersen, 1985), with Dennis Quaid in the lead role as an Earth astronaut who befriends an enemy alien who gets killed; leaving the astronaut to adopt the alien's son and become the alien youth's stepfather. More recently, that is in the early 21st century, there is the B-rated *Surrogates* (Mostow, 2009), starring Bruce Willis as a disillusioned cop who is tired of drug-induced humans, including himself and his wife, on Earth letting robotic clones take over their lives as surrogates. The most intriguing of these, as a sci-fi indie, is Neill Blomkamp's *District 9* (2009), in which a human government bureaucrat starts to change into an alien, eventually helping to liberate the more humane aliens from human oppression on Earth. It is implied that his heroism is opportunistically inspired in that he is helping them to get back to their home to find a cure for his "infection," but then again who can blame him, after he loses his wife, family, and human identity as he transmorphs into a sizable alien with a shell-less crablike head and face who continues to walk upright? But then again isn't beauty meant to be in the eye of the beholder?

In her essay "Eating the Other," hooks (1992) discusses Michel Foucault, the French philosopher and theorist:

> Though speaking from the standpoint of his individual experience, Foucault voices a dilemma felt by many in the West. It is precisely that longing for *the* pleasure that has led the white West to sustain a romantic fantasy of the 'primitive' and the concrete search for a real primitive paradise, whether that location be a country or a body, a dark continent of dark flesh, perceived as the perfect embodiment of that possibility (1992, p. 27).

She, among others, has also pointed out how these racist projections on Black Americans (and other people of color) are internalized, in what can be called "inverted racism" and "internalized colonization" (also a point made in her interview documentary, titled *Cultural Criticism & Transformation*

(Jhally & Jhally,1997). Yet anyone who reads and studies Native Americans, as in the five-part documentary series *The Great Indian Wars, 1540–1890* (by Mill Creek Entertainment), as well as scores of history books and other media, can see that Cameron took many of his "indigenous" ideas from the Native Americans, from their own indigenous experiences and perspectives, and in the historical context of U.S. conquest and colonization during and after what can be called the Indian–Settler Wars.

By recalling what some critics have claimed, this movie can be viewed as anti-U.S., anti-military, and anti-Christian, the latter from an alien indigenous perspective, as the aliens are being threatened because the Earth is dying, or in need of more petro (what else is new?). It is a movie, as has been pointed out, about race, identity, culture clash, and war. In this film scenario, it is also about U.S. colonialism on other planets. At the same time, it is also about survival and good winning over bad as well as an indigenous way of living life with nature instead of against it. One important contribution, therefore, that I argue this movie extravaganza makes, and especially in these ahistorical times, is that it reminds us of the tropes of racism and colonialism, as well as new terms like biocolonialism and biopiracy (the targeting of indigenous peoples by geneticists), and how the present is connected to the past. It is also a glimpse of the future in NASA space exploration while Earth faces the threat of global warming due to climatic change already in progress. It is therefore in this vein that I believe the iconic *Avatar* has made a backhanded contribution in reminding us of the Indigenous Way to envision an urgently needed ecological worldview, in which "Mankind is again a part of Nature" (quoting the marine biologist Dr. Rachel Carson in the PBS documentary *Earth and the American Dream* [Couturié, 1992], as a panoramic history of U.S. society). It is in this seminal movie of our times that we can remember the past in order to not repeat mistakes in the future but learn from our past errors. As hooks reminds us in her call for a "politics of cultural transformation": "Learning from the past, we need to remain critically vigilant, willing to interrogate our works as well as our habits of being to ensure that we are not perpetuating internalized racism" (1994, p. 182).

The lesson in the message is that all Humans as Earth Peoples should learn to live with Nature, and with Indigenous Peoples, both those in the historic past and presently living, as our guides. To do otherwise is to face an uncertain future with our human failings and fiascos and a growing list of "endangered species" that even includes humans, among real-life indigenous peoples and others worldwide. Sci-fi movies attempt to warn us about the future with recollections from our past in our present situations. Whether this was the intent of *Avatar* as a movie is only hypothetical. If we ignore this warning, then we may see the doom and extinction of all humans as a result of apocalyptic consequences on Earth due to escalating environmental catastrophes brought on by humans as well as nature's cycles.

There is a problematic that is highlighted in the general mix of "Hollywood" movies, and that propagandizes as well as subjugates "the other" in the eyes of the moviemaker in the U.S., as a polycultural society. Jan Nederveen Pieterse (2009) writes of a cultural mélange today:

> Globalization and culture is not an innocent theme. The intervening variable in most accounts is modernity. Three vectors—globalization, modernity, culture—come together in a package with modernization as the deciding variable. Modernity is also a polite, sociological way of saying capitalism. The sociologists Axford (1995) and Tomlinson (1999), among others, struggle with this question and in the end tiptoe over to the side of modernity (read the logics of western modernization) shaping cultural dynamics. It's difficult to argue with the combined power of modernity and capitalism, with technology and economics on their side, and therefore, it seems global (read western culture) wins out from local culture. Yet one wonders whether these accounts are actually about culture or about power (p. 141).

These cinema scenarios of culture and nature appreciation are also about conquest and colonialism, and that is evident today in the neoliberal politics of globalism underlining corporate capitalism. Consequently, there is a need to decolonize this colonizing mindset, as a normative hegemony in a dominant-subordinate hierarchy, and that includes the language issues in the theoretical thinking of "academic avatars," among them hooks, Kashani, and others, who provide us with not only their perceptive insights as cultural media critics but also with strategies to challenge and counter the Eurocentric hegemony of cultural imperialism. In this context, the U.S. is not actually a culture, in the traditional meaning of the term, but has created a "pop culture" through mass-media productions, from TV to MTV, cinema, and other propagandizing modes, for marketing commercial products, and that has to be juxtaposed with what is being seen as a globalizing world as a social and cultural theme of our times.

Note

I would like to acknowledge my research assistant Wolf Yhout Larson and my son, David Jaimes Danelowitz, who has assisted me in understanding the complexity of sci-fi science and its speculative methods in plot development.

References

Blomkamp, N. (Director). (2009). *District 9* [Motion Picture]. U.S.: TriStar Pictures.

Cameron, D. (Director). (1984). *The Terminator* [Motion Picture]. U.S.: Orion.

———. (Director). (2009). *Avatar* [Motion Picture]. U.S.: Twentieth Century Fox.

Costner, K. (Director). (1990). *Dances with Wolves* [Motion Picture]. U.S.: Orion.

Couturié, B. (Director). (1992). *Earth and the American Dream* [Documentary]. U.S.: PBS.

Favreau, J. (Director). (2008). *Iron Man* [Motion Picture]. U.S.: Paramount.

Gardiner, N. (2009, July 25). Avatar: the most expensive piece of anti-American propaganda ever made. The Telegraph. Available at http://blogs.telegraph.co.uk/news/nilegardiner/100020721/avatar-the-most-expensive-piece-of-anti-american-propaganda-ever-made/

hooks, b. (1992). *Black looks: Race and representation*. Cambridge, MA: South End Press.

———. (1994). *Outlaw culture: Resisting representations*. New York: Routledge.

Jaimes-Guerrero, M. (1999). Savage erotica exotica: Media imagery of Native women in North America. In R. Hulan (Ed.), *Native North America: Critical and cultural perspectives*, pp. 187–210. Toronto, Canada: ECW Press.

Jhally, S. (Producer) & Jhally, S. (Director). (1997). *bell hooks: Cultural criticism & Transformation* [Motion picture]. U.S.: Media Education Foundation.

Kashani, T. (2009). *Deconstructing the mystique: An interdisciplinary introduction to cinema.* Dubuque, IA: Kendall/Hunt.

Mann, M. (Director). (1992). *Last of the Mohicans* [Motion Picture]. U.S.: Twentieth Century Fox.

Mostow, J. (Director). (2009). *Surrogates* [Motion Picture]. U.S.: Top Shelf Productions.

Newitz, A. (2009, December 18). When will white people stop making movies like "Avatar" [*sic*]? *io9.com.* Available at http://io9.com/5422666/when-will-white-people-stop-making-movies-like-avatar

Petersen, W. (Director). (1985). *Enemy Mine* [Motion Picture]. U.S.: Twentieth Century Fox.

Pieterse, J. N. (2009). *Globalization and culture: Global mélange*. Lanham, MD: Rowman & Littlefield.

zoomzoom. (2009, December 27). Avatar, Native Americans, and human stereotyping. *Cinemaroll*. Available at http://cinemaroll.com/science-fiction/avatar-native-americans-and-human-stereotyping/

Appendix

A Brief Media Studies Resource List

Joanna Martinez

Marshall McLuhan wrote in *Understanding Media: The Extensions of Man* (1964):

> Today, after a century of electric technology, we have extended our central nervous system itself in a global embrace, abolishing both time and space…rapidly, we approach the final phase of the extension of man—the technological simulation of consciousness, when the creative process of knowing will be collectively and corporately extended to the whole of human society…whether the extension of consciousness…will be a "good thing" is a question that admits of a wide solution.

In the same way that McLuhan posits this critical question reflecting the social and economic changes in the world during the 1960s, one can apply this question to the ever-expanding world of new media today. Industrialization posed a great threat to the division of labor in the late 18th-century western world. Today's rapid increase of information technologies echoes a similar concern on a global scale. Information technology and the Internet, for example, have become the primary source for media consumption. The World Wide Web offers unlimited access to various forms of media all on one computer screen: music, online movies and videos, online games, academic sources, blogs, personal and corporate websites, social-virtual networks, etc., can all be viewed simultaneously due to convergence. One can virtually www-dot *anything* and find just what one is navigating for.

Yet, as open, free, and user-friendly as the Internet is, social questions and problems arise about its uses. Social scientists (particularly sociologists) must now shift their focus from the effects of television on social behavior to online social networks and their effects on the presentation of self in everyday life and the reshaping of economic, educational, and corporate institutions.

> In terms of economic and financial use, there is an opposition between those with internet connections, who have computers and software that enable them to trade and do their banking online from home and those lacking that access. And the facts clearly give lie to the myth that the internet would change relations between the North and the South: in 1997, the richest 20 percent of the world's population repre-

sented 93.3 percent of internet users, while the poorest 20 percent made up .2 percent. (Bourdieu, 2000).

For whom or what is the Internet intended? How can we use the Internet and other forms of media as tools for creating empowered communities, both virtually and physically? How do we reconcile the Internet access gap between the rich and the poor, the literate and illiterate, the young and the old, the so-called third world and the so-called first world? What can be said about the open access to free information that may lead to harm, such as the easy accessibility of pornography to youth all over the world? Should the government regulate or deregulate the flows of local, national, and international media without interfering with global public demands for consumer freedom? Is there such thing as *consumer freedom*? Lastly, are we approaching the "final phase of the extension of man" as McLuhan suggested in 1964? This appendix does not seek to answer these questions directly; rather, it provides resources, both corporate and alternative, for tackling such inquiries. In addition, it provides a list of select "Key Thinkers" for those who wish to delve into the intellectual foundations and key concepts of critical media studies.

Alternative media are necessary to augment what mainstream media do not provide, such as a wide spectrum of news coverage and multitude of perspectives. Nevertheless, clearly mainstream media, such as *The New York Times*, the BBC, and CNN are important because they play an integral role in informing people around the globe. Although not nearly comprehensive, the following list offers a multitude of media resources, both mainstream and alternative, to help the reader navigate today's media landscape.

Media Resources

Film

Films for Action: www.filmsforaction.org
Internet Movie Database: www.imdb.com
Indiewire: www.indiewire.com
Motion Picture Association of America: www.mpaa.org

Television, Cable, and Mobile Video

A.C. Nielsen: www.neilsenmedia.com
Al Jazeera Network: www.aljazeera.com
British Broadcasting Company: www.bbc.com
National Cable and Telecommunications Association: www.ncta.com

National Telecommunications and Information Administration: www.ntia.gov
National Association of Broadcasters: www.nab.org

Radio
Federal Communications Commission: www.fcc.org
National Public Radio: www.npr.org
Public Radio International: www.pri.org

Internet and Digitalization
Electronic Frontier Foundation: www.eff.org
Internet Statistics: www.internetworldstats.com
Internet History: www.isoc.org/internet/history

Newspapers and Reporting
American Society of Magazine Editors: www.magazine.org/asme/
American Society of Newspaper Editors: www.asne.org
Journalism Education Association: www.jea.org
Magazine Publishers of America: www.magazine.org
Media Activist Site: www.fair.org
National Association of Hispanic Publishers: www.nahp.org
National Newspaper Publishers Association: www.nnpa.org
Newspaper Association of America: www.naa.org
Yellow Journalism: www.yellowjournalism.net

Convergence and the Reshaping of Mass Communication
Advertising Age: www.adage.com
Broadcasting & Cable: www.broadcastingcable.com
Current TV: www.current.tv
Editor & Publisher www.editorandpublisher.com
Variety: www.variety.com
More on Kids' Media Consumption: www.kaisernetwork.org
More on Globalization: www.unesco.org

Mass Communication, Culture, and Media Literacy
Association for Media Literacy: www.aml.ca/home
Cable in the Classroom: www.ciconline.org
Center for Media Literacy: www.medialit.org
Columbia Journalism Review: www.cjr.org
IFC Media Project: www.ifc.com/mediaproject
Media Alliance: www.media-alliance.org

Media Awareness Network: www.media-awareness.ca/
Media Education Foundation: www.mediated.org
Media Education Lab: www.mediaeducationlab.com
National Association for Media Literacy Education: www.amlainfo.org
Online Kids' Media Literacy: www.pbskids.org
The Pew Research Center's Project for Excellence in Journalism: www.journalism.org
TV Critics Association: www.tvcritics.org

Media Freedom, Regulation, and Ethics

Center for Democracy and Technology: www.cdt.org
Common Dreams: www.commondreams.org
Creative Commons: www.creativecommons.org
Digital Bill of Rights: www.digitalconsumer.org/bil.htm
Electronic Frontier Foundation: www.eff.org
Electronic Privacy Information Center: www.epic.org
Fight for Fair Use: www.digitalconsumer.org
First Amendment: www.freedomforum.org
Huffington Post: www.huffingtonpost.com
Media Reform: www.freepress.net
Media Reform: www.takebackthemedia.com
Media Watchdog: www.consortiumnews.com
Organization of News Ombudsmen: www.newsombudsmen.org
Thomas Jefferson Center for Free Expression: www.tjcenter.org
Truth out: www.truthout.org

Media Watchdog

Bridge Project: www.mediamattersaction.org/transparency
Media Channel: www.mediachannel.org
Online Journal: www.onlinejournal.com
Tom Paine: www.tompaine.com

Think Tanks

Source: http://www.hks.harvard.edu/library/research/guides/think-tanks-directory.htm

National

American Enterprise Institute
American Foreign Policy Council
Ash Center for Democratic Governance & Innovation–Harvard Kennedy School
Ashbrook Center for Public Affairs (Ashland University, Ohio)
The Aspen Institute
APPAM –The Association for Public Policy Analysis and Management

Belfer Center for Science & International Affairs–Harvard Kennedy School
Brookings Institution
BRIE–The Berkeley Roundtable on the International Economy (University of California, Berkeley)
Carnegie Council for Ethics in International Affairs
Carnegie Endowment for International Peace
Carr Center for Human Rights Policy–Harvard Kennedy School
The Carter Center (Emory University)
Cascade Policy Institute
Cato Institute
Center for American Women and Politics (Rutgers University)
Center for Army Lessons Learned
Center for Civil-Military Relations
Center for Comparative Immigration Studies (University of California at San Diego)
Center for Complex Operations
Center for Congressional and Presidential Studies (American University)
Center for Democracy and Technology
Center for Economic Policy and Research
Center for Global Development
Center for Health Decision Science–Harvard School of Public Health
Center for Information & Research on Civic Learning and Engagement (University of Maryland)
Center for International and Security Studies at Maryland (University of Maryland)
Center for International Development–Harvard Kennedy School
Center for International Earth Science Information Network (Columbia University)
Center for International Trade and Security (University of Georgia)
Center for Law and Social Policy
The Center for National Policy
Center for New American Security
Center for Public Integrity
Center for Public Leadership–Harvard Kennedy School
Center for Public Policy & Administration (University of Utah)
Center for Public Policy Priorities
Center for Reproductive Rights
Center for Strategic and Budgetary Assessments
Center for Strategic and International Studies
Center for an Urban Future
Center on Budget and Policy Priorities
Centre for Development & Population Activities
The Century Foundation
Committee for Economic Development
Commonwealth Institute
Competitive Enterprise Institute
Council on Foreign Relations

Democratic Leadership Council
Demos
Eagleton Institute of Politics (Rutgers University)
East-West Center
Economic Policy Institute
Edmund J. Safra Foundation Center for Ethics–Harvard Kennedy School
Ethics and Public Policy Center
Foreign Policy Research Institute
The Free Expression Policy Project (NYU School of Law)
Freedom Forum
George C. Marshall Institute
Global Development and Environment Institute (Tufts University)
Hauser Center for Non Profit Organizations–Harvard Kennedy School
Heritage Foundation
Hoover Institution on War, Revolution, and Peace (Stanford University)
Hubert H. Humphrey Institute of Public Affairs (University of Minnesota)
Hudson Institute
The ICA Institute
The Independent Institute
Institute for Agriculture & Trade Policy
Institute for Global Ethics (IGE)
Institute for Higher Education Policy
Institute for Peace
Institute for Philosophy and Public Policy (University of Maryland)
Institute for Policy Research (Northwestern University)
Institute for Policy Research (University of Cincinnati)
Institute for Policy Studies
Institute for Public & International Affairs (University of Utah)
Institute for Research on Poverty (University of Wisconsin-Madison)
Institute for Social Research (University of Michigan)
Institute for the Study of Diplomacy (Georgetown University)
Institute for Women's Policy Research
Institute of Politics–Harvard Kennedy School
Institution for Social and Policy Studies (Yale University)
International Center for Research on Women
International Food Policy Research Institute
International Forum for Peace Operations
International Institute for Strategic Studies
Joint Center for Housing Studies–Harvard Kennedy School
Joint Center for Operational Analysis
Joint Center for Political & Economic Studies
Joint Center for Poverty Research (Northwestern University & University of Chicago)
Levy Economics Institute (Bard College)
The Manhattan Institute for Policy Research

Maryland Institute for Policy Analysis and Research (University of Maryland, Baltimore)
Massachusetts Budget and Policy Center
Massachusetts Institute for a New Commonwealth
Milken Institute
Morrison Institute for Public Policy (Arizona State University)
Mossaver-Rahmani Center for Business & Government–Harvard Kennedy School
National Academy of Public Administration
National Alliance for Civic Education (University of Maryland)
National Bureau of Economic Research
National Center for Children in Poverty (Columbia University)
National Center for Policy Analysis
National Center for Smart Growth Research & Education (University of Maryland)
National Health Policy Forum
Nautilus Institute for Security & Sustainable Development
Northeast-Midwest Institute
Pacific Research Institute
Peterson Institute for International Economics
Phoenix Center for Advanced Legal & Economic Public Policy Studies
Pioneer Institute for Public Policy Research
Political Research Associates
Program on the Economics of Crime & Justice Policy (University of Maryland)
Progress & Freedom Foundation
Progressive Policy Institute
Project on Defense Alternative
Public Agenda
Public Policy Institute of California
Public Policy Research Center (University of Missouri, St. Louis)
RAND Corporation
Rappaport Institute for Greater Boston–Harvard Kennedy School
Reason Foundation
Resources for the Future
The Nelson A. Rockefeller Institute of Government (SUNY Albany)
The Roosevelt Institution
Joan Shorenstein Center on the Press, Politics, and Public Policy–Harvard Kennedy School
Social Science Research Council
Southwest Consortium for Environmental Research & Policy
Henry L. Stimson Center
Strategic Studies Institute (U.S. Army War College)
Substance Abuse Policy Research Program
Taubman Center for State & Local Government–Harvard Kennedy School
TRAC: Transactional Records Access Clearinghouse (Syracuse University)
Urban Institute
Washington Institute for Near East Policy

Weatherhead East Asian Institute (Columbia University)
Weidenbaum Center on the Economy, Government, & Public Policy (Washington University in St. Louis)
Malcolm Weiner Center for Social Policy–Harvard Kennedy School
The Williams Institute (UCLA School of Law)
Women & Public Policy Program–Harvard Kennedy School
Woodrow Wilson Center for Scholars
World Policy Institute
World Resources Institute
Worldwatch Institute

International

Afghanistan Research and Evaluation Unit (Afghanistan)
African Centre for Economic Growth (Kenya)
African Economic Research Consortium (Kenya)
African Technology Policy Studies Network (Tanzania)
Al-Ahram Center for Political & Strategic Studies (Egypt)
Arab Planning Institute (Kuwait)
Australian Institute for International Affairs (Australia)
Bangladesh Institute for Development Studies (Bangladesh)
BioCentre (U.K.)
Cambodian Institute for Cooperation and Peace (Cambodia)
Carnegie Middle East Center (Lebanon)
Carnegie Moscow Center (Russia)
Center for Economic & Social Development (Azerbaijan)
Center for Independent Studies (Australia)
Center for International Governance Innovation (Canada)
Center for International Peace Operations (Germany)
Center for International Policy Studies (Japan)
Center for Policy Research (India)
Center for Security Studies (Switzerland)
Center for Social & Economic Research (Poland)
Center for Strategic & International Studies (Indonesia)
Center for Strategic Studies (Jordan)
Center for the Study of the Economies of Africa (Nigeria)
Centre for Development and Enterprise (South Africa)
Centre for Development & the Environment (Sweden)
Centre for Economic Policy Research (U.K.)
Centre for European Policy Studies (Belgium)
Centre for Policy Analysis (Ghana)
Centre for Strategic Research & Analysis (U.K.)
Centre for the Study of Public Policy (University of Aberdeen, Scotland)
Centre of Excellence–Defense Against Terrorism (Turkey)

Chatham House (U.K.)
China Institute of Contemporary International Relations (China)
Civilian Capacity for Peace Operations (Germany)
Clingendael (Netherlands)
Council for the Development of Social Science Research in Africa (Senegal)
East Asian Institute (South Korea)
Economic Research Institute for ASEAN & East Asia (Indonesia)
Economic & Social Research Institute (Ireland)
Emirates Center for Strategic Studies & Research (U.A.E.)
EU Institute for Security Studies (France)
European Centre on the International Political Economy (Belgium)
European Policy Centre
Group for the Analysis of Development (Peru)
Gulf Research Center (UAE)
Indian Council for Research on International Economic Relations (India)
Information & Decision Support Center (Egypt)
Institute for Defense Studies & Analyses (India)
Institute for Far Eastern Studies (South Korea)
Institute for Fiscal Studies (U.K.)
Center for International Policy Studies (Japan)
Institute for the Integration of Latin America & the Carribean (Argentina)
Institute for National Security Studies (Israel)
Institute of Developing Economies (Japan)
Institute of Development Studies
Institute of Policy Studies (University of Singapore, Singapore)
Institute of World Economics & Politics (China)
International Development Research Centre (Canada)
The International Institute for Applied Systems Analysis (Austria)
International Institute for Sustainable Development (Canada)
International Policy Network (U.K.)
Islamabad Policy Research Institute (Pakistan)
Kenya Institute of Public Policy Research & Analyses (Kenya)
LSE Ideas: International Affairs, Diplomacy, and Strategy (London School of Economics, U.K.)
Makerere Institute of Social Research (Uganda)
Malaysian Institute of Economic Research (Malaysia)
Nigerian Institute of International Affairs (Nigeria)
Overseas Development Institute (U.K.)
Oxonia: Oxford Institute for Economic Policy (U.K.)
Peace Research Institute (Norway)
Pearson Peacekeeping Center (Canada)
RAND Europe (U.K.)
Royal United Services Institute (U.K.)
Social Policy & Development Centre (Pakistan)

Stockholm International Peace Research Institute (Sweden)
Taiwan Institute of Economic Research (Taiwan)
UNEP World Conservation Monitoring Centre (U.K.)
World Institute for Development Economics Research (Finland)

Key Figures

Theodor Adorno (1903–1969)

Key works: *Dialectic of Enlightenment* (1973, with Max Horkheimer); *Negative Dialectics* (1973); *Minima Moralia* (1974); *The Culture Industry* (1991)

Key concepts: culture industry, non-identity, constellation, aesthetic theory

Website: http://plato.stanford.edu/entries/adorno/

Louis Althusser (1918–1990)

Key works: *For Marx* (1965); *Reading Capital* (1965); *Lenin and Philosophy and Other Essays* (1971)

Key concepts: ideological state apparatuses, interpellation

Website: http://plato.stanford.edu/entries/althusser/

Ien Ang (1954–)

Key works: *Watching* Dallas*: Soap Opera and the Melodramatic Imagination* (1985); *Desperately Seeking the Audience* (1991); *Living Room Wars: Rethinking Media Audiences for a Postmodern World* (1996)

Key concepts: ideology and populism

Website: http://www.uws.edu.au/ics/people/researchers/ien_ang

Roland Barthes (1915–1980)

Key works: *The Fashion System* (1967); *Writing Degree Zero* (1968); *Elements of Semiology* (1968); *Mythologies* (1972); *The Pleasure of the Text* (1975)

Key concepts: *denotation/connotation, myth*

Website: http://www.kirjasto.sci.fi/rbarthes.htm

Jean Baudrillard (1929–2007)

Key works: *The System of Objects* (1968); *The Consumer Society: Myths and Structures* (1970); *For a Critique of the Political Economy of the Sign* (1972); *The Mirror of Production* (1973); *Symbolic Exchange and Death* (1976); *Forget Foucault* (1977); *Simulations* (1983); *America* (1986*); Cool Memories* (1987); *The Ecstasy of Communication* (1987)

Key concepts: *simulation; hyper-reality*
Website: http://plato.stanford.edu/entries/baudrillard/

Walter Benjamin (1892–1940)

Key works: *The Work of Art in the Age of Mechanical Reproduction* (1936); *On the Concept of History / Theses on the Philosophy of History* (1940)
Key concepts: aura, ritual function/exhibition function, the dialectical image
Website: http://plato.stanford.edu/archives/spr2011/entries/benjamin/

Pierre Bourdieu (1930–2002)

Key works: *Outline of a Theory of Practice* (1977); *Reproduction in Education, Society and Culture* with Jean-Claude Passeron (1990); *Distinction: A Social Critique of the Judgment of Taste* (1984); *In Other Words: Essays toward a Reflective Sociology* (1990); *Language and Symbolic Power* (1991); *An Invitation to Reflexive Sociology* with Loïc Wacquant (1992); *Practical Reason: On the Theory of Action,* (1998); *On Television* (1999); *Acts of Resistance: Against the Tyranny of the Market* (1999)
Key concepts: *cultural capital, social capital, symbolic capital, habitus, taste*
Website: http://loicwacquant.net/assets/Papers/PIERREBOURDIEU-Stones2007.pdf

Manuel Castells (1942–)

Key works: *Communication Power* (2009); *The Internet Galaxy: Reflections on the Internet, Business and Society* (2001); *The Information Age: Economy, Society and Culture* (1996*); Vol. I: The Rise of the Network Society* (1996); *Vol. II: The Power of Identity*(1997); *Vol. III: End of Millennium* (1998)
Key concepts: network society, informational city, the space of flows
Website: http://www.manuelcastells.info/en/cv_index.htm

Noam Chomsky: (1928–)

Key works: *Manufacturing Consent: The Political Economy of the Mass Media* with Edward Herman (1988); *Necessary Illusions: Thought Control in Democratic Societies* (1989); *Media Control: The Spectacular Achievements of Propaganda* (1997)
***Key concepts*:** the propaganda model, manufacturing consent, necessary illusions
Website: http://www.chomsky.info/

Guy Debord (1931–1994)
Key works: *The Society of the Spectacle* (1967)
Key concepts: spectacle, spectacle society, detournement
Website: http://libcom.org/library/guy-debord-introduction

Antonio Gramsci (1891–1937)
Key works: *Selections From the Prison Notebooks* (1971)
Key concepts: hegemony, organic intellectuals, civil society
Website: http://www.victoryiscertain.com/gramsci/

Stuart Hall (1932–)
Key works: *Resistance Through Rituals* (1977); *Cultural Studies: Two Paradigms* (1980); *Representation* (1997)
Key concepts: encoding/decoding, "the work of representation," image interrogation
Website: http://changingminds.org/disciplines/sociology/theorists/stuart_hall.htm

Herbert Marcuse (1898–1979)
Key works: *One-Dimensional Man* (1964); *Eros and Civilization* (1955); *The Aesthetic Dimension* (1978)
Key concepts: one-dimensionality, pacification of existence, false needs, surplus repression, repressive desublimation
Website: http://www.marcuse.org/herbert/

Robert McChesney (1952–)
Key works: *Freedom of the Press: America's Gift to the World* (2011); *Communication and Monopoly Capital: A Reinterpretation of the Information Age and the Tribulations of U.S. Democracy* (2010); *Saving Journalism: The Soul of Democracy* (2009); *Communication Revolution: Critical Junctures and the Future of Media* (2007)
Key concepts*:* democratic reform
Website: http://www.robertmcchesney.com/

Marshall McLuhan (1911–1980)
Key works: *Understanding Media: The Extensions of Man* (1964)
Key concepts: "The medium is the message."
Website: http:/www.marshallmcluhan.com

Angela McRobbie (1952–)
Key works: *Zoot Suits and Second-hand Dress* (1989); *Feminism and Youth Culture* (1991); *Postmodernism and Popular Culture* (1994); *British Fashion Design: Rag Trade or Image Industry?* (1998); *In the Culture Society: Art, Fashion and Popular Music* (1999); *The*

Uses of Cultural Studies: A Textbook (2005); *The Aftermath of Feminism: Gender, Culture and Social Change* (2009)
Key concepts: *gender, structuralist feminism*
Website: http://www.angelamcrobbie.com/

Edward Said (November 1, 1935–September 25, 2003)
Key works: *Orientalism* (1978); *The World, the Text, and the Critic* (1983); *Nationalism, Colonialism, and Literature: Yeats and Decolonization* (1988); *Culture and Imperialism* (1993);*Representations of the Intellectual: The 1993 Reith Lectures* (1994); *Humanism and Democratic Criticism* (2004); *On Late Style* (2006)
***Key concepts*:** Orientalism, post-colonial criticism
Website: http://www.guardian.co.uk/news/2003/sep/26/guardianobituaries.highereducation

Herbert Schiller (1919–2000)
Key works: *The Mind Managers* (1973); *Communication and Cultural Domination* (1976); *Culture Inc.* (1989); *Information Inequality* (1996)
Key concepts: cultural imperialism, media corporatism
***Website*:** http://mediaresearchhub.ssrc.org/herbert-schiller/person_view

Raymond Williams (1921–1988)
Key works: *Culture and Society* (1958); *The Long Revolution* (1961); *Television: Technology and Cultural Form* (1974); *Marxism and Literature* (1977); *Keywords* (1976)
Key concepts: cultural materialism, culture: dominant, residual, emergent
Website: http://www.museum.tv/eotvsection.php?entrycode=williamsray

Contributors

Jjenna Hupp Andrews

Jjenna Hupp Andrews is an active studio artist and faculty in the Department of Communications and Visual Art at University of Michigan-Flint. She earned her BFA and MFA from Central Michigan University and is currently completing her PhD dissertation in Interdisciplinary Studies, with a humanities and visual culture concentration. Her interdisciplinary research interests focus on contemporary visual and performance art, visual and media literacy in higher education, and the intersections between the fine art and media realms.

Benjamin Frymer

Benjamin Frymer is assistant professor of sociology in the Hutchins School of Liberal Studies, Sonoma State University, and co-organizer of the Modern Media Dialogue Series at Sonoma State University. He works in the areas of critical theory, youth, education, media, and cultural studies focusing on contemporary alienation. His publications include co-editing *Cultural Studies, Education, and Youth: Beyond Schools* (2011, Lexington Books), an analysis of the Frankfurt School's contributions to the study of modern education; several pieces on the Columbine High School shootings; and *Hollywood's Exploited: Public Pedagogy, Corporate Movies, and Cultural Studies* (2010, Palgrave/Macmillan).

Ajay Gehlawat

Ajay Gehlawat is Assistant Professor of Interdisciplinary Studies, Theatre and Film in the Hutchins School of Liberal Studies at Sonoma State University. He is the author of *Reframing Bollywood: Theories of Popular Hindi Cinema* (Sage, 2010) and editor of the forthcoming collection, *The Slumdog Phenomenon*. He has also published articles in journals such as *Quarterly Review of Film & Video*, *TOPIA: Canadian Journal of Cultural Studies*, *Journal of African American Studies*, *CineAction*, and *South Asian Popular Culture*. Along with Bollywood and Indian cinema, Gehlawat is concerned with contemporary trends in film studies, postcolonial theory and popular culture. He has recently written essays exploring the racial dynamics of *The Princess and the Frog*, the erotic Orientalism of James Bond, the reception of *Slumdog Millionaire* and the shifting dynamics of whiteness in Bollywood. In addition, he has examined the construction of femininity in 1970s Bollywood, the viewing of Hindi cinema by subaltern audiences in India, and the use of media in the classroom. At the present moment he is working on a study of metrosexual masculinity and the figure of the con man in contemporary Indian cinema. He regularly teaches courses on Bollywood, film theory, multicultural musicals, and minorities in American cinema.

Henry A. Giroux

Henry A. Giroux currently holds the Global TV Network Chair Professorship at McMaster University in the English and Cultural Studies Department. His primary research areas are cultural studies, youth studies, critical pedagogy, popular culture, media studies, social theory, and the politics of higher and public education. In 2002, he was named as one of the top fifty educational thinkers of the modern period in *Fifty Modern Thinkers on Education: From Piaget to the Present* (part of Routledge's Key Guides Publication Series). In 2005, he received an honorary doctorate from Memorial University in Canada. He is on the editorial and advisory boards of numerous national and international scholarly journals, and he serves as the editor or co-editor of four scholarly book series. He has published numerous books and articles and his most recent books include: *Youth in a Suspect Society: Democracy or Disposability?*((Palgrave Macmillan, 2009); *Hearts of Darkness: Torturing Children in the War on Terror* (Paradigm, 2010), *Zombie Politics and Culture in the Age of Casino Capitalism* (Peter Lang, 2011); *On Critical Pedagogy* (Continuum, 2011), and *Education and the Crisis of Public Values* (Peter Lang, 2012), *Twilight of the Social: Resurgent Publics in the Age of Disposability* (Paradigm, 2012), and *Disposable Youth: Racialized Memories and the Culture of Cruelty* (Routledge, 2012). His forthcoming books include: *Youth in Revolt: Reclaiming a Democratic Future* (Paradigm) and *The Education Deficit and the War on Youth* (Monthly Review Press). His website is www.henryagiroux.com.

M.A. Jaimes-Guerrero

M.A. Jaimes-Guerrero is a leading Native American and Mestiza author, scholar, activist, novelist, and poet. She is a professor of Women and Gender Studies at San Francisco State University. She has worked with Women of All Red Nations and the Indigenous Women/s Network. She has taught classes on environmental justice, American Indian Studies, and Ethnic Studies. Jaimes-Guerrero is editor of and contributor to *The State of Native North America* (South End Press) and contributed the essay "Patriarchal Colonialism" to and coedited *Hypatia: A Journal of Feminist Philosophy*, Special Issue: *Indigenous Women in America,* Spring 2003: Volume 18, Number 2. Other publications include a research essay "Global Genocide and Biocolonialism," which appeared in *Violence and the Body* (Indiana University Press, 2003), and "Native Womanism: Exemplars of Indigenism and Global Genocide: A Case for Biocolonialism." Currently she is working on a manifesto that poses the question: "Is There a Nexus Between Feminisms and Indigenism for Gender Justice in Transformative Activist Movements?" with an emphasis on Latin America. She lives in San Francisco.

David Ingram

David Ingram received his PhD in philosophy from the University of California at San Diego (1980), where he studied under Herbert Marcuse. After teaching at the University of Northern Iowa (1980–87), he accepted an appointment at Loyola University of Chicago, where he currently teaches Continental and Anglo-American social and political philosophy. His research interests include human rights, philosophy of law, philosophy of social science, democratic theory, disability theory, critical race theory, and migration theory. He is author of *Habermas and the Dialectic of Reason* (1987), *Critical Theory and Philosophy* (1990), *Reason, History and Politics* (1995), *Group Rights* (2000), *Rights, Democracy, and Fulfillment in the Era of Identity Politics* (2004), *Law* (2006), and *Habermas* (2010). His edited collections include *Critical Theory: The Essential Readings* (1991), *The Political* (2002), and *From Critical Theory to Structuralism* (2010). He was recipient of the Alpha Sigma Nu Prize in Philosophy, History, and Theology in 1997 and the Casa Guatemala Human Rights Award for 1999.

Ali Kashani

Ali Kashani is a social and political philosopher who teaches at San Francisco State University in Northern California. He is currently completing his dissertation, "The Question of Radical Generosity: Ethics and Politics of Cosmopolitanism" for a PhD in Social and Political Philosophy at Michigan State University. His research interests are in critical theory, post-structuralism, and feminist theory.

Tony Kashani

Tony Kashani holds a PhD in Humanities from California Institute of Integral Studies, a Master's degree in Cinema Studies, and a Bachelor's degree in Media Studies from San Francisco State University. He is Humanities professor at Brandman University of Chapman University System, co-director of the Modern Media Project, and organizer of the Modern Media Dialogue Series at Sonoma State University. In addition to many scholarly articles on topics ranging from education to cultural studies, Dr. Kashani is the author of two editions of *Deconstructing the Mystique: An Interdisciplinary Introduction to Cinema* (2005, 2009, Kendall/Hunt), a textbook. He is also the co-editor and contributor of *Hollywood's Exploited: Public Pedagogy, Corporate Movies, and Cultural Studies* (2010, Palgrave Macmillan). Tony Kashani is a practicing black belt in Shotokan Karate and lives with his family in San Francisco. His website is www.tonykashani.com.

Douglas Kellner

Douglas Kellner is George Kneller Chair in the Philosophy of Education and Distinguished Professor at UCLA and is author of many books on social theory, politics, history, and culture, including *Camera Politica: The Politics and Ideology of Contemporary Hollywood Film* (co-authored with Michael Ryan) and *Emile de Antonio: A Reader* (co-edited with Dan Streible). Other works include *Critical Theory, Marxism, and Modernity*; *Jean Baudrillard: From Marxism to Postmodernism and Beyond*; works in cultural studies such as *Media Culture and Media Spectacle*; a trilogy of books on postmodern theory with Steve Best; and a trilogy of books on the media and the Bush administration, encompassing *Grand Theft 2000*, *From 9/11 to Terror War*, and *Media Spectacle and the Crisis of Democracy.* Author of *Herbert Marcuse and the Crisis of Marxism,* Kellner is editing the collected papers of Herbert Marcuse, four volumes of which have appeared with Routledge. Kellner's *Guys and Guns Amok: Domestic Terrorism and School Shootings from the Oklahoma City Bombings to the Virginia Tech Massacre* won the 2008 AESA award as the best book on education. In 2010, he published *Cinema Wars: Hollywood Film and Politics in the Bush/Cheney Era* with Blackwell and has recently published *Media Spectacle and Insurrection, 2011: From the Arab Uprisings to Occupy Everywhere!* (2012). Kellner's website is http://www.gseis.ucla.edu/faculty/kellner/kellner.html.

Brian Klocke

Brian Klocke is an Assistant Professor of Sociology at the State University of New York at Plattsburgh. He earned his Sociology PhD from the University of Colorado at Boulder, his MS in College Student Development from Indiana State University, and his BS in Psychology from Iowa State University. Dr. Klocke's research has involved studying the policing and surveillance of social movement organizations, the framing of the war on terrorism during the Bush administration, and the media coverage of a university scandal. He is coauthor of *The Better World Handbook*, 1st ed. His publications have appeared in *Sociology Compass, Policing and Society, Men and Masculinities, Contemporary Sociology, Bad Subjects, and Teaching Sociology*; he has forthcoming publications in *Journalism* and *The Ashgate Research Companion to Moral Panics.* Dr. Klocke has had experience as an independent reporter and photo journalist, and his work in those areas has appeared in the *Boulder Weekly,* the *Colorado Springs Independent,* the *Independent Media Center,* and *Rebellion Magazine.* Dr. Klocke teaches the Sociology of Globalization, Media and Society, Race and Ethnicity, and Gender Studies.

Joanna Martinez

Joanna Martinez is a student at the University of California, Berkeley in the sociology program, with emphasis on urban sociology and ethnography, Black feminist epistemology, and critical race theory. Martinez has worked as head coordinator of the "Li'l Bobby Hutton Literacy Campaign" for the Commemoration Committee of the Black Panther Party (2008–2012), Lead Intern for the Custodial Communications Project (2010–2012), funded by The Green Initiative Fund, and English Instructor for the federally funded UC Berkeley Upward Bound Program (2011–2012). Martinez was born and raised in Santa Rosa, Northern California, in a Mexican immigrant family.

Toby Miller

Toby Miller is a British-Australian-US interdisciplinary social scientist. He is the author and editor of over 30 books, has published essays in more than 100 journals and edited collections, and is a frequent guest commentator on television and radio programs.

His teaching and research cover the media, sports, labor, gender, race, citizenship, politics, and cultural policy, as well as the success of Hollywood overseas and the adverse effects of electronic waste. Miller's work has been translated into Chinese, Japanese, Swedish, German, Turkish, Spanish, and Portuguese. He has been Media Scholar in Residence at Sarai, the Centre for the Study of Developing Societies in India, Becker Lecturer at the University of Iowa, a Queensland Smart Returns Fellow in Australia, Honorary Professor at the Center for Critical and Cultural Studies, University of Queensland, CanWest Visiting Fellow at the Alberta Global Forum in Canada, and an International Research collaborator at the Centre for Cultural Research in Australia. Among his books, *SportSex* was a *Choice* Outstanding Title for 2002 and *A Companion to Film Theory* a *Choice* Outstanding Title for 2004. Born in the United Kingdom and brought up in England, India, and Australia, Miller earned a B.A. in history and political science at the Australian National University in 1980 and a PhD in philosophy and communication studies at Murdoch University in 1991. He taught at Murdoch, Griffith University, and the University of New South Wales and was a professor at New York University from 1993 to 2004, when he joined the University of California, Riverside. Miller is now chair of a new Department of Media & Cultural Studies and lives near the ocean in Los Angeles. His website can be found at www.tobymiller.org.

Kimberly M. Radek

Kimberly M. Radek works as a feminist cultural critic and interdisciplinary scholar as a professor of English, Film, and Gender Studies at Illinois Valley Community College in Oglesby, Illinois. Having earned her Bachelor's and Master's degrees in English from Northern Illinois University, she is currently a PhD candidate in Interdisciplinary Studies at Union Institute & University, where she is writing a dissertation that unites her passions for theory, gender, media, science, religion, and politics.

Norman Solomon

Norman Solomon is the author of a dozen books on media, politics, and social change. His book *War Made Easy: How Presidents and Pundits Keep Spinning Us to Death* (Wiley, 2005) was adapted into a documentary film produced by the Media Education Foundation. Solomon wrote the weekly syndicated "Media Beat" column from 1992 to 2009. He is founder of the Institute for Public Accuracy, co-founder of RootsAction.org, and a longtime associate of the media watchdog group Fairness & Accuracy in Reporting (FAIR). Solomon co-chairs the national Healthcare Not Warfare campaign. He is a recipient of the George Orwell Award for Distinguished Contribution to Honesty and Clarity in Public Language as well as the Annual Ruben Salazar Journalism Award. A longtime political activist and public speaker, Solomon has written for a wide array of publications ranging from the *New York Times*, *Los Angeles Times*, and *Newsday* to *The Progressive*, *The Nation*, and *Z Magazine*, as well as online outlets such as CommonDreams.org and Truthout.org. The *New York Times Magazine* has called him "a leading progressive activist." The *Los Angeles Times* has called him "a formidable thinker and activist."

minding the media

CRITICAL ISSUES
FOR LEARNING AND TEACHING

Shirley R. Steinberg & Pepi Leistyna
General Editors

Minding the Media is a book series specifically designed to address the needs of students and teachers in watching, comprehending, and using media. Books in the series use a wide range of educational settings to raise consciousness about media relations and realities and promote critical, creative alternatives to contemporary mainstream practices. *Minding the Media* seeks theoretical, technical, and practitioner perspectives as they relate to critical pedagogy and public education. Authors are invited to contribute volumes of up to 85,000 words to this series. Possible areas of interest as they connect to learning and teaching include:

- critical media literacy
- popular culture
- video games
- animation
- music
- media activism
- democratizing information systems
- using alternative media
- using the Web/internet
- interactive technologies
- blogs
- multi-media in the classroom
- media representations of race, class, gender, sexuality, disability, etc.
- media/communications studies methodologies
- semiotics
- watchdog journalism/investigative journalism
- visual culture: theater, art, photography
- radio, TV, newspapers, zines, film, documentary film, comic books
- public relations
- globalization and the media
- consumption/consumer culture
- advertising
- censorship
- audience reception

For additional information about this series or for the submission of manuscripts, please contact:

Shirley R. Steinberg and Pepi Leistyna,
msgramsci@aol.com | Pepi.Leistyna@umb.edu

To order other books in this series, please contact our Customer Service Department:
(800) 770-LANG (within the U.S.)
(212) 647-7706 (outside the U.S.)
(212) 647-7707 FAX

Or browse online by series:
www.peterlang.com